TEN DAYS
—— TO ——
SELF-ESTEEM

THE LEADER'S MANUAL

ALSO BY DAVID D. BURNS, M.D.

Feeling Good: The New Mood Therapy
(1980)
Intimate Connections
(1985)
The Feeling Good Handbook
(1990)

TEN DAYS
— TO —
SELF-ESTEEM

THE LEADER'S MANUAL

DAVID D. BURNS, M.D.

QUILL
WILLIAM MORROW
New York

AUTHOR'S NOTE

The ideas, procedures, and suggestions contained in this book are not intended as a substitute for consulting with a psychiatrist, psychologist, or other mental health professional. All matters regarding your mental health require professional supervision.

The names and personal details of the patients mentioned in this book have been changed to protect their identities.

Individuals wishing to contact the author may do so at the following address:

David D. Burns, M.D., and Associates
c/o Presbyterian Medical Center of Philadelphia
39th and Market Streets
Philadelphia, PA 19104

Burns, David D.
    Ten days to self-esteem : the leader's manual / David D. Burns.
       p.   cm.
    ISBN 0-688-12708-8
    1. Depressed persons—Counseling of—Handbooks, manuals, etc.
  2. Self-help groups—Activity programs—Handbooks, manuals, etc.
  3. Group psychotherapy—Handbooks, manuals, etc. I. Title.
RC537.B7784   1993
    616.89'152—dc20   92-38209
                                                         CIP

Printed in the United States of America

First Edition

1 2 3 4 5 6 7 8 9 10

BOOK DESIGN BY MM DESIGN 2000, INC.

PREFACE

The basic principles of cognitive therapy are quite straightforward:

- Our thoughts, not external events, create our moods.
- Distorted, illogical thoughts and self-defeating beliefs lead to painful feelings such as depression, anxiety, and anger.
- By changing these negative thoughts, we can change how we feel.

For many years in my clinical practice, I have struggled to make these principles come alive. How can we best help people to recognize the crucial connections between the ways they think, feel, and behave? How can we help them to use this new knowledge to overcome depression and lead happier and more productive lives?

Therefore, I was delighted when Dr. David Burns, my friend and colleague, asked me to collaborate with him in developing groups based on Ten Days to Self-esteem. Since the implementation of this program at the Presbyterian Medical Center of Philadelphia eighteen months ago, we have seen it blossom in ways that we could not have imagined. To date, over six hundred patients who felt discouraged and hopeless have participated in this program.

We first pilot-tested Ten Days to Self-esteem at The Residence, a short-term inpatient program with an average length of stay of seven to ten days. Many of the patients at The Residence have relatively little formal education and suffer from dual diagnoses— with severe emotional disorders as well as alcohol or drug abuse. Prior to implementing Ten Days to Self-esteem, a less-structured treatment model had been tried with only limited success. The Residence was still struggling in its infancy and many of the staff members were pulling in different directions. This setting was a real challenge to the efficacy of Ten Days to Self-esteem!

Initially, many patients and staff members expressed feelings of skepticism and often frank disbelief that the program would work. Dr. Burns and I shared some feelings of uncertainty as well. We were all concerned that the techniques might be "too sophisticated" for some of our lower-functioning patients who could not even read or write. We were also quite aware that these patients had *real* and severe problems in daily living, and might not readily accept the idea that their negative feelings resulted from distorted thinking patterns and self-defeating attitudes.

To our great surprise, the program has far surpassed our expectations. With a little bit of flexibility, creativity, and compassion, we have been able to connect with many patients who previously appeared to be unreachable. We constantly receive letters of gratitude from patients who tell us that, for the first time, they truly understand *why* they became depressed and *what* they can do to make real changes in their lives—not tomorrow, next month, or next year, but *now*! The impact on the nurses, counselors, and other staff members has been equally positive. They now work together as a team with an effective, integrated treatment program. Referrals to The Residence and the census are up, and the facility has become a source of pride for the medical center.

In addition to our inpatient experience, we have also pilot-tested Ten Days to Self-esteem in outpatient groups consisting primarily of individuals from the higher social and economic brackets. In this setting, our initial concerns were a little different. We worried that there might not be enough meaty clinical material in each session for people who were intellectually and psychologically sophisticated.

Again, *not true*! We were pleasantly surprised to discover that the individuals in the outpatient programs dug into the material enthusiastically. In fact, they frequently had so much to chew on and digest that we found ourselves running out of time at the end of each two-hour session. The issues have been so profound and exciting to the participants that, once they begin, it is difficult to get them to stop and go home! In almost every case the outpatient participants, like the inpatients at The Residence, have reported dramatic reductions in depression scores, new insights into the nature of self-esteem, and profound changes in their attitudes and beliefs.

A unique gift of Ten Days to Self-esteem is that it takes the ideas and techniques of cognitive therapy from the dry intellectual level to a more emotional and personal level. As the participants in these groups discover how to modify their own negative thinking patterns, they feel a sense of excitement and develop a new philosophy of living that is more vibrant and compassionate. Observing and directing this process has been inspirational for me as a group leader and equally rewarding for the participants. It is this contribution that patients and group leaders will find the most rewarding and long lasting.

With the current movement toward briefer psychotherapies and managed care in the delivery of mental health services, there is great pressure to develop cost-effective, time-limited treatment programs. Instead of regretting what we *can't* do because of limited funding, those of us who are involved with Ten Days to Self-esteem see this as a challenge to focus on what we *can* do. These are exciting times for change. This program will be treasured by any clinician or educator who is looking for new, creative ways to help individuals who are suffering from emotional problems such as depression and anxiety.

The experience that we have accumulated by running Ten Days to Self-esteem for a wide variety of populations has greatly enriched this *Leader's Manual*. Whether you are an experienced or novice group leader, the guidelines, tips, and suggestions here will prove invaluable. We anticipate that each group leader will re-invent this basic program by adding his or her talents and insights. However, even if one follows this program literally "by the book," it has been our experience that the group will take on a momentum of its own that will make for an exciting and rewarding experience.

With these tools in your hands, you are about to embark on an exciting journey, guiding people from all walks of life toward greater self-esteem and happiness. You will find that the exercises in Ten Days to Self-esteem are so numerous and so varied that they will fit most of your clinical needs. You can use these exercises like a musician working with a rich score. I anticipate that as you add your own unique contributions and style when interpreting this program, you will discover a beautiful melody unfolding and experience the immense satisfaction of bringing greater self-esteem to others.

—BRUCE S. ZAHN, M.A.
Director of Psychological Services
Presbyterian Medical Center of Philadelphia

ACKNOWLEDGMENTS

I would like to thank my close friend and colleague Bruce S. Zahn, M.A., director of psychological services at the Presbyterian Medical Center of Philadelphia, for invaluable assistance in the preparation of this manual. Bruce has provided numerous creative suggestions as well as incredible moral support.

I would like to thank Diane Kiddy, M.S.S., vice president of behavioral medicine, and I. Donald Snook, Jr., president of the Presbyterian Medical Center, for persistent encouragement in the development of this program. I am also indebted to Carol Persons, M.D., medical director of The Residence at the Presbyterian Medical Center, and Elizabeth Dean, program administrator at The Residence, for support of my efforts.

I would like to thank the Reverend Dick Hamlin, Dr. Dennis Hunter, and Jan Robinson at the Shepherd of the Valley Lutheran Church in Phoenix, who helped to pilot-test a prototype of this program with the members of their congregation. I am also grateful to Michael Greenwald, Ph.D., a clinical psychologist in Pittsburgh, for consultation and for supervision of several additional pilot tests of this program throughout the country.

Finally, I would like to thank Melanie Burns, my wife, colleague, and friend, for brilliant suggestions about the editing and tone of this manuscript.

The contributions of all of these individuals have been invaluable and deeply appreciated. Thank you!

CONTENTS

INTRODUCTION

This *Leader's Manual* will show you how to develop a short-term, structured group program entitled Ten Days to Self-esteem. Ten Days to Self-esteem consists of ten sessions that focus on the causes and cures for problems such as low self-esteem, feelings of inferiority, perfectionism, and procrastination. Participants learn specific skills to overcome depression and develop greater joy in daily living.

Any qualified mental health professional or trainee can lead the groups, including psychologists, psychiatrists, social workers, counselors, mental health technicians, school counselors, psychiatric nurses, and pastoral counselors. Participants can be students, psychiatric patients, or virtually anyone else.

These self-esteem training groups can be conducted in a variety of settings:

1. **High schools and colleges:** Depression, suicide, and loneliness afflict many young people. The Ten Days to Self-esteem groups are ideal for health classes in high schools and for personal growth classes and psychology courses in colleges. The program is also ideal for counseling centers in high schools and colleges. The groups represent exciting possibilities for educating a new generation of young adults with the attitudes and skills they will need to prevent depression and enhance productivity and self-esteem throughout their lives.

2. **Graduate schools and professional training programs:** Graduate students in nursing, social work, counseling, psychology, and psychiatry can participate in these groups and subsequently lead groups for patients. This experience will give the trainees a personal growth experience as well as the opportunity to master cognitive, behavioral, and interpersonal therapy techniques.

3. **Hospitals, residential treatment facilities, and day treatment programs:** One to three group sessions can be scheduled daily to create a rich and rewarding therapeutic environment. The program can have strong positive effects on staff members' morale because they will see rapid, tangible changes in their patients.

4. **Twelve-step programs and other self-help groups:** Ten Days to Self-esteem can be easily integrated into the programs of established self-help organizations such as Alcoholics Anonymous, Recovery, Inc., Emotions Anonymous, CODA (Co-Dependents Anonymous), and others. Ten Days to Self-esteem is not intended to compete with these groups, which have been enormously helpful for so many

people suffering from alcoholism, drug addiction, or emotional disorders. Rather, the practical coping skills described here can enhance and strengthen these groups by providing a richer and more exciting menu of opportunities for the members.

5. **Managed health care:** HMOs and other managed health-care delivery systems are under increasing financial pressure. Many insurance companies now offer extremely limited reimbursement for psychotherapy. Ten Days to Self-esteem can dramatically improve the quality and quantity of therapy per dollar of available funding.

6. **Private and public outpatient clinics:** Ten Days to Self-esteem can enhance the quality of care and help to attract clients. Many people want to participate in a time-limited, upbeat training program that targets a specific problem such as depression, anxiety, marital conflict, or an addiction.

7. **Churches and synagogues:** Psychotherapy and religion have been at odds during much of the twentieth century. However, the ideas and techniques in Ten Days to Self-esteem are highly compatible with nearly all religions. Any congregation can offer them as a part of the outreach program for its members as well as for the surrounding community. It will be relatively easy for leaders to point out the connections between what the participants are learning and various scriptural passages.

8. **Corporations:** Ten Days to Self-esteem can be invaluable for employee assistance programs to help individuals with emotional and interpersonal problems. The program can also be offered in a workshop format for professional training and personal growth for the staff.

9. **Prisons and correctional facilities:** Ten Days to Self-esteem can be offered in prisons and in the psychiatric hospitals that serve them. The techniques are easy to understand, based on common sense, and down-to-earth. The groups convey a nonjudgmental message and directly address the deficiencies in self-esteem and interpersonal relationships that are so common in this population.

10. **Nursing homes:** Although severely impaired individuals with Alzheimer's disease would not be good candidates for Ten Days to Self-esteem, many people in nursing homes can benefit greatly from the groups. The groups can boost morale and break the cycle of loneliness and isolation that afflicts so many older people. Weekly groups for patients and their families together can help to improve communication and reduce feelings of guilt, frustration, and rejection.

Ten Days to Self-esteem is the first of three modules that I have developed. The leader's manuals and participant's workbooks for the two additional modules will be published subsequently.

The second module focuses on intimacy and personal relationship problems. The group members receive intensive training in self-expression and listening skills that can help them develop more satisfying relationships with their spouses, family members, friends, and colleagues at work.

The third module focuses on anxiety disorders. Participants learn how to overcome

- chronic worrying and nervousness
- anxiety and panic attacks
- shyness and social anxiety
- public speaking anxiety
- test and performance anxiety
- phobias such as agoraphobia or the fear of heights
- obsessive-compulsive illness
- and more

This is a challenging time for mental health professionals. We are faced with significant cutbacks in funding for psychological and psychiatric services from insurance companies, HMOs, Medicare, and Medicaid, as well as other managed health care programs. Therapists are often told to discharge severely disturbed inpatients after only five to ten days of treatment and to limit outpatient therapy to just a handful of sessions. At the same time, we must provide solid evidence to prove that the therapy is effective! Instead of fearing or resisting these sweeping changes, we can take this as an opportunity to develop innovative, cost-effective short-term treatments that will offer real help to the great majority of patients.

I am pleased that you are interested in Ten Days to Self-esteem. As you develop this program, you will be breaking new ground for people suffering from depression, loneliness, anxiety, and addictions who wish to enrich their lives and feel good about themselves once again.

ABBREVIATIONS OFTEN USED IN THIS MANUAL

Abbr.	Meaning	Definition
BDC	Burns Depression Checklist	A test measuring how depressed a person feels
BAI	Burns Anxiety Inventory	A test measuring how anxious a person feels
RSAT	Relationship Satisfaction Scale	A test measuring an individual's satisfaction with his or her personal relationships
NT	Negative Thought	A negative thought that goes through a person's mind when he or she feels upset
PT	Positive Thought	A more positive and realistic thought
SDB	Self-defeating Belief	An attitude such as "I must always try to be perfect."
CBA	Cost-Benefit Analysis	A form to list the advantages and disadvantages of a negative thought, feeling, or belief
DML	Daily Mood Log	A form for recording upsetting events, feelings, and thoughts

GENERAL INSTRUCTIONS FOR LEADERS

This *Leader's Manual* contains clear and detailed instructions for every session in this program. As a result, your very first experience running Ten Days to Self-esteem should be reasonably smooth and successful, even if you do not have extensive previous experience with these methods.

This section tells you how to set up the Ten Days to Self-esteem groups. You might want to begin by reading the descriptions of several of the sessions, beginning on page 44 of this *Leader's Manual*, and then come back to this section. As you read, you will be able to picture yourself leading a group. This experience will place the administrative details discussed here in a live context.

The instructions for each step are easy to follow and have been applied by my colleagues and me in many different settings. Once you have run a group, you will get a feeling for what works and what does not work for your particular group. As you lead the group, you will probably have many creative ideas on how to modify the format to meet the needs of the population you are serving.

SUPPLIES YOU WILL NEED

All you will need to run a group successfully is a quiet room with comfortable chairs for the participants and a coffeepot for the break. The room should ideally be large enough so you can break up the group into small teams of two to six members at times for specific exercises. You will also need a flip chart, blackboard, or overhead projector.

SUPPLIES THE PARTICIPANTS WILL NEED

The participant's workbook is called *Ten Days to Self-esteem*. This workbook includes all the exercises, self-assessment tests, self-help forms, and other supplemental materials that the participants will need. Participants will use this workbook during each session and will do the self-help assignments in it between sessions. The exercises and charts in the workbook will make it easy for you to run the groups smoothly and professionally.

This workbook is widely available in bookstores. You can order a copy of the *Ten Days to Self-esteem* workbook with the order form at the end of *The Leader's Manual*, or you can order copies in quantity for your group at a discount by calling the publisher at 1-800-821-1513.

MEMBER MIX

You will need to think about the types of individuals who will participate in your group. Although the groups can be adapted effectively for men and women with a broad range of ages, diagnoses, intelligence levels, and social and economic backgrounds, a reasonable degree of uniformity within any group is desirable. Participants should have enough similarity to permit bonding and rapport to develop. For example, it is not wise to mix individuals with extremely severe emotional difficulties (such as schizophrenia) together with people with very mild problems who are taking the group for personal growth purposes.

INCLUSION AND EXCLUSION CRITERIA FOR THE GROUPS

The following guidelines can help you decide which participants may need individual therapy outside the group. The guidelines will also help you identify applicants who may not be suitable for Ten Days to Self-esteem.

These guidelines apply primarily to groups in *outpatient* settings. You can include more seriously disturbed individuals when you run the groups in inpatient or residential treatment settings or day treatment programs. For example, at the Presbyterian Medical Center of Philadelphia we have had excellent success in using these groups with extremely disturbed inpatient populations, including individuals with schizophrenia, drug abuse problems, and severe mood and personality disorders. Many of these patients have been enthusiastic about the program and have expressed gratitude to the staff who run the groups. However, you may have to simplify the groups and use your creativity when you are working with more disturbed populations, as described on page 34.

In an outpatient setting, you generally should not include people with these problems:

1. **Psychotic symptoms:** This includes individuals who are delusional, out of touch with reality, hearing voices, hallucinating, or behaving inappropriately.

   However, there are exceptions to this rule. In day treatment programs, or in outpatient groups consisting entirely of schizophrenics, you can run a simplified version of this program quite successfully, as long as the patients have individual psychiatric management so that medications can be prescribed if indicated.

2. **Chronicity:** People who have long-standing problems with depression or anxiety are excellent candidates for the groups but may also need individual psychotherapy and/or medication treatment.

3. **Severity:** If someone has overwhelming difficulties with feelings of depression, anxiety, guilt, or anger, then one-to-one therapy may be indicated.

4. **Low capacity to function:** If a mood problem significantly interferes with an individual's capacity to relate to others or to function adequately at home, school, or work, professional treatment is indicated. For example, if someone is so depressed that he or she refuses to get out of bed, that individual would not be likely to benefit from the group and would be a burden to the other members.

5. **Low motivation:** The groups are intended for people who want to be in them. Anyone who feels coerced to attend will feel resentful and may sabotage the group. This is why people are asked to make a significant commitment to the group at the beginning. For example, the Self-help Contract on page 33 of the participant's workbook makes it clear that members will have to work hard doing self-help assignments between sessions.

6. **Hopelessness and suicidal impulses:** Some depressed people feel like giving up because they are convinced that there is no solution to their problems. Anyone who is actively suicidal needs immediate one-to-one therapy and may require hospitalization. Such individuals may be a danger to themselves and would be a continual source of distress to the group and to the leader.

   Most people with feelings of depression have the thought at times that life is not worth living or that they'd be better off dead. These thoughts are perfectly natural and need not exclude anyone from the group. The crucial issue is whether an individual has actual intentions and plans to commit suicide. If a person has a strong desire to die, and there are no strong reasons (such as religious beliefs or a commitment to the family) preventing him or her from committing suicide, then immediate evaluation and treatment by a psychiatrist or psychologist is needed.

7. **Drug or alcohol intoxication:** Individuals who are being treated for drug or alcohol abuse are good candidates for the groups, but participants who are intoxicated may not attend any sessions. Recovering alcoholics and drug abusers should be encouraged to attend AA or NA (Narcotics Anonymous) meetings along with Ten Days to Self-esteem.

Some participants may already be receiving individual therapy. It is a good idea to ask them to obtain consent from their therapists to join Ten Days to Self-esteem. You can enhance the effectiveness of both treatments by consulting with the other therapist. The participant's perception of teamwork between the two therapists will be extremely helpful. This can prevent splitting, and the participant will find it more difficult to play you off against each other.

INITIAL SCREENING OF PARTICIPANTS

I have included a Personal History Form in Appendix B, which you may want to use for the initial evaluation to determine whether individuals are suitable for the groups. This form can be administered in about one hour and includes these subjects:

- **Basic data:** In the opening sections, you will record the individual's name, age, marital status, education, income, insurance coverage, and so forth. You will also ask how he or she was referred to you.

- **Initial psychological testing:** You will record the individual's scores on the three self-assessment tests, which measure depression, anxiety, and relationship satisfaction, respectively. This will give you an immediate reading of the severity of symptoms.

- **Reason for seeking treatment:** What are the problems this person is seeking help for? Why is he or she seeking help at just this particular time? How motivated is he or she to be in treatment?

- **Perception of group therapy:** How has this person perceived past group therapy experiences? Have there been any negative experiences? It can be useful to point out how this program is different from most group therapy. In Ten Days to Self-esteem, individuals will *not* be confronted or put on the spot; there will be no long, awkward silences. This will be an upbeat, time-limited, supportive training program.

- **Medication survey** and **summary of prior psychotherapy:** You will record current and past medications and inquire about the effectiveness of previous psychotherapeutic treatments.

- **Family history:** Has any blood relative ever had any psychiatric disturbance?

- **Sexual history:** You will inquire about sexual orientation and any sexual problems.

- **Sexual, physical, or psychological abuse:** You will ask about any abuse the individual may have experienced as a child or as an adult.

- **Quality of information during the history:** Do you think this person was completely candid?

- **Goals for therapy:** You will ask the individual to list his or her specific goals for the treatment. What does he or she hope to accomplish? If you had a magic wand and could solve all of his or her personal problems, what would be on the wish list? Developing greater self-esteem and productivity at work? Better personal relationships? How hard is this person willing to work to try to achieve these goals?

- **Diagnostic summary:** You will record *DSM-III-R* Axis I and Axis II diagnoses, along with Axes III, IV, and V.

● **Administrative checklist:** You will spell out your administrative requirements and expectations. This will include issues such as whether there is a charge for missed sessions or for premature termination from the group, when fees for the group should be paid, doing homework between sessions, emergency coverage, and so forth. Read the sample administrative checklist on page 226 now. Although some mental health professionals prefer to avoid these sensitive issues, I believe you will be *far better off* if you negotiate them clearly with each participant ahead of time. Your group will respect you more and there will be much less room for misunderstanding.

DOES SELF-HELP REALLY WORK?

Although the benefits of self-help are quite controversial, recent research studies by Dr. Forrest Scogin and his colleagues at the University of Alabama have confirmed the antidepressant effects of a good self-help book. In their studies, which were published in the *Journal of Consulting and Clinical Psychology*, they observed that two thirds of depressed older adults who were asked to read my *Feeling Good: The New Mood Therapy* or a book on depression by Dr. Peter Lewinsohn recovered or showed substantial improvement in just four weeks without any psychotherapy or medication therapy. In contrast, a control group of depressed older adults who were placed on a waiting list during this four-week period failed to improve. Then the researchers asked the subjects on the waiting list to read one of the self-help books, and two thirds of them improved. What was even more impressive was the discovery that these individuals maintained their gains and even continued to improve during a two-year follow-up period. The investigators concluded that bibliotherapy (reading a self-help book) alone, without psychotherapy, can have significant mood-elevating effects for many people who feel depressed. I believe this was the first time that this has ever been demonstrated in a well-controlled scientific investigation.

Although these studies were very encouraging, it was not possible to know whether the improvement was simply from reading, or if there was something specific about these particular self-help books that helped people to overcome depression. To find out, Dr. Scogin and his colleagues did further studies on depressed individuals who were asked to read Viktor Frankl's *Man's Search for Meaning*. This is a highly acclaimed book that does not contain any information on how to develop greater self-esteem. The depressed people who read this book did not improve. The researchers concluded that bibliotherapy can be extremely beneficial, but not just any book will do. The book has to contain helpful information about recovery from depression.

I find Dr. Scogin's pioneering research on self-help quite exciting. The results of his investigations inspired me to develop Ten Days to Self-esteem. I reasoned that if simply reading a book like my *Feeling Good* could help people to recover from depression, then the combination of bibliotherapy plus group training sessions might be even better because people would additionally benefit from the systematic structure of the group, from the specific, step-by-step training and experiential practice at each session, and from the rapport and bonding with the other group members and with the group leader.

HOW EFFECTIVE ARE THE GROUPS?

It is difficult to make generalizations about the effectiveness of this program in specific settings because groups and leaders may vary considerably. In most groups, the majority of your participants should show significant improvement on the self-assessment tests that measure depression, anxiety, and satisfaction in personal relationships. In many of our groups at the Presbyterian Medical Center, we have seen high response rates, even with very severely disturbed populations. However, the inpatients participate in two or more groups every day and so the program is quite intensive. This intensity probably enhances the effectiveness of Ten Days to Self-esteem at our center.

No matter how effective your groups are, some members will still be experiencing symptoms of depression at the end of the tenth session. This is not unusual. Some people respond very rapidly to practically *any* intervention, whereas others are more resistant and slow to change, no matter how good the therapy might be.

This idea is explained at the beginning of the participant's workbook so that the participants will not develop unrealistic expectations. However, it can be helpful for you to discuss this at the initial screening for the groups and at the first session. If you are frank and set up realistic expectations for the participants, you will have greater credibility. This will minimize any feelings of hopelessness or resentment among those who respond more slowly.

There are many good options for any members who need more treatment at the end of the module:

- They can be referred for individual psychotherapy and/or antidepressant drug therapy.

- They can continue with the module on anxiety or the module on personal relationship conflict. (See page 14.)

- They can repeat this module.

- They can join a self-help group such as the local chapter of the National Depressive and Manic Depressive Association.

The most important thing is to be enthusiastic and compassionate and to inspire hope. Ten Days to Self-esteem can be an important step along the road to recovery for every member, but you should not view the groups as the *only* approach or the *last* resort for any member. Persistence and determination are the keys to change. I believe that, with time and effort, virtually every depressed individual can eventually experience joy and self-esteem again.

FEES FOR THE PROGRAM

Since Ten Days to Self-esteem is time-limited, I would recommend that you charge a set fee for the program. Try to obtain a 50% deposit prior to the first session whenever possible. In addition, you may want to charge for the entire program whether or not a participant attends all the sessions or drops out prematurely. Make these policies clear during the initial evaluation so there will be no misunderstanding.

Although these arrangements might sound overly tough, there is an unfortunate tendency for people in outpatient therapy groups to cancel sessions at the last minute, to drop out prematurely, or to fail to do the self-help assignments between sessions. Firm, clear financial arrangements can enhance compliance, because people will be more accountable to the group.

Churches, hospitals, schools, prisons, self-help groups, and other community organizations may wish to offer this program free of charge. Overhead expenses can be defrayed through voluntary contributions, as in Alcoholics Anonymous and many of the twelve-step programs. The absence of a fee conveys a powerful and compassionate message to the participants that the techniques are genuinely helpful and that the goals are not exploitive or entrepreneurial.

You may want to apply for a grant to support Ten Days to Self-esteem. Since systematic data collection is built into the program, you will easily be able to prepare statistical reports documenting the effectiveness of the groups for the sponsoring agency.

THE DEPOSIT SYSTEM

One potential disadvantage of a free group is that some participants may devalue the program and feel less committed if they do not have to pay to attend. As mentioned above, some members will attend inconsistently and fail to do the self-help assignments between sessions, feeling they can get by with a passive attitude and simply go along for the ride. This will reduce the benefit they receive and may demoralize the other group members who attend faithfully and work hard on the self-help assignments between sessions.

I cannot overemphasize the importance of these problems! This is likely to be one of your *most significant* problems in running the groups. Unless you take the proper steps to prevent this difficulty, it will demoralize you. Sooner or later you'll get frustrated and simply run out of gas. You'll begin to ask yourself, "Why am I doing all the work?"

It takes lots of enthusiasm and dedication to develop these groups. You will need to get something back from the members to maintain your motivation and to keep your gas tank full! If you feel good about what you are doing, you'll have a great deal more to offer!

One innovative approach is to ask each member for a deposit at the beginning of Ten Days to Self-esteem. It could be any amount, such as one hundred dollars for people of average means, or a smaller deposit for people with modest incomes. The participants can receive up to 2 points for attending each subsequent session on time and up to 3 points for completing the homework assignment (depending on how much they have completed). A rating system for attendance and homework is explained on page 68. I have created a Leader's Data Sheet (see pages 69–72) so you can conveniently record these data at the beginning of each session, along with each member's scores on the three mood self-assessment tests.

Since there are ten sessions, each member can earn up to 50 points. At the end of the program, each participant will receive a refund that will depend on how many points he or she earned during the sessions. For example, if each member gives you a one-hundred-dollar deposit, each point earned will be worth two dollars. This Deposit System reinforces the idea that consistent attendance and active involvement in the homework are absolutely crucial to the success of the group and to the personal growth of every member.

The advantages of this system are quite striking. No matter what people say when they first sign up for the group, many of them will *not* do the homework and will arrive late or attend inconsistently. The Deposit System turns this perennial problem into an asset, since the people who drop out or fail to do the homework will help to defray the expenses of the group! This will tend to lift your morale as well as that of the other members who are putting more effort into the group. You won't feel so frustrated and annoyed with the people who do not comply. You are saying to them, "You can participate in a passive manner if you want, but in this case you will have to pay a small fee. On the other hand, if you are willing to do the self-help assignments and attend consistently, then you will be rewarded financially and emotionally for your efforts."

The Leader's Data Sheet will make it easy to calculate how much money each participant has earned by the end of the program. In addition, you can easily track the progress of each participant and evaluate the effectiveness of the groups. You will be able to determine precisely how much improvement each member has experienced in depression, anxiety, and personal relationship satisfaction.

Many group leaders who ran pilot studies for Ten Days to Self-esteem initially resisted this suggestion. They voiced concerns such as these: "It wouldn't be right in our church (or synagogue)." "The federal government won't permit us to charge for treatment." "The students at our university are supposed to get free treatment at our counseling center." "The inmates at our prison are poor and cannot afford a deposit."

This resistance is sometimes based on the belief that the Deposit System will appear overly crass or controlling. You may fear that people will get angry if you ask them to be accountable. As mental health professionals, we often feel that if we are nice and kind to our patients, they will be grateful and will work hard to do their part to recover. Unfortunately, this philosophy of niceness simply does not work for a significant number of people!

Many leaders who initially resisted the Deposit System were disappointed with client compliance. The next time they ran the program, they were more willing to use the

Deposit System. I strongly recommend this approach if it is feasible within your mental-health-care delivery system.

The sponsors of the pilot program at the Shepherd of the Valley Lutheran Church in Phoenix did not ask the participants for a deposit. Instead, they gave points at each session for punctual attendance and for completion of the assignments. They gave awards at the end of each program to the participants who had earned the most points.

This creative and friendly approach will not really solve the compliance problem, for several reasons. First, the participants who fall behind early in the program will not have much motivation because they cannot catch up. Furthermore, the point system rewards only the highly committed participants, and does not motivate the ones who resist doing homework. Finally, it does not make the members accountable.

I do not mention the fee and deposit arrangements in the participant's workbook. This will give you the flexibility to choose the approach that is the most appropriate for your group.

HOMEWORK ASSIGNMENTS

The self-help assignments between group sessions consist of reading as well as writing assignments. The written assignments include keeping a journal of negative thoughts on the Daily Mood Log and filling out self-assessment tests to determine how much depression, anxiety, and interpersonal conflict the participants have felt since the last session. In addition, you may ask them to experiment with new and more effective behavior patterns at times.

You will find a list of the self-help assignments for the next session at the end of each step in the participant's workbook. For example, the list of self-help assignments for Step 2 is located at the end of Step 1 on page 36 of the participant's workbook. You can read each assignment out loud and ask the participants to put a check in the column labeled "Check (√) if assigned." You will see that the right-hand column is labeled "Check (√) when finished." You can ask the participants to put a check in this column after they have completed each assignment. This will make it easy for you to evaluate how much of the homework they have completed at the beginning of each step.

The self-help assignments are *not optional*. They are one of the most important components of the program. People in therapy are presumably trying to learn new problem-solving skills and more productive ways of thinking, feeling, and relating to others. With active practice and effort, it is far more likely that this growth and learning will occur.

Can you imagine trying to learn tennis simply by talking to a coach and watching other players, but without ever hitting the ball or practicing between tennis lessons? Your game wouldn't improve much!

In spite of the importance of the self-help assignments, some participants will resist them. There are many reasons for this resistance. Some participants may believe that the warmth and support of the other members (or the charisma of the group leader) will be sufficient to make them feel good. They may feel comforted to think that a respected authority figure will listen to them, care for them, and solve their problems, much like a loving parent.

This problem can be compounded by group leaders who are reluctant to ask patients to complete the homework assignments between sessions. These leaders may feel insecure and fearful of the disapproval of the members. You may not want the participants to think of you as the "bad guy" who has to police them to do their homework. You may feel awkward about confronting the members who are not doing their homework. This concern is understandable.

In addition, some leaders may feel the homework is unnecessary, believing that the inspiration and support of the group should be sufficient. While it is true that some groups may be quite inspirational and cause a substantial mood lift, as in an evangelistic revival meeting, this improvement is likely to be quite temporary. The best learning usually comes from the members' active participation during and between sessions.

Although you will never achieve perfect homework compliance, there are three things you can do to motivate your participants. First, make sure that every participant reads and fills out the section entitled The Price of Happiness in Step 1, which begins on page 29 of the participant's workbook. This section explains the rationale for the homework, describes the types of homework participants will do, and asks them to fill out the Self-help Contract on page 33. This contract asks whether they understand that the homework assignments are required, and whether they are willing to do self-help assignments between sessions. Participants should indicate how many minutes per day they are willing to spend doing the assignments. Individuals who will not make a clear-cut commitment to the self-help assignments when they complete this contract probably should not be permitted to participate in the program.

In my individual psychotherapy practice, I do not accept patients for treatment who indicate an unwillingness to do homework after reading and discussing a similar memo. Instead, I refer them to another therapist whose method and orientation are more compatible with their expectations.

Fortunately, this is a rare occurrence. The few who have chosen not to continue in therapy with me because of the homework requirement were severely disturbed and were not good candidates for an active approach such as cognitive-behavioral therapy.

In the first session, the participants will also fill out a self-assessment test beginning on page 31 called Fifteen GOOD Reasons for NOT Doing the Self-help Exercises. This test describes many reasons why they may not want to do the assignments. They are asked to check the attitudes that best describe the way they think and feel. This test can stimulate a productive group discussion about why some participants may resist doing homework.

The second thing you can do to encourage homework compliance is to spell out the assignments at the end of each step and review the participants' homework at the beginning of the subsequent step. This sends out a clear message that the homework is important, that you are interested in the participants' efforts, and that they are accountable for completing the assignments.

The third thing you can do to improve compliance is to implement the Deposit System described on page 25. With this system, the participants will earn money for attending the sessions on time and for doing the self-help assignments between sessions. Although you may feel idealistic and turned off by the Deposit System, I recommend it. It is fair and it makes the participants accountable in a tangible way. Money is powerful! You can use it creatively and constructively.

At the first session or at the preliminary screening, ask the participants if they have any misgivings about the homework requirement. Encourage people with doubts to discuss their concerns with you. Many participants may not realize that you will ask them to work hard during the sessions and between sessions.

This is not surprising, since our society loves passive forms of entertainment such as television. Many people want a quick and easy fix. The popular stereotype of psychotherapy depicted in the media is quite passive. People fantasize that therapy consists of free association or ventilation of feelings while lying on a couch, as a kindly, pipe-smoking therapist offers profound, illuminating insights. You need to make it clear that your skills are more humble than this, and that the type of program you are offering involves persistent hard work!

Although these measures do not guarantee subsequent compliance with homework assignments, they are a useful first step. If you spell out your expectations about homework assertively and clearly, participants will have the chance to decide whether your program is suitable for them.

Although your policy may differ, if people are not comfortable with making a commitment to attend regularly and do all the homework assignments, I suggest you encourage them to drop out before the first session. This position will empower you and establish clear boundaries that the participants will respect. (The same considerations apply to the other administrative issues on the checklist at the end of the history form on page 226.)

If any participants drop out at the beginning due to the homework requirements, you can give them a list with some alternative referrals, including psychiatrists and psychologists in your community; free self-help groups such as Alcoholics Anonymous, Emotions Anonymous, or Recovery, Inc.; or community mental health clinics. Obviously, any fee they paid for the remainder of the program should be refunded.

PARTICIPANT'S CONSENT FORM

You can ask all participants to sign a consent form prior to or during the first session. This form tells them about the nature of the group and asks whether they will agree to participate along the lines that are described. Two sample consent forms are contained in Appendix D beginning on page 230. Participant Agreement A refers to the Deposit System; Participant Agreement B does not.

LENGTH OF THE SESSIONS

This is flexible and depends on the type of clients you will be working with as well as your setting. I would recommend a minimum of one and a half hours per session, and a maximum of two and a half hours.

If you are running a group for severely disturbed individuals on an inpatient ward of a mental hospital, you may have to schedule even shorter groups because of the limited attention span of some of the patients. In this case, you will have to compromise on the amount of material you can hope to cover in any one session. Instead of trying to get across many exciting ideas in an hour-and-a-half to two-hour session, you may have to focus on getting across just one idea in a one-hour session. In addition, the techniques and ideas may have to be simplified if your patients have little formal education or are severely disturbed. (See page 34 for a discussion of how to do this.)

If your group meets for an extended period, you can schedule a coffee or stretching break halfway through. This break will give the members a chance to unwind and talk informally with each other.

Outpatient groups can meet at any time, but 7:00 to 9:00 P.M. weekdays is ideal. Saturday mornings and Sunday afternoons are also good options.

THE LENGTH OF THE PROGRAM

Ten Days to Self-esteem consists of ten sessions that are called steps. You will see that the agenda for each session is jam-packed. If you have the chance, you can extend the program to fifteen or twenty sessions. This might be possible if you are offering it in a school, prison, outpatient clinic, or nursing home where time is not limited. This will give you more time to do more of the exercises and the role playing. The participants will also have more time to talk and to share their feelings and ideas about all that they are learning.

In an inpatient setting, you will also have to adjust to the rapid turnover of patients. Since a newly admitted patient could join the group at any point in the program, I have created each session so it can stand on its own. Although one would ideally participate in the program from beginning to end (Step 1 through Step 10), this is not absolutely necessary.

You can make the program effective in practically any setting if you modify it with the spirit of flexibility, creativity, and compassion. Although in some settings you may have to settle for less than what you ideally want, the impact of what you do offer can nevertheless be extremely positive. Sometimes just one idea can have a big impact on someone's life.

PROCESS GROUPS VS. PSYCHOEDUCATIONAL GROUPS

Ten Days to Self-esteem is a psychoeducational program, because you will be teaching specific skills and ideas in a systematic manner. This is unlike a more traditional "process therapy" group, in which there is no specific agenda or theme for each session and no homework. In a process therapy group, the members are encouraged to share their feelings and interact with one another. These spontaneous interactions become a major focus of the treatment.

In a psychoeducational group, the aims are quite different. You will have a *full* agenda at every meeting, with many exciting ideas and techniques to teach. You will find it difficult to complete the agenda for each step, even if you are selective and move along rapidly.

There are several predictable problems in every group that can slow you down and cause you to wander from your agenda. The first problem is the tendency of many group members to want to talk at great length about their own personal problems.

This difficulty is complicated by the equally distracting problem of other members who will want to assume the role of "helper." These "helpers" will offer all kinds of advice to the members who describe personal problems. This intense and unproductive relationship between one person who is committed to complaining and remaining stuck and another person who is addicted to saving the disturbed one is sometimes called codependency.

How can you reconcile your need to stick to the agenda with the legitimate needs of the members to relate to each other and to talk about their feelings and problems? One approach is to budget some time at the beginning of each step for ventilation and sharing. You can encourage the members to say anything they want for a fifteen- or thirty-minute period. Keep in mind that if you do this, you may need to extend the length of each session. Many self-help groups, such as Alcoholics Anonymous, discourage the members from commenting on what anyone says during this period of sharing. This policy prevents excessive interactions among the members. It also makes it easier for some members to open up, since they know that no one will play the role of therapist or say anything judgmental.

Regardless of which approach you use, the important thing is to allow a modest but reasonable amount of time for members to talk and open up. They will need to share and receive emotional support. This will enhance feelings of trust and hope, which will promote healing. However, you will need to keep this limited and maintain the proper balance between ventilation of feelings and learning specific techniques through hard work and personal effort.

You will notice that there are many structured exercises for each step in the participant's workbook. It will be easy for the participants to complete these exercises successfully because they will be working on someone else's problems. They will be more objective when they are not personally involved. It is easier to see someone else's irrationality than to recognize your own.

These exercises will give the members mastery experiences and will systematically build up their skills as they progress through the program. This will make it easier for them to apply the techniques successfully when they work on their own negative thinking patterns. Their success with the structured exercises will create an upbeat feeling that will inspire confidence and enthusiasm.

When you demonstrate the techniques, you will at times focus on the personal problems of the members of the group. In the participant's workbook, they are advised that it is usually more difficult to change their own negative thinking patterns because it is harder to see one's own irrationality than someone else's. Nevertheless, you will sometimes run into the problem of resistance when the members are working on their own negative thinking patterns. They may say, "Oh, that doesn't work," or "I still feel like I'm a loser."

If you get into a debate or power struggle with a member who feels stuck or who becomes oppositional, it may make you look inept. The other members may become frustrated or demoralized. It is often preferable simply to say something like this:

> You know, it's often really hard to turn your Negative Thoughts around at first. Sometimes it seems like all those Negative Thoughts are absolutely true and you feel like things will never change. In fact, the hopelessness is one of the worst symptoms of depression. How many of the rest of you sometimes feel stuck or hopeless?

Of course, many hands will go up. Then you can ask how they think and feel when life seems hopeless. This will create a feeling of group unity, sharing, and support instead of a debate. You can reassure them that with patience and persistence, nearly everyone can develop self-esteem once again.

GROUP DYNAMICS

Some knowledge of group dynamics will be helpful for group leaders. If you have had any experience with groups, this will make it easier for you to keep things moving smoothly. If you have not had any group training, you may wish to seek some supervision from a colleague.

You will need to think about how to handle certain predictable difficulties that can occur in any group. You may have to deal with the individual who tries to monopolize the discussion, the individual who says "yes, but," the individual who is afraid to speak up, the individual who feels disappointed because all his or her expectations are not being met, the "helper" who continually gives advice to others, the discouraged member who needs an occasional pat on the back, the complainer who continually insists on how bad life is, the competitor who tries to take over your role of leader, the angry or mistrustful individual who attacks and sabotages the group's morale, and the passive, dependent member who fails to do the homework.

Most group leaders will already be familiar with these problems in their roles as psychiatrists, psychologists, counselors, social workers, nurses, or clergy. These issues will not be discussed in detail in this manual. When you feel concerned about the dynamics of the group, I would strongly urge you to consult a colleague. The suggestions you receive can be surprisingly helpful.

You may want an assistant leader or co-leader who helps you direct the sessions. You can meet with your assistant after each session and discuss what worked and didn't. These discussions will nearly always give you good ideas on how to correct any difficulties and make the next session more rewarding. You may wish to discuss your concerns and proposed solutions with the group at the beginning of the next session. This will allow the group members to participate in the problem-solving process and will encourage them to ventilate any concerns they may be afraid to express.

The following two sources will also give you suggestions on how to deal with resistant, uncooperative participants:

1. "Managing Difficult Behaviors," in *Preparing, Designing and Leading Workshops,* by Susan Cooper and Cathy Heenan (Boston: C.B.I. Publishing Co., 1980).

2. "How to Deal with Difficult Patients," Part VI (Chapters 24–27) in *The Feeling Good Handbook,* by David D. Burns, M.D. (New York: Plume, 1990).

PROFESSIONAL VS. LAY LEADERS

At the current time, only qualified mental health professionals should run Ten Days to Self-esteem groups as therapy groups. However, it is possible that compassionate and dedicated lay leaders who work in conjunction with a responsible self-help organization such as the National Depressive and Manic Depressive Association (NDMDA) can run these groups effectively as support groups. (The NDMDA has chapters throughout the country. For information about chapters in your area, write to the organization at 730 N. Franklin Street, Suite 501, Chicago, Illinois 60610. You can also call toll free at 1-800-826-3632.)

I am currently collaborating with Dr. Bob Neimeyer and his associates at Memphis State University in a study to compare the effectiveness of groups run by mental health professionals with groups run by members of the local chapter of the NDMDA. In this study, mental health professionals will screen all the participants and will provide consultation to the lay leaders in case of emergencies or other difficulties. Although this study is still in progress, I would not be surprised if the groups run by lay leaders prove to be as helpful as the groups run by mental health professionals.

The advantage of groups run by lay leaders who are members of local self-help groups is that these groups can be absolutely free of charge, just like AA. This could make these techniques available to huge numbers of people who cannot afford psychotherapy, as well as those who are reluctant to seek therapy.

On the other hand, there is the very real danger that the techniques could backfire if the group leader has not been properly trained. Because of these concerns, I recommend that the groups be conducted only under the supervision of qualified mental health professionals until we gain further information about other applications through systematic, responsible research.

TRAINING FOR GROUP LEADERS

It is desirable for group leaders to have some training in cognitive behavioral therapy. We are currently developing one-week training programs for group leaders at the Presbyterian Medical Center of Philadelphia. If you are a qualified mental health professional or educator and you would like to learn more about these programs, please write to me at the address on page 235.

BE CREATIVE! HOW TO DEVELOP THE PROGRAM FOR SPECIAL POPULATIONS

Some people think that only very intelligent, sophisticated adults can benefit from cognitive behavioral therapy. Nothing could be further from the truth! These techniques can be applied successfully to virtually any population in a wide variety of settings. This is because the basic principles of cognitive behavioral therapy apply to people of all ages, cultures, and walks of life. However, you may have to adapt the techniques, language, and format of the groups if you are working with

- severely disturbed or psychotic individuals
- the elderly
- children and adolescents
- individuals with minimal education who are psychologically unsophisticated
- individuals with strong ethnic or religious identifications

This may require some imagination and creativity but can be very rewarding. My colleagues and I have experienced considerable success in pilot studies with this program in many different outpatient and inpatient settings.

Our first application of the program was at The Residence, a short-term residential facility at the Presbyterian Medical Center that specializes in the treatment of individuals with "dual diagnosis"—drug abuse plus significant psychiatric disability. Most of the patients receive public medical assistance and many have had little formal education.

Although we were not confident that the methods would be helpful in this setting, the program has been extremely rewarding. Patients at The Residence participate in several cognitive-therapy group sessions per day, making for an intensive therapy experience.

Although I expected the patients to have problems that were quite different from those in my private practice, I was surprised to find that there were very few differences. The concerns and problems were the same as those I encounter every day. Some patients were concerned about the lack of employment. Some felt inferior because they had not achieved a great deal in life. One man said he was angry because he had been treated in a condescending way at the welfare office. I told him that I had sometimes been treated that way, too, and asked how many people in the group sometimes got angry at how others treated them. Nearly every hand went up.

Many patients were concerned about problems in their families and love relationships. A woman named Charlene described calling her fiancé one night when she was upset and needed support. He said he'd come and see her. When he was walking to her apartment, he was struck by a hit-and-run driver and his legs were mangled. Charlene had enormous grief and guilt and was telling herself, "It's my fault because I called him. If I hadn't called, he never would have been crippled."

I asked how many people felt guilt about loved ones. Again, nearly every hand went up. A woman named Rita said that she felt guilty because she had relapsed and had to be hospitalized again. Rita said she felt like a bad mother and was afraid her children would hate her and feel abandoned.

I was surprised to discover that many of these hospitalized patients were easier to work with than those in my outpatient practice, even though the patients at The Residence had extremely severe levels of depression and anxiety. Most of them had never had a chance to get exposure to effective, compassionate treatment before coming to The Residence, and they seemed eager to learn. Many improved quite rapidly.

For example, I asked Rita, who was self-critical about her relapse, to sit on a chair in the middle of the circle facing a woman named Janice. I told Rita to imagine that Janice was just like her, and felt like a bad mother because she had been hospitalized for depression and had to be separated from her kids. I told Rita to say the same things out loud to Janice that she'd been thinking about herself. I said, "Tell her that she's a bad mother, that her children will hate her, and so forth."

Rita resisted, and protested that she'd *never* say things like that to someone else, because they were mean and not really true. She said she wouldn't want to hurt anybody by saying things like that.

Then I asked, "What would you say to Janice?" Rita said that she would reassure Janice that her children did love her and emphasize that getting treatment was the responsible thing to do.

Then I asked, "If you wouldn't want to hurt someone else, would you be willing to stop hurting yourself? Would you be willing to talk to yourself in the same compassionate way you would talk to a friend who was depressed?" Then Rita and Janice role-played this situation for several minutes with a number of role reversals. At the end, Rita reported a dramatic change in her thinking and in her mood, which I confirmed by having her take a depression self-assessment test. The scores confirmed that during the role playing her depression score fell from 39 (indicating an extremely severe level of depression) to 11 (which is just slightly above the range considered normal). In my outpatient practice, this amount of improvement often requires weeks or months of intensive treatment.

Following the session, a man named Charles asked to speak to me confidentially. He said he had AIDS and was concerned that other people might look down on him if they found out. For about three minutes, we role-played how to handle these concerns using the Feared Fantasy technique. I told Charles that I would play him, and he could play the role of a group of imaginary people who were rejecting him in the most brutal way because he had AIDS. I showed him how to deflect the criticisms without getting defensive or upset.

This was a real eye-opener for Charles, since no one had ever shown him how to handle criticism or rejection, and he did very well in a role reversal. Then we briefly talked about the idea that whoever you are and whatever your station in life—whether you are African-American or white, Jewish or Moslem or Christian, tall or short—some people will like you and others will not. This is something we all have to deal with.

Charles found this interaction very helpful. It was also very rewarding for me, since he was very warm and eager to learn. His depression score fell from 17—indicating a mild level of depression—to 8, which is in the normal range.

Because of the success of the program at The Residence, the hospital administration wanted similar programs developed on several additional inpatient units, including Wright 5. This locked ward specializes in the treatment of the most severely psychotic, disturbed patients. Many are psychotic and hallucinating at the time of admission. Very few of these patients have private insurance and many have only a grammar school or high school education. They are frequently confused and very concrete in their thinking and have a short attention span, especially when first admitted. George Collette, the director of therapies at the unit, and Bruce Zahn, director of psychological services at the Presbyterian Medical Center, have done a brilliant job of adapting the program on Wright 5. Many of these patients enjoy the groups greatly.

For example, in one of the sessions the patients identify the distorted thinking patterns that lead to depression and anxiety. One of these distorted thinking patterns is called jumping to conclusions. There are two basic types. "Mind reading" is the belief that others are looking down on you when you have no definite evidence. This distortion is common among people with social anxiety as well as depression. "Fortune-telling" is the tendency to predict that bad things will happen when you have no definite evidence. Fortune-telling is common among people who feel hopeless ("I'll never get better; I'll be depressed forever") as well as people with anxiety and phobias ("If I get on that plane it will probably crash").

To introduce this distortion on Wright 5, the patients were seated at a table and asked to write something nice about each of the other group members on pieces of paper. Then each patient collected all the comments about himself or herself and placed them in an envelope without looking at them.

George Collette, the group leader, asked all the patients to guess what the others had written about them. Because many of these patients were acutely schizophrenic and severely depressed, most of them imagined that the other patients had said very negative things about them. Typical comments were:

Most people don't like me because they think I think I'm better than they are.

People are just trying to be friendly to me so they can trick me out of the rights to my gold mine.

Then they opened their envelopes, one by one, and read the contents out loud. They were all quite taken aback by the warm and complimentary comments the others had written about them. These are typical:

Carol is a kind and friendly person. She's always willing to listen when I feel bad.

John is very quiet. He always helps me if I have a question or a problem.

This exercise, which is almost on the level of a psychotherapeutic game, has two beneficial results. First, the patients feel good, as we all do, to hear so many compliments all at once. Second, the exercise demonstrates just how irrational our negative thoughts can be when we are feeling inadequate and depressed.

At the end of the exercise, the leader asked the patients to talk about times when they felt inferior or believed that people were talking about them or looking down on them. If you were doing this exercise with children or adolescents, you could even bring in a tall, pointed fortune-teller's hat decorated with stars and half-moons. Ask if any of them are really mind readers or fortune-tellers and want to wear it!

George Collette recently received a heartwarming thank-you letter from a schizophrenic man who had been discharged from the unit. Although this man had attended only two of the Ten Days to Self-esteem sessions during his brief admission, he emphasized how helpful the experience had been. In fact, he was overflowing with gratitude and admiration.

This type of enthusiastic response means a great deal to the morale of the staff. They can easily become burned out when working with disadvantaged people who have severe and chronic disorders, such as drug addiction and schizophrenia. A small ray of hope and optimism can often make a large difference.

Because of the success of these groups on Wright 5, we have also begun to introduce Ten Days to Self-esteem on WestHaven. This is a long-term residential facility for very severe, chronic schizophrenics in the Presbyterian Medical Center. Many of these clients will be living on this unit indefinitely. Most of them are poor and have very little education. Many also have extremely difficult social backgrounds, including drug abuse. You might think that cognitive therapy could *never* be helpful for a group like this.

Nevertheless, the preliminary experience with the groups on this unit has also been extremely encouraging. The first group, which was conducted by George Collette and Bruce Zahn, was called "Hey, George!" At the beginning of the group, Bruce and George acted out a scene that might occur in a moderately rough business district in downtown Philadelphia. They pretended to be walking down opposite sides of the street when Bruce called out, "Hey, George!" George did not respond and continued walking down the street.

At this point, Bruce and George asked the members what they would have been thinking if they had been the one who called out, "Hey, George!" How would they interpret the fact that George ignored them? A number of the patients had very negative thoughts, such as these:

1. George is avoiding me because he thinks I'm soliciting him for prostitution.

2. George thinks I'm trying to sell him drugs or get money from him.

3. George thinks I said something bad about him and he's holding it against me. He's ignoring me on purpose.

Others had responses that were not so negative:

4. Maybe George didn't hear me.

5. Maybe George is worrying about something and not paying attention to what's going on.

After all the members had a chance to say how they would interpret the event, Bruce and George pointed out that they couldn't *all* be right, since they all had different theories about why George did not respond. Then the leaders asked, "How could you find out? What experiment could you do to see whether or not your interpretation is true?" Several group members came up with the idea that they would have to talk to George to find out.

Then they asked the group members to process the experience. What had they learned? What was the point of it? What did they like and dislike about this experience?

Although this might seem like a very humble demonstration, the group members were quite enthusiastic. Many of them said they enjoyed the role playing. One woman, who had a borderline personality disorder, said she had never before considered the possibility that her thoughts about a situation might sometimes be wrong. She had always simply assumed that her thoughts and feelings were true. Although this is a very obvious and basic concept, it can seem quite illuminating if you have never before considered it.

Bruce and George found the co-therapy model invaluable with this population. One of them focused on the content of the group while the other leader focused on the group process. If a schizophrenic patient began regressing and talking incoherently, one of the leaders reframed this and made an interpretation, such as "I wonder if you're feeling tired or upset with what we are talking about just now?" Often this jarred the patient, who again became engaged with the group. This co-therapist model also prevented the leaders from getting burned out, since one leader could take over when the other became stuck or encountered a logjam.

The "Hey, George!" session illustrates a number of principles that are important if you are working with adolescents or children, or with severely disturbed adults who have difficult mood disorders or schizophrenia:

1. Keep the sessions short.

2. Keep the sessions focused on one simple idea.

3. Make the sessions entertaining and fun.

4. Keep the clients actively engaged in the group so they are not just sitting and observing passively.

Remember that the principles of cognitive therapy apply to *all* human beings, not just to people who are especially brainy and sophisticated. No matter whom you are working with, you have to communicate these principles in language that your clients will understand. I believe strongly that good therapy involves education, persuasion, and communication. This is partly an entertainment business! Use illustrations, demonstrations, and metaphors that your members can understand and identify with. Allow yourself to be creative.

If you keep these ideas in mind, I believe you will be pleasantly surprised by how helpful and useful the groups can be for practically any population.

HOW TO PROMOTE AND ADVERTISE THE PROGRAM

Your outpatient groups will not be very effective if no one attends! You may need a marketing and public relations campaign to make people in your community aware of your Ten Days to Self-esteem program. As mental health professionals, many of us have been trained to express ourselves in the most boring way possible. We sometimes use big words and long, convoluted sentences when simple words and short sentences would be more vivid.

While you can usually get by with professional jargon in an academic environment, it tends to turn nearly everyone else off. People are constantly bombarded by short, grabby advertisements on television and radio. Unless your promotion stands out and appeals to people, it will be ignored. By the same token, you will want your promotion to be dignified and ethical. It is sometimes hard to find the proper balance.

On page 40 you will find a sample advertisement for Ten Days to Self-esteem aimed at the general public. Similar wording could appear in a newspaper, brochure, mailing, poster, or radio announcement. It could be accompanied by an artist's sketch of smiling faces or someone leaping in the air for joy. Notice that the wording is brief, upbeat, and understandable. You may want to modify the ad to make it more suitable for your audience. Try to maintain a bright and lively tone.

When people call for more information or come in for their screening interview, you can provide them with the program summary on pages 41–42, which describes the program in greater detail. This summary of Ten Days to Self-esteem will help them decide whether they want to make a commitment to the group.

TEN DAYS

── TO ──

SELF-ESTEEM

- Do you wake up dreading the day?
- Do you feel discouraged with what you've accomplished in life?
- Do you want greater self-esteem, productivity, and joy in daily living?

If so, you will benefit from this revolutionary way of brightening your moods *without drugs or lengthy therapy*. The only tools you will need are your own common sense and the easy-to-follow methods clearly spelled out in this innovative program developed by David D. Burns, M.D., a renowned psychiatrist and expert on mood problems.

In ten exciting group sessions you will learn

- how to defeat depression
- how to break out of a bad mood
- how to develop self-esteem, productivity, and joy in daily living

The groups will meet on ten consecutive Wednesdays from 7:00 to 9:00 P.M. beginning on January 27 at the Presbyterian Medical Center of Philadelphia. Call Bruce Zahn at 215-662-8955 for more information. **You owe it to yourself to feel good!**

FEELING GOOD FEELS WONDERFUL!

Ten Days to Self-esteem

Ten Days to Self-esteem is an innovative program that can help you develop greater self-esteem, productivity, and joy in daily living. The program was developed by David D. Burns, M.D., a clinical psychiatrist and one of the country's foremost authorities on mood and relationship problems. Ten Days to Self-esteem is not at all like traditional group therapy, where you just sit and talk about how you feel. Instead, you will receive systematic training in techniques that can help you change the way you think, feel, and behave. The ideas are based on common sense and are easy to apply.

This is some of what you will learn in each step:

Step 1: The Price of Happiness: You will learn how to measure your moods and define your goals for the program. Do you want greater self-esteem and better personal relationships? Do you want to learn how to break out of bad moods? You will discover the price you will have to pay to achieve these goals.

Step 2: You FEEL the Way You THINK: You will learn that negative feelings like guilt, anger, and depression do not actually result from the bad things that happen to you, but from the way you think about these events. This simple but revolutionary idea can change your life!

Step 3: You Can CHANGE the Way You FEEL: You will learn the difference between healthy and unhealthy feelings. Is healthy sadness the same as clinical depression? What's the difference between healthy and unhealthy anger? Between neurotic guilt and healthy remorse?

Step 4: How to Break Out of a Bad Mood: You will discover why you get so moody and learn how to brighten your moods when you're in a slump.

Step 5: The Acceptance Paradox: You will learn about two dramatically different mood-elevating techniques called Self-defense and the Acceptance Paradox. The Self-defense technique is based on Western religions and scientific thinking. In contrast, the Acceptance Paradox is based more on Eastern philosophies such as Buddhism. When used together, these two methods can transform the way you think and feel about yourself, the world, and the future.

Step 6: Getting Down to Root Causes: You will pinpoint self-defeating attitudes that have robbed you of happiness, productivity, and intimacy.

Step 7: Self-esteem—What Is It? How Do I Get It? In this step, you will learn the answers to these questions:

● When people say they have low self-esteem, what do they really mean?

● What are the consequences of low self-esteem?

● Can a person have too much self-esteem?

● What is the difference between self-esteem and self-confidence?

● Should you base your self-esteem on your accomplishments?

● Should you base your self-esteem on love and approval?

● How can you develop unconditional self-esteem?

Step 8: The Perfectionist's Script for Self-defeat: You will learn about the price perfectionists pay for this mind-set—along with the hidden benefits.

Step 9: A Prescription for Procrastinators: You will discover why people procrastinate and learn the strategies of people who are tremendously productive and creative.

Step 10: Practice, Practice, Practice! You will learn how to prevent future mood swings and enjoy greater happiness for the rest of your life. You will examine the similarities between what you have learned in this program and your own spiritual beliefs and values.

A Note of Caution
to Group Leaders

It will not always be possible—or even desirable—to complete every exercise in every step. If you try, you may appear too rigid and controlling. People may be turned off because they won't have the opportunity to ask questions and process what they are learning.

In any session, your group may suddenly become excited about an idea and want to discuss it for a while. When that happens, *go for it*, instead of steamrolling over them! Your job is to light a fire and to balance structured learning with spontaneous interaction. People need to learn the specific techniques, but they also need to open up so they can get personally involved and excited about what they are learning.

When you are planning each step, remember that the members will be working on their own between sessions, so you're not obligated to illustrate each and every exercise in every step. Choose the exercises that appeal to you the most and vary the program each time you run it. This will help you identify the teaching methods that work the best in your particular setting. You will find that some exercises create tremendous excitement, while others may be less effective. This trial-and-error process will allow you to develop your skills as a leader, and the overall quality of your program will improve over a period of time.

STEP 1

THE PRICE OF HAPPINESS

LEADER'S PREPARATION FOR STEP 1

Activity	Check (√) when done
1. Read the Introduction to the participant's workbook (*Ten Days to Self-esteem*).	
2. Read Step 1 beginning on page 17 of the participant's workbook.	
3. Study the Checklist for Step 1 on the next page of this *Leader's Manual* and the Tips for Leaders beginning on page 46.	
4. Read Chapters 1 and 2 of *The Feeling Good Handbook*.	

CHECKLIST FOR STEP 1

Activity	Optional or required?	Minimum time (min.)	Check (√) when done
1. Introduce yourself and the participants.	req.	5	
2. Discuss the participants' personal goals for Ten Days to Self-esteem.	req.	10–15	
3. Explain the administrative procedures and how to use the participant's workbook.	req.	10	
4. Interpret the participants' scores on the Burns Depression Checklist, the Burns Anxiety Inventory, and the Relationship Satisfaction Scale.	req.	10	
5. Discuss the importance of self-help assignments.	req.	15	
6. Discuss stressful events that can trigger depression or anxiety.	req.	10	
7. Do the exercise on helping vs. listening.	opt.	30+	
8. Ask for positive and negative feedback about Step 1.	req.	15	
9. Assign the homework for Step 2.	req.	3	

OVERVIEW OF STEP 1

The main focus of the first session is to clarify the structure of the group, to make sure each participant is aware that self-help exercises will be required, and to begin to develop rapport among the members of the group. These items are important, because recent research indicates that the active effort patients make on their own to change their negative thinking patterns and self-defeating behaviors can speed recovery considerably. In addition, patients who feel cared about and understood by their therapists (or by other people) typically make the biggest improvements, regardless of what school of therapy is being used.

First, you will break the ice by asking the members to introduce themselves. Next, ask the members to define their personal goals for the experience. You will find out how hard they are willing to work to accomplish these goals when you ask them to make a commitment to the self-help assignments between sessions. At the same time, you will make them aware of the many reasons they may have for resisting these assignments. You will also describe the Deposit System, explaining that the participants can earn points at each session for attending on time, for doing the self-help assignments between sessions, and for bringing along the participant's workbook, which is titled *Ten Days to Self-esteem*.

Then you will show the members how to interpret the three mood tests, which measure depression, anxiety, and relationship satisfaction, respectively. These three tests will help the members identify their own emotional and interpersonal problems and chart their progress from step to step.

Finally, you will encourage the participants to talk about some of the stressful events in their own lives. You will encourage them to share their feelings, ideas, and personal problems, and to give you specific negative and positive reactions at the end of every session.

TIPS FOR LEADERS

GETTING STARTED

After you introduce yourself, ask the group members to introduce themselves and describe briefly what they do and how they learned about the program.

Then ask the members about their goals for Ten Days to Self-esteem. Why are they here? What do they hope to accomplish? Suitable goals would include developing greater self-confidence and better personal relationships, overcoming depression, or learning to become more productive and less perfectionistic.

Ask them to write down their goals in the participant's workbook on page 28. You will review these goals during the last session to see how much each member has accomplished.

You can record the members' goals on the flip chart or blackboard as they describe them. Many of their goals will fall into one of three categories:

1. **Personal:** The participants will develop greater productivity and joy in daily living.

2. **Interpersonal:** They will get the chance to open up and to get to know others in a trusting and friendly atmosphere.

3. **Philosophical and spiritual:** They will examine their own personal philosophies and develop more positive and realistic attitudes and values.

You should be a little suspicious about any member who cannot write down any personal goals for the group, as well as any member with goals that sound vague or insincere. Although such an individual may simply feel shy or nervous when put on the spot, it is also possible that he or she does not really want to be here or has a hidden agenda to sabotage the group. Maybe someone else coerced that person to join the group. If in doubt, you can explore these issues with that member individually after the session. As a general rule, people should not be encouraged to continue with the group if they do not seem reasonably motivated to be there.

If they received the participant's workbook for Ten Days to Self-esteem ahead of time, ask how many people read the Introduction and Step 1. Ask what they liked and disliked about this material. Was there anything they did not understand or disagreed with? Was there anything that was particularly helpful or interesting? Ask how many of the people who did the reading actually wrote things down on the pages and filled out the three self-assessment tests. This will give you an immediate reading of how compliant or resistant your group may be! You will discuss resistance to the self-help assignments in depth later in today's session.

Emphasize that this program is designed to help the members with *their own* mood problems. They should *not* try to apply these techniques to others, because the methods will backfire. For example, if a man in the group points out his wife's distorted thinking patterns during an argument, she will simply become angrier! You can remind the participants that they will learn how to solve difficulties in personal relationships in the forthcoming module on communication and intimacy.

ADMINISTRATIVE ISSUES

Explain the group's administrative procedures, including the fees and the Deposit System. Answer any questions the participants may have about the procedures or purposes of the group.

Emphasize that the participants will be learning general principles and techniques, and that you will not be doing extensive individual therapy during the sessions, except for the purpose of demonstrating how the techniques work. However, you anticipate that many of them will experience significant improvements in their self-esteem and outlook on life as a result of their participation in the group.

As you discuss these issues, it is important to allow participants to raise their own questions and concerns. Try to respond in an open and empathic way without getting defensive. Suppose, for example, that a participant provokes you by saying, "My other therapist is a psychoanalyst. She said that cognitive therapy is just a Band-Aid and we need to get at the deeper issues." How would you respond to this criticism? Write down your answer here before you read on!

_____

_____

_____

_____

_____

Did you do it? No? Hey, I'm a little disappointed! How do you expect your clients to do the written assignments if you aren't willing to do them yourself? Remember the biblical passage "Physician, heal thyself." This applies to all therapists, not just physicians! Now, go back and write down the most effective response you can think of. Then you can turn to page 66 to see how I would typically respond to a confrontational client.

DESCRIPTION OF THE PARTICIPANT'S WORKBOOK

Remind the group members to bring *Ten Days to Self-esteem* to each session. Ask them to open the book to the Table of Contents. Point out that at the beginning of each of the ten steps they will find three self-assessment tests called the Burns Depression Checklist, the Burns Anxiety Inventory, and the Relationship Satisfaction Scale. (For example, the depression test for the first step can be found on page 21 of the participant's workbook.) Tell them to take these three tests *before* every group session to monitor their progress. They can report their total scores to you at the beginning of each session.

Explain that each step in the workbook contains a description of the ideas and techniques they will learn at that session. They should read each step and do as many of the exercises as possible *before* the session. If they feel intrigued by a topic and want to do some supplementary reading, they can find suggestions at the end of each step below the list of self-help assignments. (For example, the supplementary reading for Step 1 appears on page 36 of *Ten Days to Self-esteem*.) The complete references for the recommended reading appear on page 317 of the participant's workbook.

Remind the participants that this is a workbook and they should write in it. In fact, this written homework is an important part of the program. The more they write in their workbooks, the better.

The Appendix beginning on page 273 of *Ten Days to Self-esteem* contains several extra copies of all of the self-help forms and self-assessment tests, along with brief instructions on how to use them. Tell the participants that they should *always leave one copy of each form in the Appendix blank*. Then they can reproduce these forms any time they need additional copies. They may need numerous copies of forms that they find especially useful, such as the Daily Mood Log.

Although this warning to leave one copy of each form blank is spelled out in the Appendix instructions, most people will *not* read it or pay attention to it. That is why you will need to reinforce this idea in the first session.

SELF-ASSESSMENT TESTS

If they have not already done so, all the participants should fill out the Burns Anxiety Inventory, the Burns Depression Checklist, and the Relationship Satisfaction Scale at this time. Give them about two minutes for each test. These three tests can be found on pages 21, 23, and 27 of the participant's workbook. Ask them to total their scores on each test. Explain that the scoring keys for these three tests can be found on pages 22, 25, and 28 of the participant's workbook.

Encourage the members of outpatient groups to take all three tests once or twice each week so they can chart their progress. If you are conducting the groups in an inpatient psychiatric hospital setting or a day treatment program, then the participants should take these tests once a day.

This focus on the precise measurement of progress throughout the treatment is one of the keystones of cognitive therapy. There are many reasons for using good assessment devices throughout the therapy. One reason is that some clients do a good job of disguising their feelings and therapists often cannot very easily estimate how well their clients are doing. I recently treated a professional woman who said she'd been pretty unhappy since childhood. She was attractively groomed, personable, and extremely enthusiastic about the treatment. In spite of her chipper appearance, her scores on the Burns Depression Checklist revealed extraordinary levels of depression and active suicidal impulses. Had I relied on my clinical judgment, I would have been way off base in assessing how she really felt inside.

A second reason for session-by-session measurement is that it can show you precisely how much people are improving, and how much they have recovered by the end of therapy. This is a form of consumer advocacy that keeps therapists honest, because feeling better inside is what nearly all clients really want.

If we tell ourselves that a client is making great strides but the scores on the tests do not reflect this improvement, then we are probably fooling ourselves. An honest assessment of the client's scores can tell you when your therapy is right on target, and when a change of strategy may be needed.

Clinical experience indicates that these instruments are well received by clients, and statistical analysis confirms they are surprisingly accurate. For example, Cronbach's coefficient alpha, a statistical measure of the reliability of a psychological instrument, is .97 for both the Burns Anxiety Inventory and the Relationship Satisfaction Scale. This means that these tests measure how the client is actually feeling within a 3% range of error. Although I have not done a statistical analysis of the Burns Depression Checklist, other similar tests, such as the Beck Depression Inventory, are widely accepted in the research journals as valid and accurate measures of a depressed individual's mood.

The idea of using weekly or daily self-assessment tests is still somewhat new, and this practice is rapidly gaining the approval of many mental health professionals, as well as accrediting agencies such as the Joint Commission on Accreditation of Healthcare Organizations (JCAHO). For example, there was a site visit by the JCAHO to The Residence at the Presbyterian Medical Center of Philadelphia, shortly after we had developed Ten Days to Self-esteem on this unit. The psychiatrist who conducted the evaluation was favorably impressed and specifically commented on the value of requiring all patients to complete the three mood tests in their workbooks every day so that progress (or the lack of it) could be measured objectively. In fact, he said he wished that every psychiatric facility in the country would adopt a similar approach! The Residence subsequently received Accreditation with Commendation, the top level of certification granted by the JCAHO.

These three mood tests will be part of the participants' self-help assignments outside of the group. You can ask them to report their scores to you confidentially at the beginning of each meeting. You can record this information on the Leader's Data Sheet on pages 69–72. This will help you track the progress of each member of the group. You can also record whether they attended on time and how much of the homework assignment they completed, using the rating scale described on page 68.

If you are using the Deposit System described on page 25, the Leader's Data Sheet will make it easy to calculate how much money each member has earned by the end of the program. You can also analyze the data at the end of the program so you can answer questions such as these:

- How much actual improvement in depression, anxiety, and personal relationship satisfaction did the participants experience during the program?

- Did the individuals who attended consistently and who worked the hardest between sessions experience the greatest improvement?

- How many of the participants completed the program, and how many dropped out prematurely?

- How many participants are still depressed and in need of more therapy?

Interpreting the Burns Depression Checklist (BDC)

The fifteen items on the BDC evaluate the most common symptoms of depression, such as sadness, hopelessness, and low self-esteem. Review the BDC on page 21 of the participant's workbook now. Participants are asked if they have been feeling each symptom in the past few days, on a scale ranging from "Not at all" (scored 0) to "A lot" (scored 3). Total scores on the BDC can range from 0 (the best possible score) to 45 (the worst possible score). The scoring key on page 51 will help you interpret scores on this test.

This test is like an emotional thermometer. It measures how bad people feel. It does not diagnose *types* of depression or identify the *causes* of the depression.

SCORING KEY FOR THE BURNS DEPRESSION CHECKLIST

Total score	Degree of depression	Action
0 – 4	happy, with no depression	No treatment is usually needed.
5 – 10	normal but unhappy	
11 – 20	borderline to mild depression	Treatment is usually recommended.
21 – 30	moderate depression	Treatment is almost always needed.
31 – 45	severe depression	
Note: Anyone who answers 1 or above on item 15 of the BDC may be feeling suicidal.		

When you record the total scores on the BDC on the Leader's Data Sheet, keep your eye on the way each participant answered item 15, which asks about suicidal impulses. Scores of 1 or above indicate some suicidal urges, and scores of 2 or 3 may indicate moderate to strong suicidal impulses. You will need to ask about this. People who feel depressed often feel discouraged and have thoughts that life is not worth living, but they usually have no actual intention of committing suicide. However, some participants may be struggling with the urge to act on these feelings.

You can ask the participants if they feel hopeless and if they have an active desire to make a suicide attempt. Ask if they have a specific plan, if they have the means to carry it out (such as sleeping pills or a gun), if they have a strong desire to live, if they have a past history of suicide attempts, and so forth. If the answers to these questions suggest that they may be considering a suicide attempt, then you must take appropriate action. Immediate individual therapy and/or hospitalization may be needed. When in doubt, it is wise to obtain expert consultation from a colleague who specializes in mood disorders. Be sure to document your assessment and the rationale for your actions so that you will be protected legally.

I have developed a two-page Suicide Assessment Sheet, which begins on page 53. Feel free to photocopy it so that you will have copies available in case you need them.

Although the Suicide Assessment Sheet cannot guarantee a perfectly accurate assessment of suicidal impulses, it will help to protect you and your clients. You are not legally required always to be right—but it is important to document a responsible, thorough assessment in the client's chart.

Pages 40 to 41 of *The Feeling Good Handbook* provide further information on how to evaluate suicidal impulses. You can also review the comments on this topic on page 21 of this *Leader's Manual*.

Interpreting the Burns Anxiety Inventory (BAI)

The thirty-three items on the BAI evaluate the most common symptoms of anxiety and panic, such as worry, fears of dying, and a racing heart. Patients are asked if they have been feeling this way in the past few days, on a scale ranging from "Not at all" (scored 0) to "A lot" (scored 3). Total scores on the BAI can range from 0 (the best possible score) to 99 (the worst possible score).

This scoring key will help you interpret scores on this test.

SCORING KEY FOR THE BURNS ANXIETY INVENTORY

Total score	Degree of anxiety	Action
0 – 4	minimal or no anxiety	No treatment is usually needed.
5 – 10	borderline anxiety	
11 – 20	mild anxiety	Treatment is usually optional.
21 – 30	moderate anxiety	Treatment is usually needed.
31 – 50	severe anxiety	
51 – 99	extreme anxiety or panic	

Interpreting the Relationship Satisfaction Scale (RSAT)

The RSAT evaluates how satisfied a person feels about his or her most intimate relationship. It is suitable for heterosexual or homosexual relationships. Although this test assesses a person's marriage or most intimate relationship, it can also be used to evaluate a relationship with a friend, family member, or colleague. If the participant does not have any intimate relationship at this time, he or she can simply think of people in general when taking the test. This test will help you identify group members who do not feel cared about and close to others.

The seven items on the RSAT ask about seven basic relationship areas, such as communication and openness, resolving conflicts and arguments, and the degree of affection and caring in the relationship. For each item, patients are asked how satisfied they have recently been feeling on a six-point scale, with response options ranging from "Very dissatisfied" (scored 0) to "Very satisfied" (scored 6). Total scores on the RSAT can range from 0 (the worst possible satisfaction score) to 42 (the best possible score).

The scoring key on page 55 will help you interpret the Relationship Satisfaction Scale.

SUICIDE ASSESSMENT SHEET*

Name		Date	
	Not at all	Somewhat	Moderate	A lot
Degree of hopelessness				
Desire to live				
Desire to die				
Actual suicidal impulses?				
Are these impulses hard to resist?				
Any deterrents? What are they? Are they strong?				
Any previous suicide attempts?				
Any suicidal plans?				
Has he or she decided on a method?				
Any preparation (e.g., obtained a gun or sleeping pills)?				
Has he or she made a specific plan?				

SUICIDE ASSESSMENT SHEET (Continued)

Any current alcohol or drug abuse?	
Does this individual desire hospitalization?	
Will this individual call if he or she feels suicidal?	
Does this individual have a support network?	
Does he or she seem reliable?	

Conclusions and recommendations

SCORING KEY FOR THE RELATIONSHIP SATISFACTION SCALE

Total score	Level of satisfaction	Action
0 – 15	extremely dissatisfied	Therapy is usually needed.
16 – 25	moderately dissatisfied	
26 – 30	somewhat dissatisfied	
31 – 35	somewhat satisfied	Therapy is usually optional.
36 – 40	moderately satisfied	No therapy is usually needed.
41 – 42	very satisfied	

The RSAT does not measure how "good" or "adequate" any marriage or relationship is. It simply measures how satisfied or dissatisfied a person feels with the relationship.

The guidelines for therapy in the right-hand column of this key should be treated more flexibly than the guidelines for treating depression and anxiety. Some people may be satisfied with very low scores on the relationship test because they do not desire greater intimacy, whereas other people with high scores may want to make their relationships even better.

It is useful to monitor relationship satisfaction in Ten Days to Self-esteem because a lack of intimacy is one of the causes of depression. Nearly all of us feel discouraged when we do not feel cared about by others, and our moods tend to improve when we feel loved. Although this module is not intended to treat troubled relationships, a number of the participants will feel more positive about their relationships as they develop greater self-esteem. Members with low scores on this test would be excellent candidates for the forthcoming module on personal relationship problems.

All three tests appear at the beginning of each of the ten steps, so it will be easy for the participants to fill them out as they proceed through the program. Tell them that there are additional copies of the three tests in the Appendix (which begins on page 273 of the participant's workbook), along with a separate answer sheet for each of the three tests. These have been included in case members wish to continue taking the tests after the completion of the program.

SELF-HELP ASSIGNMENTS

The nature and purpose of the homework assignments are described in the section entitled The Price of Happiness beginning on page 29 of the participant's workbook. Ask the participants how they answered the four items in the Self-help Contract on page 33 of the participant's workbook. If they have not already answered these items, tell them to do so now.

If any participants appear ambivalent about the self-help assignments, this is an important time to deal with their concerns. Emphasize that these assignments are not optional but are requirements.

Let's suppose that a participant says that he or she will *try* to do the self-help assignments but feels overwhelmed because he or she already has too much to do. This participant may be a busy executive, a student, or the mother of five children. I would respond along these lines: "I can understand how pressured and overwhelmed you feel. It may not be good for you to participate in this group just yet. If you prefer, I would be happy to provide a referral list of excellent colleagues who do not require their patients to do homework between sessions.

"Of course, I hope you will decide to continue with Ten Days to Self-esteem. If you do, you should be aware that participants are not permitted to 'try' to do the homework. 'I will try' is usually just a polite way of saying that you are not really willing to do the homework just now. If you may feel that the self-help assignments are just too much for you, I would love to have you participate at some future time when you feel that you can do the self-help assignments."

Your way of delivering this message may differ, depending on your personality, the setting, and the type of group you are running. Regardless of how you say it, I feel it is crucial to get this message across. Your authority and commitment are being subtly challenged. If you give in, it could demoralize the group and you may lose control.

You should present this message in a friendly, respectful tone. Very few participants will choose to drop out, and most will respect you more because you have set clear, reasonable limits.

Homework Cost-Benefit Analysis

You can ask the members to complete a Homework Cost-Benefit Analysis together as a group. Draw a vertical line down the middle of your flip chart. Label the left-hand column "Advantages" and the right-hand column "Disadvantages," like the form on page 59. First, ask the members if they can think of any disadvantages of doing the self-help assignments between sessions. As they mention the disadvantages, such as "It takes time," or "It's boring," write them in the right-hand column of the flip chart.

If you like, you can ask the members to make a written list of the advantages and disadvantages of homework while you are conducting this exercise. Tell them to divide a piece of blank paper into two vertical columns by drawing a line down the middle from top to bottom, or you can photocopy the Homework Cost-Benefit Analysis form, which appears on page 59 of this *Leader's Manual*.

Then ask the members about the advantages of doing the homework. List them in the left-hand column of the flip chart. Tell the group to write the advantages on the Homework Cost-Benefit Analysis at the same time.

What are the benefits of doing the exercises? The participants might think about advantages like these:

- *I might learn a whole lot more.*
- *I might recover more quickly.*
- *It might make the group more interesting.*
- *I might feel more like a part of the group.*
- *I'll earn my deposit back!*

This exercise will get the participants used to the idea that they are to write things down in their workbooks. After they have listed the advantages and disadvantages, ask them which ones seem to be greater. Do the benefits outweigh the costs, or vice versa? Tell the participants to put two numbers that add up to 100 in the circles at the bottom of the Homework Cost-Benefit Analysis to indicate the results of their evaluation. For example, if the disadvantages of doing the homework assignments feel slightly greater, they might put a 40 in the left-hand circle and a 60 in the right-hand circle. If, in contrast, the advantages feel quite a bit greater, they might put a 65 in the left-hand circle and a 35 in the right-hand circle.

You can administer this exercise (as well as any other Cost-Benefit Analysis) in a straightforward way or in a paradoxical way. When you do a straightforward Homework Cost-Benefit Analysis, you assume that the advantages of homework are greater, and that this rational insight will motivate the participants. The straightforward technique is often sufficient for high-functioning, motivated individuals.

In contrast, when you do it in a paradoxical way, you assume that the disadvantages of homework are greater, but these disadvantages are hidden and repressed. For example, some participants will resist the homework because they feel angry and blame others for their problems. They feel like innocent victims and are strongly convinced that the world should change. Other participants may feel needy and dependent, and have the hidden agenda that others are supposed to care for them and magically solve their problems. Your goal when you do the exercise paradoxically is to bring this hidden resistance to conscious awareness. For uncooperative, unmotivated individuals, the paradoxical approach is often far more powerful.

If you choose the paradoxical approach, first get the group to list all the disadvantages of doing the homework. For example:

- *The self-help assignments will take time.*
- *I already have too much to do.*
- *It might not help.*
- *It might be confusing or frustrating.*
- *It's too hard.*
- *It's unfair that I should have to change, since my husband (or wife) is to blame for our problems.*
- *The homework is too mechanical.*

- *It's too much like being in school.*
- *It probably won't work anyway because I feel hopeless.*
- *It will be easier just to attend and get to know the other members.*
- *I'm basically a lazy person and I can't do things like this.*
- *I have too many other commitments right now.*

The key to the paradoxical approach is that you become the *advocate* of the members' resistance. You encourage them to come up with reasons for not doing the assignments and you cheer them on. Do not subtly imply that these are poor excuses or rationalizations.

Once they list all these reasons for not doing the assignments, you can say something along these lines: "It appears that you have lots of good reasons not to do the homework, and I can see that they are all pretty darn valid. I'm feeling puzzled—is there any reason for you to participate in these groups, since *lots* of homework will be required? Certainly there are other fine groups you could attend without this requirement. Of course, I strongly hope you will stay, since I would enjoy working with you. But that is just my own selfish motive. I want you to know that if you do decide to drop out now, you will get your entire deposit back with no penalty."

Reasons for Resisting Self-help Assignments

If they have not yet filled out the list of Fifteen GOOD Reasons for NOT Doing the Self-help Exercises on page 31, ask the the participants to do so now. Ask them to discuss their responses on these fifteen items. Pay particular attention to any attitudes they may have agreed with strongly.

You should not try too hard to persuade the members to do the self-help assignments. This will put you in the position of a salesperson, and they will simply resist. Your role is simply to uncover many of the reasons for resistance—such as dependency, feelings of hopelessness, a lack of belief in the program, or feelings of bitterness and entitlement. You can encourage them to express these feelings and empathize with them. However, the bottom line is that if they choose to stay, the assignments are required, not optional.

If the members do not feel they can do the exercises, or if they do not want to do them, then they can choose to leave the group and participate in some alternative form of therapy. If they choose to continue with the group but fail to do the assignments regularly, they will not earn back their deposits. Keep in mind that the deposit should be significant so that they will take it seriously.

LEADER'S DATA SHEET

On the Leader's Data Sheet on page 69 you can record whether the participants attended sessions on time and how much of the assigned homework they have completed since the last step. You can use a rating scale like this one to record how much homework they did:

HOMEWORK COST-BENEFIT ANALYSIS*

Advantages of doing the self-help assignments	Disadvantages of doing the self-help assignments

0—no homework at all

1—a minimal amount of homework, such as taking the self-assessment tests only

2—a moderate amount of homework, such as taking the tests and doing some of the reading and written assignments

3—nearly all the homework, including the reading, the self-assessment tests, and the written assignments

If you use the Deposit System, you can use the data on the Leader's Data Sheet to calculate how much money the participants have earned by the end of the ten steps. (They can earn up to 3 points for homework and up to 2 points for attending on time.) There are 50 possible points in the ten sessions. If they have given you a one-hundred-dollar deposit, then each point will be worth two dollars.

I would recommend that you also give out a bonus point for bringing the participant's workbook to each session. The members will need their workbooks for many of the exercises and it will be a great advantage if they have them available.

Notice that the Leader's Data Sheet contains extra columns before Step 1 to record the participants' initial scores on the three mood tests, in case you've done preliminary testing. In addition, there is a follow-up section after Step 10 in case you have the opportunity to obtain data from your clients after they have completed the program.

DISCUSSION OF STRESSFUL EVENTS

Encourage the members to discuss the kinds of stressful events that make them feel depressed or anxious. These could include difficulties such as criticism from a spouse or boss, rejection by a lover, a divorce, career reversals, concerns about health or aging, and problems with children or other family members. The goal of this discussion is to get the participants to open up and break the ice. The purpose is not to provide therapy or helpful advice, but simply to send out the signal that it is safe for them to share their problems and feelings openly in the group.

As the group leader, you can model the listening skills presented on page 61 of this *Leader's Manual*. Paraphrase what the members say and acknowledge their feelings. Suppose that a participant says her husband is never on time. You could say, "Thank you for sharing that. It can be really frustrating when that happens. You might feel sad, lonely, hurt, or angry. How do you feel when he's late?" This response illustrates the Disarming Technique, Feeling Empathy, and Inquiry. Notice that you have *not* given any advice or tried to help in any way.

Then, after she tells you that she feels unappreciated and unloved, you can say, "Do any other group members ever get upset with friends or family members who fail to follow through on their commitments?" Ask for a show of hands. Then ask if anyone else would like to describe a similar problem.

This type of response will keep the dialogue moving along and will make it easy for the members to contribute to the discussion. You won't get bogged down with any

THE THREE SECRETS OF EFFECTIVE LISTENING*

1. **The Disarming Technique.** You find some truth in what the other person is saying, even if it seems totally unreasonable or unfair.

2. **Empathy.** You put yourself in the other person's shoes and try to see the world through his or her eyes.
   - **Thought Empathy.** You paraphrase the other person's words.
   - **Feeling Empathy.** You acknowledge how he or she is probably feeling.

3. **Inquiry.** You ask gentle, probing questions to learn more about what the other person is thinking and feeling.

*Copyright © 1991 by David D. Burns, M.D., from *Ten Days to Self-esteem: The Leader's Manual*, copyright © 1993.

GOOD VS. BAD COMMUNICATION*

Bad communication	Good communication
1. **You fail to express your feelings**—instead, you pout or attack with "you" statements (such as "*You're* such a jerk!" or "*You're* making me mad!").	1. **You express your feelings openly and directly**—with "I feel" statements (such as "I'm feeling annoyed" or "I'm worried about you").
2. **You fail to acknowledge the other person's feelings**—instead, you blame or "help" or insist that the other person is wrong.	2. **You acknowledge the other person's feelings**—"You seem to be frustrated and sad. Are you?"
3. **Your attitude is not respectful**—instead, you sound patronizing, defensive, or hostile.	3. **Your attitude is respectful and caring**—even if you feel angry or upset.

*Copyright © 1992 by David D. Burns, M.D., from *Ten Days to Self-esteem: The Leader's Manual*, copyright © 1993.

participant who talks too much, and you will prevent the other participants from entering into time-consuming dialogues with members who describe their problems.

Most people enjoy open sharing in a group. Do not encourage participants to "help" or offer advice to the other members of the group. These "helpers" may be subconsciously competing with you for leadership. If you allow the participants to give each other advice, you will probably lose control of the group and end up feeling in a one-down position.

If members do offer advice, you can simply thank them politely. Explain that all they need to do is describe stressful events in their own careers or families, and that you will work on solutions to these problems later on.

Of course, you should watch out for this codependency tendency in yourself. Try to practice the three listening skills instead of giving advice on how to solve problems. Even though you may have the best intentions, helping often sounds intrusive. People will frequently resist what you say because you have not acknowledged how they feel inside.

Most people who feel angry, worried, or discouraged simply want someone to validate their feelings. When you resist the urge to help and use the three listening skills instead, you will paradoxically end up being very helpful, because they will feel understood.

OPTIONAL EXERCISE: HELPING VS. LISTENING

This exercise is quite challenging and you should be sure you have adequate time if you decide to pursue it. It may even require the lion's share of an entire session. You should also be aware that this is probably the most difficult exercise in the entire program. It is not described in the participant's workbook, so you can skip it the first time you run the program if you do not feel comfortable with the methods.

If you are familiar with the techniques and feel your group can handle them, this exercise can be extremely rewarding. When it is done properly, it is a great favorite and nearly always stirs up a great deal of excitement and involvement.

If you do this exercise, you may want to study Part IV (Chapters 18–22) of *The Feeling Good Handbook* first. These five chapters will clarify the techniques and the underlying principles you will be demonstrating in this exercise.

Ask for a volunteer to play the role of Betty; you will play the role of Mary. Tell Betty to complain about a problem in her life, like the one illustrated in the following script. (If you like, you can simply ask Betty to read her lines from your *Leader's Manual*.) Betty speaks first:

Betty: I feel really depressed because my son is smoking pot and getting D's and F's at school. I feel like it's my fault. I feel like I'm a bad mother.

You will play the role of Mary. Explain that Mary wants to cheer Betty up, so she replies:

Mary: You're not such a bad mother, you're a *good* mother. Raising kids can be difficult. I know you're doing the very best a person could do under the circumstances.

Ask them whether Mary's attempt to help Betty is an example of good or bad communication. Read the definitions of good and bad communication on page 61, or photocopy and distribute them. Review the three characteristics of good and bad communication one by one. The participants should be able to see why Mary's response is a prime example of bad communication:

- She has not expressed her own feelings. She may be feeling concerned or frustrated with Betty's complaining.

- She has not acknowledged how upset Betty feels.

- Her attitude is patronizing and not respectful. She's talking down to Betty.

Although this analysis may seem obvious, many of the members of your group will have difficulties with this notion. They may find if difficult to resist getting into unproductive "helping" or "advice-giving" interactions with friends and family members who feel depressed.

Next, repeat the role playing this improved version of the Betty and Mary interaction. In this version, Mary will use active listening skills:

Betty: I feel really depressed because my son is smoking pot and getting D's and F's at school. I feel like it's my fault. I feel like I'm a bad mother.

Mary: I'm sure you must feel very worried about your son. Can you tell me a little more about what's going on?

Ask the group to discuss the differences between this dialogue the previous one. Is this a more effective way for Mary to respond? Why?

If time permits, you can break up the group into small teams of two or three members to practice the three listening skills described on page 61. One member can be "the complainer." He or she will say things such as "Life stinks," and "the listener" can respond with one of the three listening techniques. Here's a list of things the complainer can say:

They spend all our tax money on foreign aid, and the little guy never gets a break.

I've really got to get my life together. I don't know *what* to do. What should I do?

I lost my job. It's all politics.

My husband can't express his feelings. He's such a cold fish.

My hemorrhoids are aching and none of the doctors are doing anything about it.

Nobody *really* understands me or cares about me.

Each listener should try to use only *one* of the three listening skills when responding, beginning first with the Disarming Technique. After all the participants have mastered the Disarming Technique, then you can ask them to practice Thought Empathy and Feeling Empathy. Finally, they can practice responding with Inquiry.

You can emphasize that this is like karate practice, where you practice one technique at a time so that you can master it. Once the participants have learned each of the separate techniques separately, then they can integrate them so they will sound more natural.

When you do this exercise, the following structure will make it far more successful. Tell the participant who plays the role of the complainer that he or she is permitted to make only *one* complaint. After speaking once, the complainer is not allowed to say anything else or to enter into a dialogue with the person who plays the role of the listener.

Tell the participant who plays the role of the listener that he or she is permitted to make only *one* response. After speaking once, the listener is not allowed to say anything else or to enter into a dialogue with the person who plays the role of the complainer.

After this one exchange, ask the complainer and the other members to critique what the listener said according to these criteria:

1. Did he or she use the listening skills properly?

2. Did the listener avoid helping or giving advice?

3. Did the response sound natural and genuine? Was the listener patronizing or sarcastic?

4. Did the listener make the complainer feel supported and understood?

Here are four examples that illustrate the use of different listening skills.

Example 1 illustrates the Disarming Technique:

Complainer: Life stinks!
Listener: You're right! Life can sure be stinky at times.

Example 2 illustrates Thought Empathy, Feeling Empathy, and Inquiry:

Complainer: Life stinks!
Listener: You say life stinks. It sounds like you're feeling pretty frustrated. Are you?

Example 3 illustrates Inquiry:

Complainer: Life stinks!
Listener: What happened that made you feel so ticked off?

The fourth example illustrates how all three listening skills can be integrated into one response:

Complainer: Life stinks!
Listener: You're right! Life can be darn stinky at times. It sounds like you're feeling pretty upset. Can you tell me what happened?

Tell the participants to use frequent role reversals in their teams so that everyone gets the chance to practice the listening skills.

There are two potential benefits from this exercise:

1. The participants may find these listening skills useful in their personal lives.

2. This exercise may help to undercut the tendencies of some participants throughout this program to "help" or give advice when other members talk.

Walk around so you can answer questions and provide supervision during the exercise. Try to keep the members focused on the task and not gossiping in a general way. After fifteen to twenty minutes, reconvene the group as a whole and ask how the members felt about the experience. Were they able to use the listening skills? Were they tempted to give advice?

FEEDBACK ABOUT STEP 1

At the end of each session, ask for positive and negative reactions to the group. Ask questions like "What did you find helpful? Was there anything that turned you off? Was there anything you disagreed with or didn't understand?"

Ask the members to read the Evaluation of Step 1 on page 34 of the participant's workbook and write down several things about the session that turned them off. Then they can write down several things they did like about Step 1.

It's important to get any negative feelings out in the open so you can deal with them. Otherwise, the participants may express their feelings indirectly, by arguing with you, dropping out, or "forgetting" to do the self-help assignments.

When participants express negative reactions, it's important not to get defensive. Otherwise, they will feel awkward about being honest and open. This will hurt the morale of the group. Instead, try to find some truth in each criticism. A simple response such as "That's a good point; thank you for sharing it" will often be sufficient.

If you have a co-leader or a consultant, you can process the group's comments after each session when you write your progress notes for the session. (You can find a sample progress note on page 73 at the end of Step 1.) This can be an invaluable learning process. Often small changes can lead to dramatic improvements in the quality of the next group.

Many of the members will feel inhibited about criticizing you or the group. Ask if they can think of any reasons why someone might be reluctant to ask questions, to criticize you or other participants, or to open up in the group. Write down what they say on your flip chart. If you like, you can photocopy and distribute the table entitled

Ten *Good* Reasons *Not* to Express Your Feelings, which follows. Ask the participants to complete it. When they are done, ask which attitudes they agreed with "moderately" or "a lot." Encourage them to discuss these concerns.

Finally, ask if they have any questions or concerns about today's session or future sessions.

SELF-HELP ASSIGNMENTS FOR STEP 2

Discuss the self-help assignments for Step 2 on page 36 of the participant's workbook before the members leave. If they have not yet read and completed Step 1, tell them to do that as well.

If you have included the optional exercise on helping versus listening (or if you plan to include it in a future session), tell the participants that they can read more about this topic on pages 435–440 of *The Feeling Good Handbook* (in Chapter 21, "How to Deal with Difficult People").

ANSWER TO THE EXERCISE ON PAGE 48

You could say: "I agree strongly with your therapist. It can be very important to get at the deeper issues. I have great respect for the psychoanalytic method, and for your thoughtfulness in raising this good question. In fact, cognitive therapy was originally developed by a psychoanalyst, and I believe we can all work together as a team. Would you like me to call your therapist and discuss what we are trying to accomplish, so that we can open up a line of communication in case you get contradictory or confusing messages from us?"

Notice that this response illustrates the Disarming Technique: You find some grain of truth in what the other person is saying. This is far more effective than arguing and getting into a power struggle. This response also illustrates a communication technique known as Stroking: You find something genuinely positive to say about the other person. You express respect for him or her, even in the heat of battle. In this example, you are Stroking the participant (praising him or her for thoughtfulness) as well as the other therapist.

These two communication techniques can help you deal with resistance throughout this program. The philosophy is to avoid arguments or power struggles with the participants. Much of what you are teaching is controversial, and some participants will challenge you *over* and *over* throughout the program. This is good—it shows they are fired up, challenged, interested. You will need to decide whether you want to spend time fighting with them. Your style of responding will determine the outcome!

HOW TO USE THE LEADER'S DATA SHEET

At the beginning of each session, ask each member to tell you his or her score on the BDC (Burns Depression Checklist), BAI (Burns Anxiety Inventory) and RSAT (Relationship

TEN *GOOD* REASONS *NOT* TO EXPRESS YOUR FEELINGS

	This attitude describes me			
	not at all	somewhat	moderately	a lot
1. I may hurt people's feelings if I say something negative.				
2. I usually try to avoid conflicts with other people.				
3. I'm afraid that I'll look stupid or foolish if I ask a question.				
4. I am basically a nice person and I don't like to upset other people.				
5. People may get mad at me if I say something negative.				
6. I don't really trust other people very much.				
7. I need everyone's approval in order to feel good about myself.				
8. I don't believe that what I have to say is really important.				
9. I don't really want to get very close to the other people in the group.				
10. I don't believe it would do any good for me to say how I feel.				

Satisfaction Scale). You can find these three tests on pages 21, 23, and 27 of the participant's workbook.

Record how much assigned homework each member has done since the last session, using this rating scale:

0—no homework at all

1—a minimal amount of homework, such as taking the self-assessment tests only

2—a moderate amount of homework, such as taking the tests and doing some of the reading and written assignments

3—all the homework, including the reading, the self-assessment tests, and the written assignments

Record whether each member attended on time using this rating scale:

0—did not attend at all

1—attended but was more than five minutes late

2—attended on time

Optional bonus point (add to the "on time" column, if desired):

0—did not bring the participant's workbook to the session

1—did bring the participant's workbook to the session

Note: You can find an extra set of Leader's Data Sheets in Appendix A beginning on page 207. Save that set for making photocopies to use with future groups.

SAMPLE PROGRESS NOTE

On page 73 you will find a blank progress note that you can use to keep records on individual members after each session for your files. On the page after that, you will find a filled-in progress note on a fictitious participant. This will give you an idea of one way to keep notes for your files. If you are a mental health professional, some type of record keeping will be clinically useful. It is also necessary for insurance and for legal purposes. You will find several extra copies of the progress note in Appendix C beginning on page 227. Feel free to photocopy a sufficient number for your group.

LEADER'S DATA SHEET

Name of participant	Preliminary testing date: _____			Step 1 date: _____						Step 2 date: _____					
	BDC (0–45)	BAI (0–99)	RSAT (0–42)	BDC (0–45)	BAI (0–99)	RSAT (0–42)	HOME-WORK (0–3)	ON TIME? (0–2)		BDC (0–45)	BAI (0–99)	RSAT (0–42)	HOME-WORK (0–3)	ON TIME? (0–2)	

LEADER'S DATA SHEET (Continued)

Name of participant	Step 3 date: ____					Step 4 date: ____					Step 5 date: ____				
	BDC (0–45)	BAI (0–99)	RSAT (0–42)	HOME-WORK (0–3)	ON TIME? (0–2)	BDC (0–45)	BAI (0–99)	RSAT (0–42)	HOME-WORK (0–3)	ON TIME? (0–2)	BDC (0–45)	BAI (0–99)	RSAT (0–42)	HOME-WORK (0–3)	ON TIME? (0–2)

LEADER'S DATA SHEET (Continued)

Name of participant	Step 6 date: _____					Step 7 date: _____					Step 8 date: _____				
	BDC (0–45)	BAI (0–99)	RSAT (0–42)	HOME-WORK (0–3)	ON TIME? (0–2)	BDC (0–45)	BAI (0–99)	RSAT (0–42)	HOME-WORK (0–3)	ON TIME? (0–2)	BDC (0–45)	BAI (0–99)	RSAT (0–42)	HOME-WORK (0–3)	ON TIME? (0–2)

LEADER'S DATA SHEET (Continued)

Name of participant	Step 9 date:___						Step 10 date:___						Follow-up date:___				
	BDC (0–45)	BAI (0–99)	RSAT (0–42)	HOME-WORK (0–3)	ON TIME? (0–2)		BDC (0–45)	BAI (0–99)	RSAT (0–42)	HOME-WORK (0–3)	ON TIME? (0–2)		BDC (0–45)	BAI (0–99)	RSAT (0–42)	HOME-WORK (0–3)	ON TIME? (0–2)

TEN DAYS TO SELF-ESTEEM
Progress Note

Patient name: _____

Date of session: _____ Session number: _____

BDC score = _____ BAI score = _____ RSAT score = _____

Goal: _____
_____

Progress toward goal: _____
_____
_____
_____
_____
_____
_____
_____
_____
_____
_____
_____
_____
_____
_____
_____
_____
_____
_____

_____
signature

TEN DAYS TO SELF-ESTEEM
Progress Note

Patient name: *Bruce Simpson*

Date of session: *3/20/94*   Session number: *1*

BDC score = *18*   BAI score = *31*   RSAT score = *17*

Goal: *(1) Orientation to the program. (2) Obtain a commitment to the self-help assignments between sessions.*

Progress toward goal: *Mr. Simpson participated openly in the session. He made a commitment to the philosophy of doing things to help himself between sessions. He discussed his fears of aging and his concerns about illness and death. He also discussed his concerns about retirement. He feels unproductive now and has little to do. He expressed remorse about a son with severe emotional problems who had shown great promise while in grammar school and high school. Although he had a very low score on the Relationship Satisfaction Scale, he said he thought he had "accommodated" to his wife.*

Bruce Zahn, M.A.
signature

STEP 2

YOU FEEL THE WAY YOU THINK

LEADER'S PREPARATION FOR STEP 2

Activity	Check (√) when done
1. Read the description of Step 2 in the participant's workbook beginning on page 37.	
2. Study the Checklist for Step 2 on the next page of this *Leader's Manual* and the Tips for Leaders beginning on page 77.	
3. Read Chapter 5 of *The Feeling Good Handbook*.	

CHECKLIST FOR STEP 2

Activity	Optional or required?	Minimum time (min.)	Check (√) when done
1. Using the Leader's Data Sheet on page 69, record the participants' scores on the three self-assessment tests, along with their points for homework and for attendance.	req.	10	
2. Ask for positive and negative feedback about Step 1.	req.	5 – 10	
3. Ask about participants' reactions to the reading and exercises they did to prepare for Step 2.	req.	5 – 10	
4. Lead the relaxation exercise, which illustrates how thoughts create moods.	req.	10	
5. Discuss stressful events and feelings, using the Feeling Words chart in the workbook.	req.	10	
6. Discuss the causes of negative emotions.	req.	5	
7. The Stick Figure Technique.	req.	5 – 10	
8. Exercise on the specific kinds of thoughts that are associated with specific kinds of negative emotions.	req.	10 – 15	
9. Discuss the ten types of cognitive distortions that are associated with unhealthy emotions.	req.	10 – 20	
10. Distorted Thinking Exercise 1.	req.	5 – 10	
11. Distorted Thinking Exercise 2.	opt.	15	
12. Identify the distortions in the Stick Figure's thoughts and substitute more positive and realistic thoughts.	req.	10 – 20	
13. Ask for positive and negative feedback about Step 2.	req.	5	
14. Assign the homework for Step 3.	req.	3	

OVERVIEW OF STEP 2

In today's step you will introduce the basic principles of cognitive therapy:

- People FEEL the way they THINK. Specific kinds of feelings result from specific kinds of thoughts.

- Most BAD feelings come from ILLOGICAL thoughts ("distorted thinking").

- People can CHANGE the way they FEEL when they develop more positive and realistic thoughts and attitudes!

Although these ideas are very straightforward, they are likely to stir up considerable curiosity and controversy. Most people are not aware of the powerful impact of their thoughts and attitudes on the way they feel and behave.

You will also introduce a number of basic skills such as how to separate an upsetting event (what actually happened) from how a person feels and thinks about that event. These skills will provide a sound foundation when the participants learn a variety of techniques for changing negative thinking patterns in future sessions.

TIPS FOR LEADERS

DATA COLLECTION

Record participants' scores on the three self-assessment tests (the BDC, the BAI, and the RSAT) on the Leader's Data Sheet on page 69. Record how much homework they completed using the 3-point rating scale on page 68. Record whether or not they arrived on time using the 2-point rating scale on page 68.

FEEDBACK AND REVIEW OF HOMEWORK

Ask about the participants' positive and negative reactions to the first session. What did they like and dislike about it?

Follow this with a brief discussion of the assigned reading (Step 2 of *Ten Days to Self-esteem*). Ask if anyone did the optional reading. Encourage the group members to ask questions about this material. Ask what they agreed and disagreed with. Were any passages or exercises particularly helpful and interesting? Was there anything they didn't understand?

IDEA 1: YOU <u>FEEL</u> THE WAY YOU <u>THINK</u>

The first principle of cognitive therapy is that negative feelings such as depression, anxiety, guilt, and anger result more from Negative Thoughts than from external events. One way to illustrate this is to ask all the participants to sit comfortably and close their eyes. Tell them to relax and think of a happy, peaceful scene such as lying on a quiet beach on a warm, mellow summer day while they listen to the waves gently breaking on the shore. As an option, they might prefer to visualize themselves sitting on the porch of a cabin in the woods on a peaceful summer day.

Tell the participants to visualize the details of the scene they have chosen. Suggest that they can see the blue sky and a few white clouds, and they can feel the warm breeze on their skin. Tell them to imagine that all the problems in their lives have been solved, and they have no worries. All the bills have been paid; all the conflicts with others have been happily resolved. Any bad habits, such as overeating, drug abuse, or drinking excessively, have been eliminated. They are no longer depressed or anxious. They feel confident and in control of their lives. It is quiet and restful here.

Give the participants a moment to settle in, and repeat similar suggestions in a friendly, hypnotic voice. Ask them to raise their hands when they feel peaceful and relaxed.

Now ask them to keep their eyes closed and change the way they feel. Tell them to try to create a different emotion. They can make themselves feel sad, worried, guilty, angry, or happy. Tell them to use any method they want to create the new emotion. Give them a few moments to do this. Ask them to raise their hands once they have generated the new feeling.

Now ask the participants what emotions they created and how they did this. How many of them made themselves feel upset? How many created a positive feeling? Some of them will probably say that they thought about something sad or frightening or annoying. They may visualize an argument with a friend, a loved one's problem, or failing an examination. You can tell them that this illustrates the first principle of cognitive therapy, that *your thoughts create your moods.*

You can emphasize this basic idea as the participants discuss the feeling they experienced during the exercise. Point out that they were all in the same room and exactly the same external event was occurring. They all heard you say the same words out loud. Nevertheless, they all experienced completely different emotions. How is this possible? Who created all these different emotions? Did you, the leader, cause Mary to feel nervous and cause Jennifer to feel angry? Or did they create these emotions themselves?

You may be able to think of other creative ways to illustrate the idea that your thoughts create your moods. George Collette and Bruce Zahn, my colleagues at the Presbyterian Medical Center, created a technique called the Pepper Shaker to illustrate the idea on one of the psychiatric inpatient units. At the beginning of the session, they told the participants that they had hidden a pepper shaker in the room in full view, and they wanted all the participants to search for it. (They had placed the pepper shaker over the Exit sign above the door, where it was easily visible.) Then the participants searched the room until one of them found it.

At this point the leaders asked the participants to discuss how they had been feeling and what they had been thinking while they were looking. A man with paranoid schizophrenia said he had felt angry because he was convinced the group was being tricked by the staff. He said he had thought that George had hidden the pepper in his pocket where it couldn't be seen.

Another man said he had kicked himself and become very self-critical during the exercise. He explained that when he hadn't found the pepper shaker on the windowsill, he had berated himself for not looking behind the refrigerator where another patient was searching. He suddenly became convinced it was stupid to look on the windowsill because the pepper shaker was more likely to be behind the refrigerator.

Other participants had had a variety of emotions as they searched for the pepper shaker—some felt amused and curious, others sad and inferior, and so forth. The group leaders pointed out that their feelings were all quite different because of the different messages they were giving themselves. Finally, they asked the participants to discuss the thoughts and feelings they have in other situations when they get upset.

Although this exercise may seem quite humble and concrete, the idea that your thoughts create your feelings is really quite revolutionary to many people. Most of us think that our *environment* makes us feel the way we do. We say, "I feel lousy because *this* bad thing (or *that* bad thing) happened to me." The idea that our thoughts play a major role in our emotions is quite empowering. Although we cannot always change what happens to us, we *can* do something to change the way we think and feel about it. That is the foundation of cognitive therapy.

Separating Thoughts, Feelings, and Events

Some people do not find it easy to separate the actual upsetting event (such as being rejected) from their thoughts ("I'm unlovable") and feelings (sad, hopeless, or worthless). To illustrate this, ask the participants to write down a brief description of a specific upsetting event that happened at some time during their lives, on page 42 of the participant's workbook. (A number of them may have already done this as part of their preparation for today's step.)

Ask several volunteers to read their descriptions out loud. When they do, use the three listening skills described in Step 1: the Disarming Technique, Thought and Feeling Empathy, and Inquiry. Do not get into helping or problem solving.

For example, let's assume that Jerome says he was arrested unfairly for drug possession. As the leader, you may doubt that his arrest was unfair, since you know for a fact that Jerome has a long police record for selling cocaine and other drugs.

Nevertheless, do not get into a confrontation with Jerome. You can simply say, "It can be real upsetting when something like that happens. How did it make you feel? Were you mad, or frustrated, or what?" This response includes the Disarming Technique, Feeling Empathy, and Inquiry. Once Jerome tells you how ticked off he felt, you can thank him for the good example of an extremely stressful event and ask the other members if they ever felt like they were treated unfairly by family members, friends, or the authorities. You can ask one or two to describe briefly what happened to them. This will help the group bond together, and it will encourage all the members to get involved.

Then ask other group members about the upsetting events they wrote down. When they describe their stressful events, ask them to describe their negative emotions. Tell them they can use the Feeling Words chart on page 43 of the participant's workbook. This chart lists common emotional categories in the left-hand column along with synonyms for each category. Make sure they actually write down the description of the event and list their negative feelings on page 42 of the participant's workbook.

Some participants will find it easy to identify their emotions, whereas others may find this more difficult. They may not be used to thinking about the names of different kinds of feelings. Depending on the needs of your group, you can spend more or less time with the Feeling Words chart.

Now ask the participants what *caused* these different negative emotions they had. You can ask, "Why do we get upset? What makes us feel angry, or worried, or sad, or inferior? Where do these negative feelings come from? What causes us to feel this way?"

Ask how many of them think the events caused their negative emotions. Then ask how many think that their Negative Thoughts created their emotions.

The Stick Figure Technique

Tell the members to look at the first Stick Figure on page 45 of the participant's workbook. Tyrone lost his job (the actual event) and felt sad and guilty (the emotions). His Negative Thoughts are in the bubble above his head. Can they see the connection between how the Stick Figure is thinking and feeling? You can ask the participants if they ever felt discouraged when something bad happened at work or at school.

Ask the members to think of the stressful event they described on page 42 of the participant's workbook. Ask them to try to tune in to the Negative Thoughts they had at that time. What were they telling themselves to make themselves feel sad, angry, or worried? Tell them to write down these thoughts in the bubble above the second Stick Figure's head on page 46 of the participant's workbook.

Ask the members to read their Negative Thoughts out loud. Ask if they can see any connections between their feelings and their thoughts. For example, if they felt sad, did they have thoughts of loss or failure? If they felt anxious, were they telling themselves that they were in danger, or that something bad was going to happen? If they felt angry, did they tell themselves that someone was treating them unfairly? If they felt frustrated, were they thinking that things *should* be different? If they felt guilty, were they telling themselves they had done something bad?

Finally, ask them why this idea that our thoughts create our emotions may be important.

You can tell the participants to keep a journal of upsetting events, negative feelings, and Negative Thoughts as one of their homework assignments for Step 3. You can illustrate this triple-column format on your flip chart:

The Event (describe what actually happened)	My Emotions (use the Feeling Words chart)	My Negative Thoughts

When the participants do this assignment, they can record upsetting events that happened at *any* time in their lives. An upsetting event can be something recent or something in childhood. It can be something major (like a serious illness) or something minor (like getting upset when the phone rings). Tell them to spend at least five minutes per day recording upsetting events, negative feelings, and Negative Thoughts in the triple-column format.

Ask if any of the participants do not understand the assignment, and if any of them think they might not be able to do it. Ask them to spend one or two minutes doing the assignment now, so they can get started. Once they're done, ask if they had any difficulties or need help. Do they have any trouble thinking of upsetting events? Do they know how to use the Feeling Words chart? Can they write down their Negative Thoughts?

Although these ideas may seem very basic and obvious to you, some people will have difficulty understanding them. Others may resist doing the written homework. You may need to spend some time answering questions and making the assignment clear to all the members.

It is also important to note that specific kinds of negative emotions result from specific kinds of thoughts. You already introduced this idea when you asked if the participants noticed any connections between their own negative feelings and the thoughts they were having at this time.

Discuss the table entitled Your Thoughts and Your Feelings on page 48 of the participant's workbook. The first emotion listed is sadness. Read the description of the kinds of thoughts that lead to sadness. Ask about the kinds of events that make the group members sad. Then ask about the kinds of Negative Thoughts they've had when they felt sad or discouraged.

Then ask the members to describe times they felt the different kinds of emotions listed on the table. Inquire about the Negative Thoughts they had when they felt that way. Ask them to write brief descriptions of the specific kinds of upsetting events and Negative Thoughts that are associated with each type of emotion. (The answers to this exercise appear on page 60 of the participant's workbook.)

If you like, you can divide the group into teams of two or three for this exercise. Each team can work on a different negative emotion. Walk around and supervise the exercise. After about five minutes, ask a spokesperson from each team to summarize their conclusions.

IDEA 2: MOST BAD FEELINGS COME FROM ILLOGICAL THOUGHTS ("DISTORTED THINKING")

The next principle of cognitive therapy is one of the most controversial and exciting: The Negative Thoughts that lead to unhealthy emotions such as depression, anxiety, and anger are nearly always illogical and distorted, even though they seem absolutely realistic when you feel upset. In other words, reality practically *never* causes unhealthy feelings such as clinical depression or anxiety. These unhealthy feelings result from wrong thoughts about reality! When you replace these distorted Negative Thoughts with others that are more positive and realistic, you can change the way you feel.

In the next step we will distinguish healthy from unhealthy emotions. A healthy emotion, such as sadness, results from a *realistic* thought. For example, if a loved one dies, you may feel a sense of grief and loss because you cared deeply about the person who died and will miss him or her. If you lose your job, it is natural to feel disappointed. In contrast, clinical depression (or neurotic anxiety or destructive anger) results from distorted thoughts about an event, such as "I'm no good" or "I'll be alone and miserable forever."

In today's session the members will learn how to identify the ten types of cognitive distortions that are associated with unhealthy feelings. These distortions, which are defined in the box on page 50 of the participant's workbook and page 83 of this *Leader's Manual,* include all-or-nothing thinking, overgeneralization, emotional reasoning, and others. Read the definition of each distortion and ask the participants if they can think of examples of that distortion in their own thinking at times when they felt upset.

If you like, you can ask the participants to identify the distortions in the thoughts they wrote in the bubble above the Stick Figure's head. You can write their Negative Thoughts on a flip chart during this demonstration. Be sure that you separate the upsetting event, the negative emotions, and the Negative Thoughts. This is crucial to the success of the exercise.

For example, a man in your group might say that he got really ticked off when someone cut in front of him on the freeway on the way to work. If you write, "I got really ticked off because the SOB cut me off," you will not be able to identify any distortions. This is because you have written down an *event* plus an *emotion.* You will do better if you write it down this way on the flip chart:

Event: Someone cut into my lane on the freeway this morning and nearly ran into me.

Emotions: 1.   Anger—99%
          2.   Frustration—99%

Next ask the group what thoughts they might have had in this situation. What would they be telling themselves? Write their Negative Thoughts on the flip chart and number them consecutively. Ask them how strongly they would believe each thought (from 0% to 100%) when it first went through their minds. What you write down might look like this:

Negative Thoughts:

1. He's got no right to cut in front of me like that! 100%

2. He must think I'm a real wimp. 100%

3. I ought to teach that SOB a lesson! 100%

4. This *always* happens when I'm in a hurry. 90%

Now you can ask the group to identify the distortions in each of these Negative Thoughts. The distortions include "should" statements, labeling, magnification, mind reading, overgeneralization, and others.

DISTORTED THINKING*

1. **All-or-nothing thinking:** You look at things in absolute, black-and-white categories.

2. **Overgeneralization:** You view a negative event as a never-ending pattern of defeat.

3. **Mental filter:** You dwell on the negatives and ignore the positives.

4. **Discounting the positives:** You insist that your accomplishments or positive qualities don't count.

5. **Jumping to conclusions:** You conclude things are bad without any definite evidence.

    (a) **Mind reading:** You assume that people are reacting negatively to you.

    (b) **Fortune-telling:** You predict that things will turn out badly.

6. **Magnification or minimization:** You blow things way out of proportion or you shrink their importance.

7. **Emotional reasoning:** You reason from how you feel: "I feel like an idiot, so I must be one."

8. **"Should" statements:** You criticize yourself or other people with "shoulds," "shouldn'ts," "musts," "oughts," and "have-tos."

9. **Labeling:** Instead of saying "I made a mistake," you tell yourself, "I'm a jerk" or "a loser."

10. **Blame:** You blame yourself for something you weren't entirely responsible for, or you blame other people and overlook ways that you contributed to a problem.

*Copyright © 1980 by David D. Burns, M.D. Adapted from *Feeling Good: The New Mood Therapy* (New York: William Morrow & Company, 1980; Avon, 1992).

After this exercise has been completed, break up the group into teams of two or three to do Distorted Thinking Exercise 1 on page 54 of the participant's workbook. (Alternatively, you can ask the participants to do this exercise individually.) After they have completed the exercise, ask them to discuss the distortions they found in Lyle's Negative Thoughts.

If time permits, you can do Distorted Thinking Exercise 2 on page 56 of the participant's workbook. In this exercise the members will have to supply the upsetting event. Then they will record their emotions and Negative Thoughts before identifying the distortions. This exercise will cement the concepts that were presented in today's session and will introduce the Daily Mood Log. (They can read more about the Daily Mood Log in Chapter 5 of *The Feeling Good Handbook* as part of their homework for the next session.)

Direct this exercise in a step-by-step manner. First, ask the members to write down a brief description of an upsetting event on page 56 of the participant's workbook. It can

can be any upsetting event that happened at any time in their lives, but it must be specific and real. After about one minute, ask several of them to read what they wrote down. This will help you find out if they are on track and doing the assignment properly. Help them focus their descriptions on an event that happened on an identifiable day of the week at a specific time and location.

For example, a member might write down "Life stinks" or "Things are overwhelming" as the upsetting event. These problems won't work very well because they are far too vague and general! Instead, they should write down a *specific* example of when life seemed stinky. Where were they when they noticed the smell? When did things feel overwhelming? What were they doing? Were they lying in bed daydreaming? Were they trying to study? Whom were they with? Were they arguing with a family member or friend?

Getting people to be very concrete about the event is really an *essential* first step. If they are not concrete and specific about the upsetting event, you run the risk of dealing with complaints that are vague and unworkable. You will go down blind alleys and end up feeling frustrated. Learning this skill sometimes takes considerable practice. As you gain experience, this task will become considerably easier.

Suppose that a participant tells you his event is that he "needs to get his life together." Another participant says, "I'm broke." A third says, "My marriage is crummy." A fourth says, "I'm a constant procrastinator." Can you see any problem here? Is your anxiety level suddenly going up? How will you respond to these vague complaints to help the participants focus the event a bit better? Think about this for a moment before you read on. You will probably be confronted by similar statements from members of your group.

You might respond to the first man in this way: "Can you be a bit more specific? You say you need to get your life together. I must admit that I don't really know quite what you have in mind. It's just a little bit too vague. What's one *specific* problem you're having that you want help with? Can you think of something bad that happened that upset you? What time of day was it? What were you doing at the time? How were you thinking and feeling?"

Once the participants have described the upsetting event, ask them to record their negative emotions and rate each of them on a scale from 0% to 100%. Tell them to use emotion words like these from the Feeling Words chart on page 43 of the participant's workbook: sad, depressed, worried, anxious, angry, guilty, ashamed, discouraged, hopeless, and so forth. After another minute ask several of them to read what they wrote down.

Although these assignments sound quite simple, you will be surprised at how difficult they can be for some people. Getting feedback and answering questions after each little step can sometimes be tremendously important. You may discover that some people have trouble doing the simplest self-help exercises in the group. I have also observed this curious phenomenon in workshops for mental health professionals who are presumably very sophisticated and highly motivated.

Next, ask the participants to write down one or two Negative Thoughts that were associated with their negative emotions. You can say, "What were you telling yourself when you felt anxious (or angry or sad)?" You may have to supervise and help them just as before.

Make sure the participants do not put emotion words or descriptions of events in the

Negative Thoughts column. Although this may seem like a minor point, it is actually quite important. Your skill at recognizing emotion words that are hidden in the Negative Thoughts will also develop over time.

Suppose someone with an airplane phobia has the Negative Thought "I'm really scared about getting on the plane." This is not a Negative Thought. It is an upsetting event (getting on the plane) plus an emotion (scared). The Negative Thought might be "The airplane will crash" or "I'll be trapped in there and go crazy" or "I'll be out of control once the plane takes off." You can easily deal with these thoughts with cognitive techniques.

Once the participants have written down several Negative Thoughts, ask them to identify the distortions in their thoughts, using the Distorted Thinking chart. Understanding these distortions is one of the most important cognitive therapy skills.

Remind the group members that there is a lot of overlap in the definitions of these distortions, and that any Negative Thought will usually contain many of the distortions. The identification of the distortions is not a precise, perfect process. For example, after her boyfriend got nervous about the prospect of getting engaged, a woman had the thought "I'm always failing at relationships." The distortions in this thought would include overgeneralization, all-or-nothing thinking, mental filter, and emotional reasoning.

Whenever the participants identify Negative Thoughts, it will be crucial to avoid these pitfalls:

1. Warn them not to put a rhetorical question (or any other question) in their list of Negative Thoughts. For example, they might say they have this Negative Thought: "Why is this always happening to me?" Ask them to change this rhetorical question into a statement before they write it down. The revised version of a rhetorical question will nearly always be a "should" statement, such as "It's unfair that this is happening to me" or "This shouldn't be happening to me." "Should" statements can be dealt with easily, but rhetorical questions cannot.

2. Do not put descriptions of emotions or actual events in the list of Negative Thoughts. The Negative Thoughts, by definition, are the distorted *perceptions* of the events that *create the emotions*.

Suppose that a group member says he had the Negative Thought "I feel crappy because Helen stood me up at the last minute." This is not a Negative Thought and it cannot be refuted or challenged. It is actually an event ("Helen stood me up") and an emotion (he says he feels "crappy," and he may also feel hurt, inferior, frustrated, discouraged, or angry).

After the member has recorded the event and the emotions appropriately, he can more easily write down his Negative Thoughts. These may include:

1. Women are always dumping me. 100%

2. I'm a loser. 100%

Some participants may be able to identify upsetting events and emotions but may have trouble identifying their Negative Thoughts. There are two methods that you can use to help them. The first method requires some therapeutic skill; the second one does not.

Method 1

You ask the question "Why is that upsetting to you?" over and over, until the participant finally begins to identify his or her Negative Thoughts. Suppose that a man has lost his job as a short-order cook. He tells you that he feels angry and depressed. He insists that he doesn't have any Negative Thoughts and says it's normal to feel like this when you lose your job and get shafted. Your dialogue with him might go like this:

Leader: Why was it upsetting to you when you got fired? What were you thinking?

Participant: I was thinking that I lost my job and I got ticked off.

Leader: What was the thought that made you angry?

Participant: (*Defensively*) Wouldn't it make *you* angry? How would you like it if you got fired? Anyone would feel lousy!

Leader: You're absolutely right! Any of us would feel lousy if we got fired. I know that I would.

We might all look at the situation from our own unique perspective, and that could vary from person to person. For example, you might be thinking, "This is unfair" or "My boss is a piece of garbage" or "It's my fault" or "I'll never get another job" or "My wife will be ticked off at me." Some people might even be feeling relief because they would be telling themselves, "It was a crummy job and I know I can find a better one."

Can you think of any of the Negative Thoughts that went through your mind when you got fired? What were you telling yourself?

The leader in this example is using two techniques:

1. The leader is using the Disarming Technique by finding truth in this man's claim that "anyone would feel lousy." As a leader, you should nearly *always* disarm antagonistic group members. This will calm them and prevent a conflict that could demoralize the group.

2. The leader is using the Multiple-Choice Technique to make this man more aware of his Negative Thoughts.

If the man who lost his job still has trouble, you could ask other group members what *they* might be telling themselves if they were in this situation. Write their Negative Thoughts on the flip chart. This nearly always works.

Method 2

Suppose another member insists that he suddenly became anxious when he was golfing but he cannot identify any Negative Thoughts. He tells you his negative feelings usually come out of the blue, without any upsetting events and without any Negative Thoughts.

Draw a Stick Figure on the flip chart like the one on page 46 of the participant's workbook. If you have a flair for art, you can even draw a golf club in the Stick Figure's hands. Tell the man that the Stick Figure is not him, but someone else much like him who suddenly got anxious on the golf course. Ask him to *make up* some Negative Thoughts so that the people who read the cartoon will understand what the anxious Stick Figure golfer is thinking. You can write what he says in the bubble above the Stick Figure's head.

He may come up with these thoughts: "I'll probably hook the ball into the lake. The stock I bought went way up in value. Why didn't I buy more? I *knew* I should have! Just think of all the money I lost by not taking a stronger position. I'm such a coward!"

After you write them in the bubble, you can say, "Are these thoughts similar at all to the ones you had?" He will almost certainly say yes. Then tell him that these were his Negative Thoughts.

IDEA 3: YOU CAN CHANGE THE WAY YOU FEEL

The final idea is that you can change the way you feel when you change your Negative Thoughts. In the next several steps you will explore this notion in great detail with the group. In today's step, you will just introduce the concept with one simple exercise.

Earlier in the session the participants worked with Tyrone, the first Stick Figure character, who lost his job. Tyrone had the thought "I'm a born loser." They will find this thought along with the distortions on the Daily Mood Log on page 52 of the participant's workbook. Tell them to turn to this page now. Ask them to substitute a Positive Thought in the right-hand column. What could Tyrone tell himself instead of "I'm a born loser"?

The Positive Thought should have these characteristics:

- It should be affirming.

- It should be absolutely valid and realistic.

- It should put the lie to the Negative Thought.

After the participants have come up with an effective Positive Thought, tell them to repeat this process with Tyrone's other two Negative Thoughts.

When they are done, tell them to put a big X through the Negative Thoughts in the bubble above the first Stick Figure's head on page 45. Then they can write more Positive Thoughts above the smiling Stick Figure's head on page 55 of their workbooks.

SUMMARY OF STEP 2

At the end of the session, summarize the ideas that were discussed today:

1. Your thoughts, not external events, create your moods. Specific kinds of emotions result from specific kinds of thoughts.

2.   Unhealthy emotions result from distorted thoughts.

3.   You can CHANGE the way you FEEL.

Then you can summarize The Steps to Feeling Good listed below, which were presented in today's session. Ask if the participants have any questions about any of these steps. Tell them that they will learn a great deal more about these ideas in the next several sessions.

EVALUATION OF STEP 2

At the end of the session, ask the participants what they liked and disliked about it. Ask them to fill out the Evaluation of Step 2 on page 61 of the participant's workbook. Tell them to write down several things about the session that turned them off. Then they can write down several things they liked about the session. Ask if they would be willing to read what they wrote down. Remember to disarm them and to respond nondefensively when they voice criticisms or negative reactions.

SELF-HELP ASSIGNMENTS FOR STEP 3

Discuss the self-help assignments for Step 3 before the participants leave. These assignments are listed on page 62 of the participant's workbook.

THE STEPS TO FEELING GOOD

1.   Write down a brief description of what happened when you got upset.

2.   Identify your bad feelings about that event. Use the Feeling Words chart if you need help.

3.   Use the Triple-Column Technique:

   •   Write down the Negative Thoughts that are making you feel bad about yourself.

   •   Find the distortions in those thoughts using the Distorted Thinking chart.

   •   Write down more positive and realistic thoughts that will make you feel better.

When you are done, *congratulate* yourself for doing a *great job*!

STEP 3

YOU CAN <u>CHANGE</u> THE WAY YOU <u>FEEL</u>

LEADER'S PREPARATION FOR STEP 3

Activity	Check (√) when done
1. Read the description of Step 3 in the participant's workbook beginning on page 63.	
2. Study the Checklist for Step 3 on the next page of this *Leader's Manual* and the Tips for Leaders beginning on page 92.	
3. Review Chapter 4 of *The Feeling Good Handbook*.	

CHECKLIST FOR STEP 3

Activity	Optional or required?	Minimum time (min.)	Check (√) when done
1. Using the Leader's Data Sheet on page 10, record the participants' scores on the three self-assessment tests, along with their points for homework and for attendance.	req.	10	
2. Ask for positive and negative feedback about Step 2.	req.	5 – 10	
3. Discuss the assigned reading for this step.	req.	5 – 10	
4. Exercise on the differences between healthy and unhealthy negative emotions.	req.	10 – 15	
5. Emotion Cost-Benefit Exercise 1.	req.	10 – 20	
6. Emotion Cost-Benefit Exercise 2.	opt.	15	
7. Review the steps in filling out a Daily Mood Log.	req.	5	
8. Daily Mood Log Exercise 1.	req.	10 – 15	
9. Daily Mood Log Exercise 2.	req.	10 – 15	
10. Discuss the Troubleshooting Guide.	req.	10	
11. Optional Daily Mood Log Exercises.	opt.	10 – 15	
12. Ask for positive and negative feedback about Step 3.	req.	5	
13. Assign the homework for Step 4.	req.	3	

OVERVIEW OF SESSION 3

In the last session you discussed these important ideas:

- Only your thoughts can create your moods.

- Healthy feelings result from realistic thoughts, whereas unhealthy feelings, like depression or anxiety or destructive anger, result from distorted, illogical, unrealistic thoughts.

In today's session you will focus on the differences between healthy and unhealthy negative feelings. It is tremendously important to distinguish them, because unhealthy feelings are destructive and can usually be changed with cognitive therapy techniques. In contrast, healthy feelings do not need to be changed. Healthy feelings can be accepted and expressed.

Many people are confused about their negative feelings. They make one of two mistakes when they get upset. The first mistake is to suppress their feelings. People who do this are frequently emotion-phobic. They think that most negative emotions are bad, without distinguishing healthy from unhealthy feelings. They sweep their feelings under the carpet and tell themselves, "I *should not* feel this way."

I call this attitude "emotophobia." Emotophobia is the belief that a person should always feel happy and in control, and never feel upset, sad, anxious, angry, or vulnerable. I have also coined the terms *anger phobia* and *conflict phobia* to refer to the belief that it is best to avoid any conflict in personal relationships.

You may encounter these emotophobic attitudes when you ask the participants about their positive and negative feelings at the end of each group. Some participants will find it extremely difficult to say anything negative, believing that "if you can't say something nice, you shouldn't say anything at all." They may see themselves as "nice" and deny that they feel angry or upset. People with this mind-set sometimes behave in a passive-aggressive manner, denying their hostile feelings and then acting them out indirectly so as to maintain a facade of innocence. For example, if they are unhappy with the group, they may complain, come late, fail to do homework, or simply drop out prematurely instead of discussing their concerns more assertively.

Other people make the opposite mistake. They believe that their negative feelings are always realistic and justified. People with this mind-set may become addicted to negative emotions, falling into a pattern of chronic depression, anger, self-pity, bitterness, or resentment. They may resist changing their feelings, even when those feelings are clearly destructive to their self-esteem and personal relationships. They often blame others for their problems, telling themselves that life *should* be different and that they deserve better treatment.

Both types of people have adopted equally simplistic solutions to a complex problem. All of us must make this decision when we feel upset: Should I *accept* this feeling or should I try to *change* the way I feel? This session will help the participants think about this issue in a practical, helpful way.

In today's session you will have three goals:

- You will show the group how to distinguish healthy from unhealthy emotions: What is the difference between healthy sadness and clinical depression? Between healthy, constructive anger and unhealthy, destructive anger? Between healthy fear and neurotic anxiety?

- You will show the group how to perform an Emotion Cost-Benefit Analysis. Members will ask themselves, "Do I want to feel this way? What are the advantages and disadvantages of this feeling? How will this feeling help me and how will it hurt me?" This motivational strategy is quite powerful and is different from all the other cognitive therapy techniques. It is extremely useful for dealing with resistance to change.

- You will show the group how to change unhealthy negative emotions with the Daily Mood Log, which was introduced in Step 2.

If you want to study this topic in greater detail before the group meets, read Chapter 4 of *The Feeling Good Handbook*. The discussion in this chapter will provide greater clarification of the differences between healthy and unhealthy emotions and will make it easy for you to lead the discussion.

TIPS FOR LEADERS

DATA COLLECTION

Record the participants' scores on the three self-assessment tests (the BDC, the BAI, and the RSAT) on the Leader's Data Sheet on page 70. Record how much homework they completed using the 3-point rating scale on page 68. Record whether or not they came on time using the 2-point rating scale on page 68.

FEEDBACK AND REVIEW OF HOMEWORK

Ask about the participants' positive and negative reactions to the second session. What did they like and dislike about it?

Follow this with a brief discussion of the assigned reading. Encourage the group members to ask questions about this material. Ask them what they agreed and disagreed with. Were any passages particularly helpful and interesting? Was there anything they didn't understand?

EXERCISE ON HEALTHY VS. UNHEALTHY FEELINGS

To introduce today's topic, ask the members if they have ever thought about the differences between healthy and unhealthy emotions. What is the difference between healthy sadness and depression? What is the difference between neurotic guilt and healthy remorse? What is the difference between healthy anger and unhealthy anger? What is the difference between healthy fear and neurotic anxiety?

Ask the group to describe as many differences between healthy sadness and depression as possible. Draw a line down the middle of your flip chart and label the left-hand column "Healthy sadness." Label the right-hand column "Depression." You can ask, "When would it be appropriate to feel sad? What is the difference between healthy sadness and depression? When does healthy sadness turn into depression?" As the participants describe the differences, record them on the flip chart. (A list of six differences between healthy sadness and depression can be found on page 68 of the participant's workbook.)

After the group has come up with at least three or four characteristics that distinguish healthy sadness from depression, you can repeat this exercise with healthy and unhealthy anger. Ask the group to do it together while you write on the flip chart, just as before. You can ask, "What's the difference between healthy and unhealthy anger? What would be an example of excessive or inappropriate anger? What would be an example of healthy anger? When we feel angry, how can we tell whether or not our feelings are reasonable? When should we express our angry feelings, and when should we try to change these feelings?" (A list of ten differences between healthy and unhealthy anger can be found in the participant's workbook on page 69.)

For many members, this distinction between healthy and unhealthy feelings will be new and confusing, and the discussion should help them comprehend this idea.

One group leader recently told me that his group spent the entire two-hour session discussing the list of ten differences between healthy and unhealthy anger. He was disappointed that he was unable to complete the entire agenda for the session, but said this theme had triggered a great amount of discussion. I think this type of involvement in the group process is good and should be encouraged. As a leader, you will want to be flexible and responsive to techniques and themes that turn your members on, as well as times when you begin to lose the group due to boredom or other problems.

The involvement of his group in this topic is not surprising. There is a great deal of concern these days about anger because of media descriptions of hostility, family violence, and abuse, but people get very little constructive information on how to deal with anger. I hope your group will find this topic intriguing and helpful. I have been fascinated by the distinctions between healthy and unhealthy anger for the past ten years!

Once the distinctions between healthy and unhealthy emotions appear reasonably clear to your group, you can divide it into teams of two to six members. Ask each team to list the differences between the healthy and unhealthy versions of a different emotion. If you have three groups, you could assign them like this:

Team 1:   Healthy Fear vs. Neurotic Anxiety

Team 2:   Healthy Remorse vs. Neurotic Guilt

Team 3:   Healthy Self-esteem vs. Arrogance or Self-centeredness

You can ask, "What's the difference between healthy fear and neurotic anxiety (such as a phobia, chronic worry, or panic attacks)? What's the difference between healthy remorse and neurotic guilt? Between healthy self-esteem and narcissism?"

While completing this exercise, members can fill in the blank forms on pages 70 (healthy fear/neurotic anxiety), 71 (healthy remorse/neurotic guilt), and 72 (healthy self-esteem/arrogance) of the participant's workbook. Tell them to think of specific instances when they felt the emotion they are discussing in this exercise. This will help them to develop guidelines for distinguishing the healthy from the unhealthy version of the emotion they are working on. (The answer to the exercise on healthy fear and neurotic anxiety appears on page 70 of the participant's workbook, as an example.)

While the participants are doing this exercise, you can walk around and make yourself available to answer questions and to keep them focused on the assignment. Do not encourage them to talk or gossip in a general way. After five or ten minutes, reconvene the group as a whole. Ask a spokesperson from each team to summarize the conclusions of his or her members. This should stimulate considerable discussion.

At the conclusion of this exercise, you can ask why we are bothering to make this distinction between healthy and unhealthy emotions. What are the practical consequences? Is this just a philosophical question, or something that affects the participants on a daily basis? If an emotion is healthy, what should they do about it? If an emotion is unhealthy, what should they do about it?

RATIONALE FOR THE EMOTION COST-BENEFIT ANALYSIS

People sometimes have mixed feelings about giving up certain kinds of negative emotions. This is frequently the case with anger and resentment. It can feel good to be angry and to harbor a grudge. We often tell ourselves, "I have the *right* to be angry." Anger is often a choice we make, even though we don't always think about it like this. We may feel like victims and tell ourselves, "That self-centered SOB is ticking me off. What he's doing is unfair!" We are not always aware that our anger results from our own thoughts, because we feel so strongly convinced that the other person is making us mad. In addition, we may feel very committed to hostile, vindictive feelings.

It can sometimes be difficult for people to let go of anxiety, guilt, or depression as well. We may tell ourselves, "I *deserve* to feel guilty because I'm such a rotten person," or "My fears of flying are *entirely justified*," or "If I worry a lot, I'll study harder and do a better job on the examination."

This phenomenon of hanging on to negative emotions is sometimes called resistance. Some people will say they really *want* to change but then dig in their heels when you show them how. There is an inner battle between the self that wants to change and feel happy, and the self that is committed to feeling miserable.

The Emotion Cost-Benefit Analysis can help people overcome this resistance to change. The participants will list the advantages and disadvantages of a negative feeling. Tell them to ask themselves, "How will it *help* me and how will it *hurt* me to feel this way? What are the *benefits* and what are the *costs* of this feeling?"

If the advantages of a negative feeling are greater than the disadvantages, the participants can simply accept the feeling, they can take constructive action based on the feeling, or they can express the feeling tactfully. If, in contrast, they decide that the disadvantages of the feeling outweigh the advantages, then they will usually be more receptive to using cognitive techniques such as the Daily Mood Log.

Suppose that a woman is angry with her husband for being late. She may have the Negative Thought "He's a self-centered bum. All he cares about is himself!" Although this thought involves two familiar cognitive distortions, labeling and mind reading, she will probably resist using cognitive techniques to change the way she is thinking and feeling. She probably feels that her anger is justified and that her husband is to blame.

If she does an Emotion Cost-Benefit Analysis, she may decide that she wants to be angry with him. Instead of encouraging her to change her Negative Thoughts and feelings, which would lead only to resistance, it would be far better to thank her for describing a personally upsetting situation and to move on to another problem. Otherwise you will get stuck in an uncomfortable power struggle with someone who will resist therapy.

The Emotion Cost-Benefit Analysis empowers clients as well as therapists. You will empower the members of the group because you are telling them: You do have the right to feel this way. Let's examine the consequences and see if this is the way you really want to feel.

At the same time you empower yourself, because you no longer have to struggle with therapeutic resistance. Instead, you surrender to the resistance and examine it collaboratively. You give the participants the ultimate responsibility of defining their problems and deciding whether they want to solve them.

EMOTION COST-BENEFIT EXERCISE 1

Ask the group members to do the Emotion Cost-Benefit Analysis exercise on page 75 of the participant's workbook. Their assignment is to list the advantages and disadvantages of getting angry when they discover that their fourteen-year-old daughter, Julie, has been cutting classes in high school and failing to do her homework. Ask the members to think about these questions when they do the Emotion CBA: "How will your anger help you? Will it help Julie? How will your anger hurt you or your daughter?"

As the participants describe the advantages or disadvantages of getting angry, write them on the flip chart in the front of the room. Ask the participants to list them in their workbooks.

After you have listed several advantages and disadvantages, ask the participants to put two numbers that add up to 100 in the circles at the bottom of the page. These numbers will show how they weighed the advantages and disadvantages against each other. For example, if the advantages of getting angry seem greater, they might put a 60 in the left-hand circle and a 40 in the right-hand circle.

This would mean that they view the anger as healthy. In this case, ask how they might express these feelings most effectively. What would be a destructive way to express angry feelings to Julie? What would be a constructive way? Remember that when the advantages of a negative feeling appear greater than the disadvantages, it is inappropriate to use cognitive therapy techniques to change that emotion.

EMOTION COST-BENEFIT EXERCISE 2

Divide the group into teams of three to six members. Ask each team to do a Cost-Benefit Analysis of the advantages and disadvantages of feeling upset in one of the following situations. Each team should choose a different situation. (More of these situations are listed on page 72 of the participant's workbook.)

- You overeat when you are on a diet.

- You are nervous about an upcoming presentation you have to give.

- A policeman stops you for speeding.

- A friend is late for a meeting.

- Your child runs out into the street to chase a ball.

- Your boss is irritable and criticizes you in a disrespectful, insulting way in front of your co-workers.

- Your spouse makes a rude remark about you at a dinner party.

After ten or fifteen minutes, ask the group as a whole to reconvene. Ask a spokesperson from each team to summarize the advantages and disadvantages that his or her group listed.

The Cost-Benefit Analysis can be used to evaluate a Negative Thought (like "I'm hopeless" or "I'm a loser"), a self-defeating attitude (like perfectionism), or a behavior (such as procrastination). In future steps, you will show the group how to do this.

DISCUSSION OF THE DAILY MOOD LOG

When a negative emotion is unhealthy, you can often change that feeling with cognitive techniques. Explain that today the members will learn more about how to use the Daily Mood Log to change their Negative Thoughts. (This method was introduced in the last step and is described in detail in Chapter 5 of *The Feeling Good Handbook*, "How to *Change* the Way You *Feel*.")

Begin by reviewing the three steps in filling out a Daily Mood Log:

Step One: Write a brief description of the upsetting event.

Step Two: Record your negative emotions and rate their intensity from 0% (the least) to 100% (the most).

Step Three: Use the Triple-Column Technique:

- Write down your Negative Thoughts and rate how much you believe each of them, from 0% (not at all) to 100% (completely).

- Identify the distortions in each Negative Thought, using the Distorted Thinking chart.

- Substitute more positive and realistic thoughts in the right-hand column of the Daily Mood Log. These are called Positive Thoughts.

In this session, the group will learn how to complete a Daily Mood Log.

DAILY MOOD LOG EXERCISE 1

You can illustrate these steps with the exercise beginning on page 79 of the participant's workbook. Read the description of the upsetting event and the negative emotions. Ask if any of the group members ever had a similar experience when they were dating. Did any of them ever get depressed or angry when a friend, family member, or colleague criticized them or rejected them?

Ask the members to put themselves in the shoes of Doug, the man who got the brush-off from Laura, his lady friend. Ask if any of them ever got depressed or discouraged because they were rejected in an important love relationship. Probably most of the hands will go up. Ask several of them to describe what happened to them and how they were thinking and feeling. This is a good way to get the group involved in a personal and emotional way, since nearly everyone can identify with rejection.

Ask the members to identify the distortions in the thought on page 81 of the participant's workbook, "I'll be alone forever." They can do this either as a group or individually. (The answer to this exercise is on page 89 of the participant's workbook.)

Next, ask the members to write a Positive Thought (PT) in the right-hand column of the form on page 81 of the participant's workbook. Remind them to record how strongly they believe their PT, from 0% to 100%. Ask several of them to read their PTs.

Now ask the participants to reestimate how strongly they believe the NT, "I'll be alone forever." Has the percentage gone down? Tell them to draw a line through the original estimate of 100% and put the new, lower estimate next to it. (There is an example of how to do this on page 83 of the participant's workbook.)

Ask them to repeat this process with the second NT, "I'm unlovable," on page 83 of the participant's workbook. They will complete these steps:

1. Identify the distortions in the thought.

2. Substitute a PT and estimate the percentage of belief in it (0% to 100%).

3. Estimate how strongly they now believe the NT (0% to 100%). Draw a line through the original estimate and put the new, lower estimate next to it.

You will notice there is a lot of attention to detail and to the correct format. This is not just a compulsive preoccupation with the methods of cognitive therapy! The success of the Daily Mood Log frequently depends on using the technique correctly.

For example, a PT will not be helpful unless you believe it 100% or nearly 100%. Rationalizations and vague, optimistic statements almost never help. You won't know whether or not a participant is convinced by the PT unless he or she estimates how much he or she believes it (using the 0%-to-100% rating system). If it is a halfhearted PT, you can tell the participant it's a good first effort that is not likely to help at the gut level. Ask the individual to try to come up with a Positive Thought that is more convincing and believable.

After the members have reduced their belief in both NTs, ask them to reestimate how upset they now feel, as illustrated on page 84 of the participant's workbook. Ask them to draw a single line through each of the percentages and to record the new, lower estimates.

Explain that when they work with their own Negative Thoughts and feelings, it will usually be more difficult. It is hard to be objective when you are the one who feels upset. Emphasize that it sometimes takes many weeks to put the lie to your own NTs in a convincing and helpful way. Patience and persistence are the keys to success.

DAILY MOOD LOG EXERCISE 2

Ask the members to do Daily Mood Log Exercise 2 beginning on page 84 of the participant's workbook. It describes a man named Bob who felt anxious and inferior when he was invited to play cards with his buddies. Ask the members if they ever felt nervous or insecure when playing cards or sports or when socializing with friends.

You can ask them to complete the exercise individually or in teams. They will identify the distortions in Bob's Negative Thoughts, substitute Positive Thoughts, and reestimate how strongly they now believe the NTs, on a scale from 0% to 100%. Then ask them to reestimate the negative emotions on a scale from 0% to 100%. Give them at least five to ten minutes for this exercise, and then lead a discussion of their work.

HOW TO TROUBLESHOOT

Make sure you emphasize the following points when you describe the Daily Mood Log (DML), because they are crucial to the success or failure of the procedure:

1. The participants must separate the actual event (for example, a woman's ex-husband gets engaged) from the feelings (sad, anxious, jealous, angry, hopeless) and the distorted Negative Thoughts ("I can never be happy without him"; "The divorce was all my fault") that accompany it.

2. They must not put descriptions of their feelings, such as "I feel sad" or "I felt upset," in the Negative Thoughts column. Negative emotions are recorded in Step Two of the Daily Mood Log, where it says "Record your negative feelings."

3. Positive Thoughts will improve their moods only if they believe the thoughts 100% *and* they put the lie to their Negative Thoughts (their belief in the Negative Thoughts is reduced nearly to 0%).

When the Daily Mood Log does not seem to be working properly, the Troubleshooting Guide on page 87 of the participant's workbook can be useful. Discuss it with the members. Ask if they have any questions about it. Let them know that they will be learning more about the Daily Mood Log in the next several sessions.

TWO OPTIONAL DAILY MOOD LOG EXERCISES

If you have plenty of time and would like to do another exercise with the DML, you can divide the group up into teams of three to six members. Ask each team to fill out a Daily Mood Log together, using one of these upsetting events:

- You get upset when a family member, colleague, or teacher criticizes you.

- You feel nervous about a presentation you have to give.

- You do not achieve an important personal goal. This could be a good grade on a paper you wrote for a class, making a sale or getting a promotion at work, sticking to a diet, and so forth.

- Someone you care about is critical of you or angry with you.

You can probably think of many other negative events that nearly everyone experiences that would be suitable for this exercise. The members can fill in the blank Daily Mood Log on page 290 of the participant's workbook as they do this exercise.

Ask each team to choose one upsetting event. Tell each team's members to write a brief description of the event on the DML. This is Step One of the DML. Next, they can identify and rate the negative emotions they might have in that situation on a scale from 0% to 100%. This is Step Two of the DML. Then they will write down the Negative Thoughts they would have in that situation. This begins Step Three of the DML. Ask them to record the percent they believe each Negative Thought (0% to 100%) and identify the distortions in it. Next, ask them to substitute Positive Thoughts and reestimate how strongly they believe each of them (0% to 100%). Finally, they reestimate how strongly they believe each NT (0% to 100%) and rerate the intensity of their negative feelings (0% to 100%). This completes the DML. When they are done, reconvene the group as a whole and ask a spokesperson from each team to summarize the work that was completed.

You can select one Negative Thought from one team's Daily Mood Log and write it on a flip chart. After the participants have identified the distortions in the thought, ask how many Positive Thoughts they can come up with. Write down each Positive Thought. Ask how strongly they believe each Positive Thought, from 0% to 100%. Ask them if the Positive Thought reduces their belief in the Negative Thought.

In these exercises, the members are working on Negative Thoughts that are not their own. This will keep the group moving smoothly and rapidly and will give them greater confidence when they later move ahead to the more difficult task of challenging their own Negative Thoughts.

At the end of today's session, you can direct an exercise with the DML using an example of an upsetting event supplied by a group member. The members can fill in one of the blank Daily Mood Logs beginning on page 290 of the participant's workbook as they do this exercise. Remind them to keep one copy of the DML (as well as every other form) blank so they can make photocopies when they run out.

This exercise is more challenging and should be attempted only by leaders who feel reasonably confident about their cognitive therapy skills. The danger is that the member who supplies the personal problem may be angry or resistant to change. He or she may get bogged down in complaining and the group may get sidetracked by giving advice or trying to "help." This could be time-consuming and could demoralize or bore the other group members. It may be easier for them to work with examples of other people's problems at this stage, since they are still just learning.

If you do work with an example of an upsetting event supplied by a member, you can ask the group as a whole, "How would you be feeling if this happened to you?" Tell them to record the emotions and NTs they would have in that situation. Then they can identify the distortions in their own thoughts, substitute PTs, and so forth.

This procedure will prevent you from having to treat an individual while the rest of the group watches nervously to see whether or not you will succeed. Some of the pioneers in cognitive therapy, like Dr. Albert Ellis, can comfortably do live demonstrations with ornery individuals in front of large groups. Most of us, who are not quite so experienced, may find this a little nerve-racking!

FEEDBACK ABOUT STEP 3

At the end of the session, summarize the ideas that were discussed. Ask the participants what they liked and disliked about it. Tell them to fill out the Evaluation of Step 3 on page 90 of the participant's workbook. Ask if they would be willing to read what they wrote down. Remember to respond nondefensively when they voice criticisms or negative reactions.

SELF-HELP ASSIGNMENTS FOR STEP 4

Discuss the self-help assignments for Step 4 before the participants leave. These assignments are listed on page 91 of the participant's workbook.

STEP 4

HOW TO BREAK OUT OF A BAD MOOD

LEADER'S PREPARATION FOR STEP 4

Activity	Check (√) when done
1. Read the description of Step 4 in the participant's workbook beginning on page 92.	
2. Study the Checklist for Step 4 on the next page of this *Leader's Manual* and the Tips for Leaders beginning on page 103.	
3. Read Chapters 6 and 8 in *The Feeling Good Handbook*.	
4. Study the table called Fifteen Ways to Untwist Your Thinking on page 299 of the participant's workbook.	

CHECKLIST FOR STEP 4

Activity	Optional or required?	Minimum time (min.)	Check (√) when done
1. Using the Leader's Data Sheet on page 70, record the participants' scores on the three self-assessment tests, along with their points for homework and for attendance.	req.	10	
2. Ask for positive and negative feedback about Step 3.	req.	5	
3. Review the steps in filling out an Emotion Cost-Benefit Analysis and discuss the written homework assignment with the CBA.	req.	5 – 10	
4. Review the steps in filling out a Daily Mood Log, which were presented in the last session, and discuss the written homework assignment with the Daily Mood Log.	req.	10	
5. Discuss the assigned reading for this step.	req.	5 – 10	
6. Introduce Fifteen Ways to Untwist Your Thinking.	req.	5 – 10	
7. Attitude Cost-Benefit Analysis Exercise 1.	req.	10	
8. Attitude Cost-Benefit Analysis Exercises 2, 3, and 4.	opt.	10 – 15	
9. Experimental Method Exercise 1.	req.	10 – 15	
10. Experimental Method Exercise 2.	opt.	10 – 15	
11. Examine the Evidence Exercise.	req.	10 – 15	
12. Survey Method Exercise.	opt.	5 – 10	
13. Daily Mood Log Exercise 1.	req.	10 – 15	
14. Daily Mood Log Exercises 2 and 3.	opt.	10 – 15	
15. Daily Mood Log Exercise 4.	opt.	10 – 15	
16. Ask for positive and negative feedback about Step 4.	req.	5	
17. Assign the homework for Step 5.	req.	3	

OVERVIEW OF STEP 4

Changing one's Negative Thoughts is often the key to emotional change. The moment group members see that their self-critical thoughts are not valid, they will feel an uplift in their moods and self-esteem. However, it may sometimes be quite difficult to guide them in a successful challenge of their Negative Thoughts, because these thoughts can seem overwhelmingly convincing.

Cognitive therapists have developed many techniques to help people challenge their distorted Negative Thoughts so they can develop more positive and realistic thoughts. If one method doesn't work, clients can try another, and then another, until they finally see that their self-critical thoughts are not valid.

In today's session you will teach the members of your group how to use a number of the techniques on a table called Fifteen Ways to Untwist Your Thinking. This table lists fifteen of the most basic cognitive techniques. Although experienced cognitive therapists routinely use many more techniques than this, the fifteen methods on the table can be thought of as a beginner's toolkit. Participants will be using this table from now on in conjunction with the Daily Mood Log. The table will provide them with lots of ideas about how to talk back to their Negative Thoughts. In future steps, you will teach them more of the techniques listed on this table, as well as a number of additional techniques that are not listed there.

TIPS FOR LEADERS

DATA COLLECTION

Record the participants' scores on the three self-assessment tests (the BDC, the BAI, and the RSAT) on the Leader's Data Sheet on page 70. Record how much homework they completed using the 3-point rating scale on page 68. Record whether or not they came on time using the 2-point rating scale on page 68.

FEEDBACK AND REVIEW OF HOMEWORK

Ask about the participants' positive and negative reactions to the previous session. What did they like and dislike about it? What are the differences between healthy and unhealthy negative emotions? Is this an important distinction? Why?

Ask the participants if they understand how the Cost-Benefit Analysis can be used to examine the positive and negative consequences of a negative feeling such as guilt, anxiety, or anger. Ask them to discuss any homework they did with the Emotion Cost-Benefit Analysis. How did it work for them?

Review the steps in completing a Daily Mood Log that were presented in the last session. Ask about the written homework assignments using the Daily Mood Log. What problems did they encounter? Ask if any participants would be willing to describe their written homework to the group.

Follow this with a brief discussion of the assigned reading. Encourage the members to ask questions about this material. Ask them what they agreed and disagreed with. Were any passages particularly helpful and interesting? Was there anything they didn't understand?

INTRODUCTION TO FIFTEEN WAYS TO UNTWIST YOUR THINKING

The participants have already learned two techniques that can help them talk back to their negative thoughts:

1. **Identify the Distortions:** The participants use the list of ten cognitive distortions to identify the distortions in their Negative Thoughts. Although this usually won't be sufficient to change the way they feel, it's a helpful first step. Once they see that their Negative Thoughts are not realistic, it becomes easier to replace them with thoughts that are more positive and realistic.

2. **The Straightforward Approach:** The participants simply ask themselves if they can think of a more realistic and positive thought.

In today's session, several additional techniques for talking back to Negative Thoughts will be illustrated. These techniques are listed on the table called Fifteen Ways to Untwist Your Thinking in the participant's handbook. There are two versions of this table. The short version of the table can be found on page 109 and the long version can be found on page 299.

3. **The Attitude Cost-Benefit Analysis:** In Step 3 the participants learned how to do an Emotion Cost-Benefit Analysis. Today they will learn how to do an Attitude Cost-Benefit Analysis for a Negative Thought (such as "I'm an inferior person") or attitude (such as "I must always try to be perfect"). In doing an Attitude Cost-Benefit Analysis, they list the advantages and disadvantages of the Negative Thought. They ask themselves, "How will it help me, and how will it hurt me, to think like this?"

4. **Examine the Evidence:** The participants ask themselves, "What is the evidence that this thought is true? What is the evidence that it's not true?"

5. **The Survey Method:** The participants do a survey to find out if their thoughts and attitudes are realistic. For example, if they believe that public speaking anxiety is unusual or abnormal, they could ask several friends if they ever felt that way.

6. **The Experimental Method:** Participants will discover that they can often test the accuracy of a Negative Thought scientifically. They ask themselves, "What experiment could I perform to find out if this thought is really true?"

In future sessions you will illustrate many more techniques for talking back to Negative Thoughts. The list that follows is similar to the list in the participant's workbook.

If you like, you can briefly discuss these techniques so the members will get a preview of some of the methods they will learn in upcoming sessions.

7. **The Double-Standard Technique:** People are often much harder on themselves than others. After participants write down their Negative Thoughts, they can ask themselves, "Would I say this to a friend with a similar problem? Why not? What would I say to him or her?" They will often discover that they operate on a double standard—they have a realistic, fair, compassionate set of standards that they apply to other people whom they care about. They encourage friends or loved ones who are suffering. In contrast, they may have a harsh, unrealistic set of standards that they apply to themselves. They beat themselves up relentlessly, as if this would somehow help them achieve perfection or become better human beings. One secret of self-esteem is simply to make the decision to talk to yourself in the same way you would talk to a beloved friend who was upset.

8. **The Pleasure-Predicting Method:** Participants predict how satisfying various activities will be on a scale from 0% (the least) to 100% (the most). After completing each activity, they record how satisfying it actually turned out to be. This technique can help people get moving when they feel discouraged and lethargic. It can also be used to test Self-defeating Beliefs such as "If I'm alone, I'm bound to feel miserable."

9. **The Vertical Arrow Technique:** Instead of disputing a Negative Thought, participants draw a vertical arrow under it and ask themselves, "If this thought was true, why would it be upsetting to me? What would it mean to me?" This process, when repeated over and over, will generate a series of Negative Thoughts that will lead to their Self-defeating Beliefs.

10. **Thinking in Shades of Gray:** This is particularly helpful for all-or-nothing thinking. Instead of looking at life in black-and-white categories, participants learn to evaluate things in shades of gray. For example, instead of thinking of themselves as total failures when they're having trouble in their marriages or careers, they could ask themselves, "What are my specific strengths and weaknesses? What are my positive qualities? What deficiencies could I work on?"

11. **Define Terms:** Participants ask themselves, "What does this Negative Thought really mean?" For example, if they call themselves "total losers," they can ask themselves what the definition of a "total loser" is. Does this definition really make sense? Is there any such thing as a total loser? Is a total loser someone who loses at everything all the time? Or someone who loses at some things some of the time? They will discover that we all experience losses and disappointments at times, but there's really no such thing as "a loser." Would they think of themselves as "breathers" simply because they breathe?

12. **Be Specific:** Participants learn to stick with reality and to avoid global judgments about reality. Instead of thinking of themselves as totally defective, they can focus on their specific strengths and weaknesses.

13. **The Semantic Method:** Participants use words that are more objective and less emotionally charged. This is especially effective for "should" statements and for labeling. For example, when they are upset they may beat themselves up and think, "I'm *such a jerk. I shouldn't* have made that mistake. How could I *possibly* be so stupid?" Instead, they could use the Semantic Method and tell themselves, "*It would be preferable* if I hadn't made that mistake. The world won't come to an end, so let's see what I can learn from this. I'm a human being, not a jerk, and I will sometimes screw up, like all other human beings." When they use the Semantic Method, they ask themselves, "Could I use kinder, gentler language when I think about my shortcomings?"

14. **Reattribution:** Instead of blaming themselves entirely for a problem, participants can identify the many factors that may have contributed to it. Then they can focus on solving the problem instead of using all their energy feeling guilty. They ask themselves, "What caused this problem? What did I contribute and what did other people (or fate) contribute? How long am I expected to suffer? At what point am I permitted to let go of the guilt and continue living in a productive, joyous, loving way once again?"

15. **The Acceptance Paradox:** Many of the cognitive techniques are based on the idea of Self-defense—because their Negative Thoughts are usually illogical and distorted, participants learn to challenge these thoughts and talk back to them. They defend themselves and try to build up their self-esteem. This approach is based on Western philosophy and on the scientific method. The idea is that "the truth shall make you free." In contrast, the Acceptance Paradox is based on Eastern philosophies such as Buddhism. Instead of defending against their own self-criticism, they find some truth in it. They accept their deficiencies with inner peace and tranquility, instead of feeling self-hatred and shame.

If you read the definitions of several of these methods, ask the group members if they can think of concrete examples of how one or two of them would work. Here's a brief example of the Acceptance Paradox. Let's assume that a man in your group has the thought that "there must be something wrong with me," because he has had a lifelong tendency toward recurrent depression. This sense of global, inherent defectiveness is actually quite common among people who feel depressed. What methods could he use to talk back to this thought?

One approach would be to argue that there's nothing wrong with him and that he is a perfectly normal human being who's just as good as anybody else. The "power of positive thinking" people might take this approach even further and train him to repeat these words over and over: "I'm getting better and better every day in every way." The use of positive affirmations is quite common among many mental health professionals.

These strategies represent the Self-defense approach. The problem is that they sound a little defensive and don't sound realistic. If the group member has had recurrent depressions, then it's simply not true that his moods are just as good as anybody else's.

Furthermore, he may be feeling stuck and not making any tangible progress just now. Self-defense runs the risk of sounding hollow and contrived.

In contrast, if the member used the Acceptance Paradox he might tell himself, "There's actually more than just *something* wrong with me. There's *a lot* wrong with me! I have huge numbers of deficiencies. I am a human being and I am quite flawed." If he can accept this message with inner peace and objectivity, it can be quite liberating.

If you use this example, emphasize that the Acceptance Paradox should never be used as a cop-out or a way to avoid one's shortcomings. Often personal change through hard work is needed. Paradoxically, self-acceptance is frequently the crucial first step to personal change. When people accept their shortcomings, they can use their energy in a creative, productive way instead of moping and beating themselves up.

Of course, there are numerous other strategies that he could use. For example, he could do an Attitude Cost-Benefit Analysis and list the advantages and disadvantages of insisting that there's "something wrong with me." This procedure may make him more consciously aware of the hidden benefits of his chronic feelings of inferiority, as well as the many costs of this negative mind-set.

Some participants may ask why there are so many techniques for changing Negative Thoughts. There are many tools because it can be very hard for people to change their Negative Thoughts. Many people have had feelings of self-doubt and unhappiness for many years, if not for their entire lives. They are used to thinking about themselves and the world in a negative way. If it were easy to change these thinking patterns, they would have done it already!

You can illustrate these many different techniques in an entertaining way by using the example from pages 137–143 of *The Feeling Good Handbook*. This example involves Chuck, a man with a slightly deformed chest. Chuck was afraid to go to the beach because he believed he was inferior to men with better physiques. He was convinced that if he did go to the beach and take off his shirt, people would notice his sunken chest and look down on him. Chuck had these two Negative Thoughts:

1. "I'm inferior to all these other men who have such better physiques."

2. "If I took my shirt off, everyone would stare at me and think I was abnormal."

After you write these two thoughts on the flip chart, you can ask the group, "What are the distortions in these thoughts?" Then ask, "How would you use the technique called Examine the Evidence to talk back to one of them? How would you use the technique called the Experimental Method?" And so forth. This will make it easy for participants to see how many different techniques can be used to refute a Negative Thought. While you do this, you can photocopy and distribute copies of the illustration called "There Are Numerous Ways to Challenge Any Automatic Thought" from page 142 of *The Feeling Good Handbook*.

If you do this exercise, you can also act out the Feared Fantasy Dialogue on page 141 of the *Handbook* with a volunteer from the group. The volunteer can play the role of the hostile crowd at the beach and you can play the role of Chuck, the man with the deformed chest. If you do this exercise, explain that the Feared Fantasy is not intended to be realistic; it is an Alice in Wonderland adventure where your worst fears come true. The leaders of a Ten Days to Self-esteem group at the University of Georgia counseling service mentioned that the students in their group had a great deal of fun with this example when they used the Feared Fantasy.

ATTITUDE COST-BENEFIT ANALYSIS EXERCISE 1

In this exercise, ask the participants to think of a time when they had a setback in school, in dieting, or in their careers. Then ask them to describe these experiences. How did they think and feel? What messages did they give themselves?

When people fail, they may get down in the dumps and tell themselves, "I'm a total failure." Ask if any of the participants ever think like this. Tell them to list the advantages and disadvantages of believing this on page 101 of the participant's workbook. Tell them to ask themselves, "How will it *help* me and how will it *hurt* me to think this way?"

Direct this exercise with the group as a whole. When the members come up with advantages of the Negative Thought, write them on your flip chart while they list them in their workbooks. Make sure the group members do not gloss over the advantages of thinking of oneself as a total failure. Although distorted thoughts are very destructive, they may subtly reward us in many ways. One purpose of the Attitude Cost-Benefit Analysis is to make people aware of how their negative thinking patterns may secretly reward them. Some of the benefits of thinking "I'm a total failure" are listed on page 117 of this *Leader's Manual*.

After the participants have listed a number of advantages, ask them about the disadvantages of the Negative Thought. It will be easy for the group to list the disadvantages. They are more obvious than the advantages.

Once they have completed the list of advantages and disadvantages of thinking "I'm a total failure," ask the group whether the costs or the benefits are greater, using a 100-point scale. For example, the advantages may outweigh the disadvantages by 60–40, or the disadvantages may outweigh the advantages by 30–70. The participants can put their ratings in the circles at the bottom of the Attitude Cost-Benefit Analysis form.

If they decide that the disadvantages are greater, ask them what Positive Thought they could substitute for "I'm a total failure." What could they tell themselves instead?

ATTITUDE COST-BENEFIT ANALYSIS EXERCISES 2–4

You can ask the participants to do these exercises individually or in teams of two to six members. I will assume you will divide them into three teams. Assign a different Attitude Cost-Benefit Analysis exercise to each team. Tell each team to read the description of the problem you have assigned in the participant's workbook. Then they can list the advantages and disadvantages of the Negative Thoughts. Tell them not to look at the answers at the end of Step 4 in the participant's workbook while they are doing the exercise.

Here's a brief description of the problem each team will work on:

Group 1

This team will do Attitude Cost-Benefit Analysis Exercise 2, which is on page 109 of the participant's workbook. They will imagine they are Fred, a chronically depressed and angry doctor. One day Fred learned that an obnoxious colleague of his had been promoted to associate professor in the Department of Medicine. Fred felt a surge of annoyance and had these Negative Thoughts: "How can a phony like that get ahead? He's just a brownnoser. Promotions should be based on merit and original research, and not on politics. What's the world coming to? It's unfair!" Fred often feels bitter and disappointed in the world. Ask this team to list the advantages and disadvantages of Fred's Negative Thought "It's unfair!" How does it reward Fred, and how does it hurt Fred, to think like this?

Group 2

This team will do Attitude Cost-Benefit Analysis Exercise 3, which is on page 102 of the participant's workbook. The team members will imagine that they are a thirty-two-year-old single attorney named Harry. Although he is attractive and personable, Harry is extremely shy and has had very little dating experience because he gets so nervous around women. He stubbornly resisted his therapist's assignment of flirting with ten attractive women every day. Instead, he wanted to analyze *why* he had been anxious and shy all his life. His Negative Thoughts were "Dr. Burns just doesn't understand that I *can't* do this. Women are looking for men who are confident and glib. I'm not like that. If any woman found out how nervous and insecure I am, she'd dump me like a ton of bricks. Besides, I'm a *nice* and *sincere* person and I *shouldn't have to* play social games just to get dates. I'm not like that. I *shouldn't have to* wear any stupid flashy clothing. That's not *the real me*. Women should like me just the way I am. If they don't like me the way I am, that's tough!" Ask this team to list the advantages and disadvantages of one of Harry's Negative Thoughts. Two choices could be "I *can't* do this" and "Women should like me just the way I am."

Group 3

This team will do Attitude Cost-Benefit Analysis Exercise 4, which is on page 103 of the participant's workbook. It deals with a woman who experienced severe sexual abuse as a child. She suffered from chronic depression because she told herself, "It was my fault. I should have been able to prevent it. If anybody knew about what happened to me, they'd think I was a horny little girl." Although she could see rationally how unreasonable these thoughts were, she had an irrational compulsion to think them. She was terribly depressed but resisted change. The team will list the advantages and disadvantages of believing her first Negative Thought, "It was my fault." If you choose this exercise, keep in mind that it is a little raw and may upset some members of your group.

While the participants are doing the exercises, walk around and supervise. Tell them to stick with the assignment and to avoid gossiping. (The answers to these problems appear in the participant's workbook as follows: Exercise 2, page 117; Exercise 3, page 117; Exercise 4, page 118. Tell your group members not to look until they've written their own answers first.)

After each team has had about five minutes to complete the Attitude Cost-Benefit Analysis, ask a spokesperson to summarize the results of his or her team's analysis.

At the end of the exercises, you can remind the participants that the Attitude Cost-Benefit Analysis deals primarily with their motivation to believe a Negative Thought. It does not necessarily deal with whether or not the Negative Thought is true. Once they see that the disadvantages of a Negative Thought outweigh the advantages, they will usually be able to revise the thought to make it more positive and realistic.

EXPERIMENTAL METHOD EXERCISE 1

Remind the group that there are many ways to challenge Negative Thoughts. One of these techniques is called the Experimental Method. An exercise using the Experimental Method is described on page 104 of the participant's workbook. Do this exercise with the group as a whole.

A twenty-eight-year-old chemist from India named Ronny suffered from severe nervousness in social situations. While standing in line at the grocery store, he would stare at the floor anxiously and tell himself, "These people are all poised and charming and chatting with each other. When I get to the cash register, they'll expect me to say something clever or witty to the checker."

Ask the participants to identify the distortions in Ronny's thoughts. Then ask how Ronny could use the Experimental Method to challenge his thoughts. This exercise should be easy for the group.

(The answer to this problem is on page 118 of the participant's workbook. Tell the participants not to look until they've written their own answers first.)

EXPERIMENTAL METHOD EXERCISE 2

This exercise is described on page 105 of the participant's workbook. A forty-two-year-old chronically anxious, perfectionistic attorney named Bill was afraid that his colleagues would look down on him if he ever lost a case. Although he had an exceptionally successful career, Bill was a chronic worrier and could never relax because of his intense fear of failure.

Ask the participants to do this exercise individually or in teams of two or three members. While they are doing it, walk around and supervise. Answer questions and make sure that they are sticking to the assignment and not talking in a general way. After about five minutes, ask them for the results of their analysis.

(The answer to this problem is on page 119 of the participant's workbook. Tell the team members not to look until they've written their own answers first.)

EXAMINE THE EVIDENCE EXERCISE

Ask the group how to use the technique called Examine the Evidence to refute the following Negative Thoughts:

1. *I'm a total procrastinator. I can't seem to get <u>anything</u> done on time! What's wrong with me?*

2. *I just can't control my appetite. I have no willpower.*

3. *I'm so indecisive. I just can't make up my mind about anything!*

4. *I'm such a klutz. I can't do <u>anything</u> right.*

Ask each group member to choose one of these four thoughts and to circle the number of that thought on page 105 of the workbook.

Tell them to identify the distortions in the thoughts they have chosen. They can review the Distorted Thinking chart on page 50 when they list the distortions in their workbooks on page 106.

Finally, ask them how they could use the method called Examine the Evidence to refute the thought they have chosen. Tell them to write their ideas in their workbooks.

(The answer to this problem is on page 119 of the participant's workbook. Tell the participants not to look until they've written their own answers first.)

SURVEY METHOD EXERCISE

The Survey Method is similar to the Experimental Method. Instead of doing an actual experiment to test the truth of a Negative Thought, participants do a survey. For example, I once treated a psychologist with public speaking anxiety. She had to give a series of seminars for colleagues who were mental health professionals. She felt nervous and ashamed because of her belief that it was unusual for a mental health professional to have this problem. She told herself that she should "have it all together." Can you think of a survey she could do to test this belief?

I suggested that at her next presentation she could ask people in the audience with public speaking anxiety to raise their hands. She was surprised to learn that more than half of her colleagues suffered from this problem!

You could describe her problem and ask your group what survey she could perform to test her belief. In addition, there is a written exercise on the Survey Method in the participant's workbook on page 106. This exercise deals with a man who was upset with his wife. He felt she was too lenient in disciplining their son. He was moping about this, but afraid to express his feelings because of his belief that couples with happy and successful relationships should never fight or argue. Ask the participants what survey he could perform to test the validity of this belief.

(The answer to this problem is on page 120 of the participant's workbook. Tell the participants not to look until they've written their own answers first.)

DAILY MOOD LOG EXERCISE 1

This exercise, which is on page 108 of the participant's workbook, will give the members of your group some practice using a variety of techniques when they talk back to their Negative Thoughts. Tell them to imagine that they received a bad evaluation from their boss. They felt upset and had these Negative Thoughts:

1. I'm a total loser. 100%

2. There must be something wrong with me. 100%

3. This shouldn't have happened. It's unfair. 75%

Ask the participants if they ever had thoughts or feelings like these after they were criticized. Ask each participant to choose one of these three thoughts. After they choose a thought, tell them to identify the distortions in it. Then they can study the list of Fifteen Ways to Untwist Your Thinking on page 109 of the participant's workbook so they can refute the thought. Tell them to record the Positive Thought in the right-hand column.

For example, if they choose "I'm a total loser," they might go through these steps:

1. **Identify the Distortions:** The distortions in "I'm a total loser" would include labeling, all-or-nothing thinking, mental filter, emotional reasoning, and so forth.

2. **The Straightforward Approach:** Participants ask themselves, "Can I think of a way to talk back to this claim that I'm a total loser? Is this thought true? Why or why not?"

3. **Cost-Benefit Analysis:** Participants list the advantages and disadvantages of believing the thought. They ask themselves, "How will it help me to think of myself as a total loser? What are the benefits of this mind-set? And how will it hurt me?" They could also list the advantages and disadvantages of an alternative mental message, such as thinking of themselves instead as "a human being with strengths and weaknesses."

4. **The Double-Standard Technique:** Participants ask themselves, "Would I say this to a dear friend with a similar problem? Why not? What would I say to him or her instead?"

5. **Examine the Evidence:** Participants ask themselves, "What is the evidence that I'm a total loser? What is the evidence that I'm not a total loser?" Or if they were working on Negative Thought 3, they might ask themselves, "Where is it written that bosses should always be fair and reasonable? Is there any evidence that the world will always be the way I want it to be?"

6. **The Experimental Method:** Participants test the thought to find out if it is realistic. They ask themselves, "What experiment could I do to find out if this thought is true?"

7. **Define Terms:** Participants ask themselves, "What is a total loser? Does the definition make sense? Is there any such thing as a total loser?"

8. **The Semantic Method:** Participants ask themselves, "Can I think of a more kindly and objective way to describe myself than 'total loser'?"

9. **Thinking in Shades of Gray:** Participants can use Thinking in Shades of Gray on the first thought: "Can I make a list of my specific strengths and weaknesses? What are my positive qualities? What are some problem areas that I need to work on?" Or they could use Thinking in Shades of Gray on the third thought: "Is the world fair all of the time? Is the world fair none of the time? Or is the world fair some of the time?"

10. **The Acceptance Paradox:** Participants ask themselves, "Is there some truth in the criticism? Can I learn from this situation? Can I accept the fact that my performance was not up to par? Is it okay for a human being to be flawed?"

This list is not exhaustive. It's just a starting point. There are numerous other methods that could be used, such as Reattribution: They ask themselves, "How much of the problem is really my fault? Fifty percent? One hundred percent? And how much can be attributed to other factors, such as pressures on my boss that make him (or her) overly harsh at times?" They could also work on learning to use more effective verbal strategies to handle criticism at work, such as the Disarming Technique and Stroking. These communication techniques nearly always work like a charm on ornery bosses!

The main point is that when one method fails, participants can try another, and then another, until they finally put the lie to the Negative Thought.

After several minutes, ask several volunteers to read the distortions they found in the Negative Thought they chose. Then ask them to read the Positive Thoughts they wrote down to refute the Negative Thought. Ask which methods they used when generating their Positive Thoughts.

DAILY MOOD LOG EXERCISES 2 AND 3

In these exercises participants will record the event, the emotions, and the Negative Thoughts on the Daily Mood Log before they identify the distortions and substitute Positive Thoughts. However, the event, the emotions, and the Negative Thoughts are all described in their workbooks, so they will not have to create them from scratch. These exercises are intended to give them a feel for doing a complete Daily Mood Log, starting with Step One.

Divide the group into two teams for this exercise. One team will work on Daily Mood Log Exercise 2 on page 110 of the participant's workbook, and the other team will work on Daily Mood Log Exercise 3 on page 112 of the participant's workbook. Exercise 2 deals with social anxiety and Exercise 3 deals with the death of a family member. Tell each team to work together. Emphasize that every participant should fill in the Daily Mood Log in the participant's workbook while doing the exercise. Walk around and monitor the teams to make sure that every participant actually does the writing and that they are working on the exercises and not just chatting.

After about ten minutes, reconvene the group as a whole and ask a spokesperson from each team to summarize his or her team's efforts. Were they able to come up with effective Positive Thoughts to replace the Negative Thoughts? What techniques did they find the most useful?

DAILY MOOD LOG EXERCISE 4

In this solo flight, participants will create a Daily Mood Log from scratch based on their own personal experiences. The instructions for this exercise begin on page 114 of the participant's workbook. You can direct this exercise in three different ways:

1. You can lead the group as a whole while the participants do it together.

2. You can break them up into teams of three to five members and ask each team to do the exercise.

3. You can have the participants do it individually in their workbooks.

With a talented group who seem to grasp the concepts quickly and enthusiastically, the second and third options will work. If your group members are a little slower, you can choose the first option. This will be the easiest for them, because you can structure the exercise as they go along. This will help them avoid several common pitfalls, such as putting descriptions of emotions or events in the NT column.

I will assume you have chosen the first option. Ask the participants to describe upsetting events from their own lives. If they like, they can use upsetting events from their written homework with the Daily Mood Log. Jot these events down on the flip chart. This will give you time to select an event that seems suitable. Sometimes it is easier when the event involves depression rather than anger. People who feel angry often find it difficult to let go of their Negative Thoughts and negative feelings. They may *want* to feel the way they feel. In contrast, people who feel depressed and self-critical are often more flexible and more willing to change.

Once you have selected the upsetting event, ask all the participants to write it down on page 115 of their workbooks. Make sure the event is specific as to time (when did it happen?), place (where did it happen?), person (who was there?), and details (what happened that was upsetting?). Upsetting events that are vague or abstract (such as "Life stinks" or "I can't seem to get my life together" or "I think I have an identity crisis") simply cannot be dealt with in a meaningful way.

Then go through the steps outlined on page 109 of the workbook. Ask the participants to write in their workbooks while you direct the exercise. Even though you are working with an event supplied by one member of the group, tell them all to imagine it was happening to them. Ask them, "How would you be feeling and thinking if this happened to you?" Tell them to record their negative emotions and rate each one on a scale from 0% to 100%. Ask them about the Negative Thoughts they would have in this situation.

Tell them to record their Negative Thoughts and number them on the Daily Mood Log. You can record their Negative Thoughts on your flip chart. Ask them to rate how strongly they believe each NT on a scale from 0% to 100%.

This will get the participants personally involved. It will make it far easier to develop effective Positive Thoughts to refute the NTs, since this event did not actually happen to most of them. The exercise is make-believe, except for the person who actually described the event. This is a big advantage in terms of keeping the group moving along and successfully refuting the NTs. The person who supplied the event may still feel stuck at the end, but most of the members will be able to see how the Daily Mood Log works. They will also see that most of the NTs are quite unrealistic.

When the participants come up with Negative Thoughts, make sure these are not simply descriptions of emotions (such as "I feel sad") or events (such as "My wife had an affair") or rhetorical questions (such as "Why me?").

You may find it helpful to break up the group into teams after you generate the list of NTs. Ask each team to work on a Negative Thought that was generated by someone in a different team. This will prevent them from "helping" or playing the role of therapist. In addition, the person with the Negative Thought won't be in a position to offer resistance and say, "Oh, that doesn't help," or "Oh, I've already thought of that." The goal at this stage is simply to learn how the approach works, and not to do therapy on specific group members.

Remind the participants to estimate how strongly (from 0% to 100%) they believe each PT. Then they can reestimate how strongly (from 0% to 100%) they believe each NT.

After each team has had time to refute one NT, ask the group as a whole to reconvene so a spokesperson from each team can summarize the work that they did. Ask what methods they used in refuting the NT. Were they able to reduce their belief in it?

At the end of today's session, remind the participants that working on their own NTs will often take considerably more time and persistence. It is usually easy to see how illogical and self-critical someone else is being. But when they are upset, their own self-critical thoughts may seem completely realistic. The moment they suddenly see how harsh and illogical these NTs are, they will often experience a tremendous boost in self-esteem.

FEEDBACK ABOUT STEP 4

At the end of the session, summarize the ideas that were discussed. Ask the participants how many of the techniques for refuting NTs they can recall.

Ask if they know why so many different kinds of cognitive techniques were developed. Ask if they understand how to use the table called Fifteen Ways to Untwist Your Thinking on page 109 of the participant's workbook. Remind them to use this table when they are trying to refute their Negative Thoughts.

Ask the participants what they liked and disliked about the session. Tell them to fill out the Evaluation of Step 4 on page 120 of the participant's workbook. Ask if they would be willing to read what they wrote down. Remember to respond nondefensively when they voice criticisms or negative reactions.

SELF-HELP ASSIGNMENTS FOR STEP 5

Discuss the self-help assignments for Step 5 before the participants leave. These assignments are listed on page 121 of the participant's workbook.

ANSWER TO THE EXERCISE ON PAGE 108
ATTITUDE COST-BENEFIT ANALYSIS*

The Attitude You Want to Change: *I'm a total failure.*

Advantages of believing this	Disadvantages of believing this
1. *I can avoid any conflict with the other person.*	
2. *I can pout and feel sorry for myself.*	
3. *I don't have to talk about any error I actually made.*	
4. *I don't have to find out if the other person is mad at me.*	
5. *I don't have to learn or do anything differently.*	
6. *This reaction to criticism is easy and familiar to me.*	
7. *If I feel angry, I do not have to deal with these feelings.*	
8. *I can make the other person feel guilty or sorry for me.*	
9. *This thought seems valid since I feel like a failure.*	

STEP 5

THE ACCEPTANCE PARADOX

LEADER'S PREPARATION FOR STEP 5

Activity	Check (√) when done
1. Read Step 5 in the participant's workbook beginning on page 122.	
2. Study the Checklist for Step 5 on the next page of this *Leader's Manual* and the Tips for Leaders beginning on page 120.	
3. Read descriptions of the Externalization of Voices and the Feared Fantasy Technique on pages 130–136, 137–143, 173–174, 245–248, and 356–357 of *The Feeling Good Handbook*. There are several additional examples in Chapter 13 of *Feeling Good: The New Mood Therapy*, as well as Appendix C of *Intimate Connections*.	

CHECKLIST FOR STEP 5

Activity	Optional or required?	Minimum time (min.)	Check (√) when done
1. Using the Leader's Data Sheet on page 70, record participants' scores on the three self-assessment tests, along with their points for homework and for attendance.	req.	10	
2. Review Steps 1–4 of the program.	opt.	5 – 10	
3. Ask for positive and negative feedback about Step 4.	req.	5	
4. Discuss the assigned reading for this step and review any written homework with the Daily Mood Log and the Cost-Benefit Analysis.	req.	5 – 10	
5. Review several techniques for refuting Negative Thoughts listed on the table called Fifteen Ways to Untwist Your Thinking on page 109 of the participant's workbook.	req.	5 – 10	
6. Exercise on the Externalization of Voices.	req.	20 +	
7. Exercise on the Acceptance Paradox.	req.	20 +	
8. Discuss the difference between healthy and unhealthy self-acceptance.	req.	5 – 10	
9. Ask for positive and negative feedback about Step 5.	req.	5	
10. Assign the homework for Step 6.	req.	3	

OVERVIEW OF STEP 5

In this step you will have the following major goals, one of which is optional:

- You can review what the participants have learned so far in the program. This review is optional. (You will have a chance to review the entire program in Step 10.)

- You will introduce a dramatic role-playing technique called the Externalization of Voices. This technique can be used to produce emotional change at the gut level. It is one of the most entertaining and engaging ways to teach cognitive therapy in individual therapy or in groups.

- You will contrast two dramatically different mood-elevating techniques called Self-defense and the Acceptance Paradox. The Self-defense technique is based on Western religion and scientific thinking. In contrast, the Acceptance Paradox is based more on Eastern philosophies such as Buddhism. Although most therapists and clients naturally gravitate to the Self-defense method, the Acceptance Paradox is often more powerful. Once you grasp it, the impact can be quite spectacular. When used together, these two methods can transform the way people think and feel about themselves, the world, and the future.

- You will lead a discussion of the philosophical and psychological implications of these two opposing styles. This discussion need not have a spiritual dimension, but you can easily direct the discussion in this direction if the members of your group have religious beliefs they would like to integrate with the methods they are learning.

- You will discuss the distinction between healthy and unhealthy self-acceptance. When does acceptance lead to feelings of worthlessness, hopelessness, and despair? When does acceptance lead to inner joy, freedom, and personal responsibility?

TIPS FOR LEADERS

DATA COLLECTION

Record the participants' scores on the three self-assessment tests (the BDC, the BAI, and the RSAT) on the Leader's Data Sheet on page 70. Record how much homework they completed using the 3-point rating scale on page 68. Record whether or not they came on time using the 2-point rating scale on page 68.

REVIEW OF STEPS 1–4 (OPTIONAL)

You may want to spend five to ten minutes reviewing what the participants have learned so far in this program. If time permits, a review can be very useful here.

In Step 1 they defined their personal goals and learned about the importance of measuring their moods and doing the self-help assignments between sessions so as to achieve these goals.

Ask if the participants can recall some of the reasons people resist doing the assignments. Ask if any of them have experienced this resistance personally. How many of them are satisfied with the amount of homework they have done so far? How many are dissatisfied? Is this resistance to homework puzzling to them? How do they feel about this issue now?

In the first session you also discussed the importance of opening up in the group and providing positive and negative feedback at the end of each session. Do the participants recall why some people may feel reluctant to open up and talk about their negative feelings? Ask how many of them have actually tried to share their personal feelings in the group. What was this experience like for them?

You can ask if they recall the three secrets of effective listening. What are the names of these three methods? What is the difference between listening and "helping"? What is the difference between good communication and bad communication? (Do not ask these questions if you omitted the exercise on helping versus listening at the end of Step 1.)

In Step 2 the participants learned about the basic principles of cognitive therapy. What are these principles? What causes us to have feelings like anger, sadness, or fear? What is a Negative Thought? What is a cognitive distortion? Can anyone provide some examples of cognitive distortions?

In Step 3 the group learned about the differences between healthy and unhealthy emotions. What are the differences? What are the practical implications of this distinction? What is the purpose of an Emotion Cost-Benefit Analysis?

The participants also learned more about how to fill out a Daily Mood Log. What are the basic steps? Is it just as effective if you do it in your head instead of on paper? What are the characteristics of an effective Positive Thought? How can you troubleshoot if the DML does not seem to be working?

In Step 4 the participants learned several techniques for challenging Negative Thoughts. Do they recall the names of any of these techniques? What is an Attitude Cost-Benefit Analysis? What is its purpose? What is the Experimental Method? Why are there so many different kinds of techniques? Why is it sometimes so difficult to talk back to your own NTs? What is the purpose of the DML? How do you use the list of Fifteen Ways to Untwist Your Thinking?

FEEDBACK AND REVIEW OF HOMEWORK

Ask about the participants' positive and negative reactions to the last session. What did they like and dislike about it?

Follow this with a brief discussion of the assigned reading in Step 5 of the participant's workbook and the supplementary reading in *The Feeling Good Handbook*. Encourage the group members to ask questions about the reading. Ask them what they agreed and disagreed with. Were any passages particularly helpful and interesting? Was there anything they didn't understand?

Do they understand how to use the table called Fifteen Ways to Untwist Your Thinking? Do they have any questions about this table? Have they been able to use it when they prepared their Daily Mood Logs?

Were the participants successful in doing the Attitude Cost-Benefit Analysis as part of their written homework? See if any of them would like to share their CBAs with the group.

Ask about the written homework assignment using the Daily Mood Log. Were they able to refute any of their NTs successfully? If so, ask them to give examples. What problems did they encounter? Did they have some NTs they were not able to refute?

I would recommend that you deal with the DML homework briefly. If the participants want help with a Negative Thought, ask if they have done the exercise on paper. Do not offer to help any participant who has an NT that was not carefully recorded on a Daily Mood Log. If they didn't do the DML on paper, tell them to do it as homework and to ask their question again at the next session. (Of course, if you have members who cannot read, you will have to make an exception to this rule!)

If the participants have done the DML on paper, write the NT they are having trouble with on the flip chart. Ask the group to troubleshoot with you, using the chart on page 87 of the participant's workbook as a guide. First, make sure they have correctly identified the upsetting event and the emotions. Then ask them, "Is this a healthy, appropriate emotion that needs to be expressed, or an unhealthy emotion that should be changed with the Daily Mood Log?"

If it's an unhealthy emotion and the DML seems to be appropriate, ask the members if they can identify the distortions in the thought you have written on the flip chart. Then ask them to study the table called Fifteen Ways to Untwist Your Thinking on page 109 of the participant's workbook. Ask them what methods they might use to develop a more effective PT. See if they can come up with several convincing PTs. Write these on the flip chart.

If the person who supplied the NT still feels stuck, reassure him or her that this is natural and that it sometimes takes many weeks before you can refute an NT that is especially upsetting. Let the group know that today they will learn more about how to refute NTs.

It's important not to let this process take up excessive amounts of time at the expense of the other group members. Try to avoid a power struggle with one individual, because he or she may be stuck just now and determined not to let go of the negative mind-set. People need time to digest and process these new ideas. You do not need to preach or force the issue. Right now, you only need to point people in the right direction.

EXTERNALIZATION OF VOICES

In today's session you will illustrate a technique I created in the late 1970s called the Externalization of Voices. It is called that because people externalize—or act out—the negative, self-critical thoughts that make them feel so upset. This method can transform intellectual understanding into real emotional change at the gut level. This is one of the most powerful and entertaining cognitive therapy techniques.

There are two different ways you can conduct this exercise. I will describe the version using the Double-Standard Technique first. This version, which is described in the participant's workbook, is the friendlier and easier of the two. Ask for a volunteer to demonstrate a new technique in the front of the group. Explain that you will play the role of the volunteer's Negative Thoughts and he or she will play the role of the Positive Thoughts.

Let's assume that the volunteer is a woman who has Negative Thoughts similar to these, which can be found on page 127 of the participant's workbook:

1. If people knew what I was really like, they'd look down on me.

2. Other people are a lot smarter than I am.

3. I'm always screwing up.

4. I'm a loser and a failure.

5. I shouldn't be so depressed all the time. There must be something wrong with me.

6. I'll never get well.

7. I'm defective and inferior.

8. I'm not witty or clever enough. I don't have a good sense of humor.

Tell the volunteer to imagine that you are very similar to her and that you are feeling self-critical. Tell her that you will verbalize her Negative Thoughts. Tell the volunteer to talk to you the way she would talk to a dear friend who was feeling lousy.

Since you will play the role of the volunteer's Negative Thoughts, you will use the first person (for example, "*I'm* a loser and a failure; *I'll* never get well; *I'm* defective and inferior"). Since the volunteer will play the Positive Thoughts, tell her to use the second person (for example, "*You're* not a loser, *you're* a human being. *You* have strengths and weaknesses, just like everyone else").

This Double-Standard version is easy because most of us can readily see the distortions in the thoughts of another person who's feeling depressed and self-critical. It's not hard to see how harsh and illogical that person's thinking is. When you verbalize the volunteer's Negative Thoughts as if they were your own, she will probably give you more positive and realistic messages. This can provide a model for the group members, showing them how to talk to themselves in a more objective and compassionate way, just as they would talk to a friend who was feeling depressed.

Once the group grasps how the Externalization of Voices works, divide them into teams of three so they can practice it. There is a clear, brief, step-by-step summary of the instructions on page 128 of the participant's workbook.

The second way of doing the Externalization of Voices is more dramatic and confrontational. It is the one I personally prefer once I have developed a positive, trusting relationship with a client. This second approach should be attempted only by experienced leaders. It is similar to the style that is illustrated in the suggested reading on the Externalization of Voices and the Feared Fantasy listed on page 118 of this manual.

If you use this more confrontational version of the Externalization of Voices, you can tell the volunteer that you will play the role of her Negative Thoughts and she will play the role of the Positive Thoughts. Explain that you two will act out a dialogue between the positive and negative parts of her mind. Tell her that even though you will sound like another person, you will actually be the negative, self-critical part of her brain. Explain that you will therefore use the *second* person (for example, "*You're* a loser; *you'll* never recover from your depression; *you're* defective and inferior to other people").

Tell the volunteer to play the Positive Thoughts and use the first person (for example, "*I'm* not a loser, *I'm* a human being. *I* have strengths and weaknesses, just like everyone else"). Explain that she can do her best to defend against this external attack. Remind her once again that the person who attacks her is not really another person but simply the projection of her own self-criticisms. You will be playing the role of her negative, self-critical thoughts.

Use frequent role reversals whenever the volunteer gets stuck or upset. Suppose, for example, that she comes up with a defensive or ineffective response to one of your attacks, as in this example:

Leader: (*as NTs*) You'll *never* get better.
Volunteer: (*as PTs*) Well, I hope that eventually I'll get better! I'm sure this group will help me.
Leader: Well, it sure hasn't helped you any yet. Everyone else is making progress but you're stuck. You know in your heart of hearts that you'll *always* be depressed, since you've practically always been depressed in the past. Besides, you're *always* screwing up. You're a loser!
Volunteer: I'm not *always* screwing up!
Leader: No one can screw up *all* the time, dummy, but you're what we call a General Screwup, since you screw up so often. It's partially explained by your low IQ and partially by your inherent defectiveness, and primarily by the fact that you're just a loser!
Volunteer: Uncle! I can't answer these Negative Thoughts! That's what I tell myself!

Now that she's clearly stuck, you can do a role reversal and demonstrate a more effective way of talking back to the Negative Thoughts:

Volunteer: (*as NTs*) You'll *never* get better.
Leader: (*as PTs*) I've already learned a lot in the therapy and I've made some progress. I haven't always been depressed in the past, so I'm sure I won't always be depressed in the future. No matter how lousy I feel, I always seem to improve sooner or later. I'm quite excited by all the new techniques I'm learning about, too.
Volunteer: Yes, but you're *always* screwing up. You're a loser!
Leader: That's very true! I often *do* screw up and I accept it. I have a lot to learn and I suspect that I'll still be making mistakes when I'm old and gray.
Volunteer: Touché!

At this point you could continue to do role reversals until the volunteer has grasped how to talk back to her Negative Thoughts in a more effective manner.

Remind the participants once again that the Externalization of Voices is not assertiveness training. They are *not* talking back to another person, but to their own self-critical thoughts.

You may need to remind them about this several times. Even mental health professionals sometimes get confused when they practice this technique for the first time. They begin to think they are talking back to another person, such as a depressed friend or an angry colleague or parent. This subtle shift—which often occurs halfway through an exchange—will nearly always sabotage the effectiveness of the method. That's because the techniques for dealing with another person who's angry and critical, such as one's boss or spouse, are quite different. These techniques for dealing with interpersonal conflict will be covered in the forthcoming module on personal relationship problems.

After you have illustrated the version of the Externalization of Voices that you are more comfortable with, divide the group members into teams of three so they can practice it. They can use their own Negative Thoughts or the Negative Thoughts on page 127 of the participant's workbook. Person A will play the role of the Negative Thoughts, Person B will play the role of the Positive Thoughts, and Person C can be the observer. The observer can make helpful comments and suggestions. Tell the teams to use frequent role reversals when Person B gets stuck. Walk around and supervise the process. This exercise will require at least twenty minutes.

Afterward, convene the group as a whole so they can talk about their experiences. How did the exercise feel? Was it frightening? Did they feel upset? What worked and what did not work?

If the group liked the Externalization of Voices, and if time permits, you can repeat the team exercise so they will gain more experience with this method.

The following table summarizes the two methods of doing the Externalization of Voices.

	Person A, who plays the Negative Thoughts, uses:	Person B, who plays the Positive Thoughts, uses:
Double-Standard Technique	the *first* person ("I'm such a jerk!")	the *second* person
Confrontation Technique	the *second* person ("You're such a jerk!")	the *first* person

In *both* versions, Person A plays the role of Person B's Negative Thoughts at the beginning of the exercise. When Person B gets stuck, they can do a role reversal. Person A plays the Positive Thoughts and Person B plays the Negative Thoughts. They should continue doing role reversals until Person B can comfortably challenge all his or her Negative Thoughts.

THE MIRROR METHOD

You may enjoy demonstrating the Mirror Method, which is described on page 129 of the participant's workbook. This is an optional exercise that was included in the participant's workbook for readers who are not members of a Ten Days to Self-esteem group like the one you are conducting. Nevertheless, you can demonstrate this interesting and entertaining technique with your group.

Bring one or more mirrors to the group. The mirrors can be any size, but the larger they are, the better. Instead of pairing off in twos, the members look into the mirrors and talk to themselves. First they play the role of the Negative Thoughts, and then they talk back to these Negative Thoughts, as in the Externalization of Voices. They can use either version of the Externalization of Voices in this exercise. The Double-Standard version will be the easier and friendlier approach for most groups.

SELF-DEFENSE VS. THE ACCEPTANCE PARADOX

After these demonstrations, explain that there are two opposite sources of healing in cognitive therapy: Self-defense and the Acceptance Paradox. Nearly all cognitive therapy techniques fall into one of these two categories. However, the two approaches are radically different.

When participants are in the Self-defense mode, they try to disprove or challenge the distorted Negative Thoughts that make them feel so bad. Once they see that their NTs are distorted and untrue, they will usually feel better.

This approach is based on Western religious, philosophical, and scientific influences. The goal is to build up self-esteem through reason, logic, and truth. This approach is the most common and popular one because we all want to defend ourselves when we feel under attack. We all want to see ourselves as innocent, worthwhile, and special.

However, there is sometimes a significant problem with the Self-defense strategy. The moment people go on the defensive, they end up creating a battle. This is equally true whether they are getting defensive because another person is criticizing them or whether they are criticizing themselves. Then the critic becomes even more aggressive and relentlessly critical. Every defense is followed by a new attack. And so they may end up in a frustrating internal battle that they can't possibly win.

The Acceptance Paradox, in contrast, is based on Eastern philosophical influences. Instead of building up their self-esteem by talking back to their self-critical thoughts, people can learn to accept their deficiencies with inner peace. They can often transcend their shortcomings by accepting them. They give up the need for self-esteem entirely. Although both approaches have great merit, the Acceptance Paradox is often more powerful and liberating.

I will illustrate the Self-defense technique first. I once used this strategy successfully to help a woman named Cathy who had suffered for more than ten years from severe, intractable depression and unpredictable, overwhelming panic attacks. During these attacks she strongly believed these thoughts: (1) "I cannot breathe deeply enough." (2) "I will have a heart attack and die." She was actually in excellent health and many doctors assured her that her cardiovascular system was perfect. Nevertheless, she believed these thoughts during each panic attack, and consequently she was terrified. You might feel that way, too, if you thought you were about to suffocate or collapse with a heart attack!

In my office I induced a panic attack by having Cathy hyperventilate and telling her to think frightening thoughts while she closed her eyes. I told her to imagine she was suffocating and an ambulance was bringing her to a hospital emergency room. I said, "Imagine that your windpipe is closing off. Your lips are turning blue. Now they are doing a tracheotomy. The blood is spurting everywhere. It's going into your trachea. You're choking now because you cannot get enough air in your lungs."

Being quite suggestible, Cathy became terrified and started sobbing. She was convinced she could not breathe deeply enough, and told me she felt certain that she was on the verge of collapse from a heart attack.

You might want to ask the group how Cathy could disprove her Negative Thoughts with the Experimental Method. What experiment could she do in the office at that very moment to put the lie to her belief that she was about to pass out or collapse from a heart attack?

I suggested to Cathy that she could test her belief that she was about to die of a heart attack if she would stand up and run in place strenuously, and then do some jumping jacks, right there in the office.

Cathy was sobbing uncontrollably and extremely reluctant to do this. She blurted out that if she stood up, she would pass out. I persuaded her—gently but firmly—to stand up so we could check this idea out and see if she would keel over. She resisted and begged me to stop, but I was firm. She finally agreed to stand up and run in place as a way of testing her Negative Thoughts. This is the essence of the Experimental Method.

After several minutes of strenuous calisthenics, it began to dawn on Cathy that she could not possibly be having a heart attack or suffocating. While doing jumping jacks, she suddenly said, "I wonder if I could really be doing this if I were about to collapse and die of a heart attack." I replied, "Is this what you see in the emergency rooms of hospitals? People with massive heart attacks standing next to their gurneys doing jumping jacks?"

Cathy erupted in laughter, and her symptoms of panic suddenly disappeared. She sank back into her chair smiling and exclaimed, "I'm feeling much better now!" The moment that she saw her NTs were not true, she felt immediate relief.

I repeated the demonstration, with similar results. When Cathy returned two weeks later, she was completely free of any symptoms of depression or anxiety. In fact, her scores on the Burns Depression Checklist and the Burns Anxiety Inventory were both near zero, indicating a near-euphoric state.

This is a prime example of the Self-defense approach. The whole idea is to disprove your Negative Thoughts. The moment people see that their Negative Thoughts are not true, they will feel better. This is the essence of cognitive therapy.

However, many NTs can be handled far more effectively with the Acceptance Paradox. Instead of trying to disprove their Negative Thoughts with logic or evidence, clients firmly agree with them. Instead of struggling to defend themselves from their own internal attack, they simply surrender. If they can do this with inner peace and self-esteem, the results can be quite spectacular.

You can illustrate this Acceptance Paradox in many ways. One approach would be to invite a group member to attack you, using a list of NTs that different group members may have had about themselves. You can use the Acceptance Paradox when you respond. For example, let's say that one member has NTs such as these on her DMLs:

1. I'm a rotten mother.

2. I'm an addict and I've wasted my life.

3. I'm not nearly as smart and successful as other people. I've never accomplished anything that was really outstanding.

4. I'm a phony and I'm dishonest with people.

5. I'm a loser and I have no friends.

6. I'm fat and I have no willpower.

The volunteer who plays the role of the NTs will attack you, using the second person. You will be the PTs, using the first person. Remind the group that although this looks like a dialogue between two different people, it is actually the voices in someone's mind that are battling. It might go like this:

Volunteer: (*as NTs*) You're a rotten mother.
Leader: (*as PTs*) I have many shortcomings as a mother. There is much I need to improve on. I accept this.
Volunteer: Yes, but you're an addict and you've wasted your life.
Leader: That's correct. I have screwed up and wasted an awful lot of my life. I make no bones about this.
Volunteer: Well, you should feel terrible and guilty then. You're admitting what a loser and what scum you are.
Leader: Oh, absolutely, I do admit it! And believe me, I have often felt guilty and terrible about my life.
Volunteer: So you admit you're a stupid loser!
Leader: Without hesitation! Many people are smarter and more successful than I am. Millions, in fact.
Volunteer: Half the time you hate everybody, and no one gives a damn about you either.
Leader: You've hit the nail on the head again! My relationships with people have not been good either. I often get angry and irritable and that turns people off. I still have a lot of growing up to do. That's the gospel truth!

Since this dialogue can also be found on page 132 of the participant's workbook, you can ask a volunteer to read it with you. If you feel courageous enough to do it spontaneously, it will be even more effective.

After this demonstration, ask the participants to process what they have just seen.

What is the essence of the Acceptance Paradox? How does it differ from Self-defense? Which approach seems more helpful? Is there a place for both strategies?

Ask the participants to pair off in teams of two or three to practice the Externalization of Voices again. This time, they will use the confrontational style, as described in the box on page 137 of the participant's workbook.

The team members can use their own self-critical Negative Thoughts when they do this exercise. When they talk back to their Negative Thoughts, they can use the Self-defense technique as well as the Acceptance Paradox.

Afterward, ask the participants to compare the two approaches: Self-defense and the Acceptance Paradox. Which approach feels more comfortable for them? What are the philosophical and practical implications of the Acceptance Paradox? If it seems helpful to some of the members, why is it helpful? How does it tie in with the philosophy of groups such as Alcoholics Anonymous, or with their own religious beliefs?

Ask the participants about the difference between healthy and unhealthy self-acceptance. When does self-acceptance lead to self-esteem and personal change? When does self-acceptance lead to hopelessness and depression? This topic is discussed beginning on page 138 of the participant's workbook. If they cannot describe the differences, tell them to read that section as homework so you can discuss it with them at the beginning of the next session.

FEEDBACK ABOUT STEP 5

At the end of the session, ask the participants what they liked and disliked about it. How does the Externalization of Voices technique work? What are the differences between Self-defense and the Acceptance Paradox? What is the difference between healthy and unhealthy self-acceptance?

Ask the group members to fill out the Evaluation of Step 5 on page 139 of the participant's workbook. Ask if they would be willing to read what they wrote down. Remember to respond nondefensively when they voice criticisms or negative reactions.

SELF-HELP ASSIGNMENTS FOR STEP 6

Before the participants leave, summarize the ideas that were presented. Discuss the self-help assignments for Step 6, which are listed on page 140 of the participant's workbook.

STEP 6

GETTING DOWN TO ROOT CAUSES

LEADER'S PREPARATION FOR STEP 6

Activity	Check (✓) when done
1. Read the description of Step 6 in the participant's workbook beginning on page 141.	
2. Study the Checklist for Step 6 on the next page of this *Leader's Manual* and the Tips for Leaders beginning on page 132.	
3. Read Chapter 7 in *The Feeling Good Handbook*.	
4. Read Chapter 10 in *Feeling Good: The New Mood Therapy*.	

CHECKLIST FOR STEP 6

Activity	Optional or required?	Minimum time (min.)	Check (√) when done
1. Using the Leader's Data Sheet on page 71, record the participants' scores on the three self-assessment tests, along with their points for homework and for attendance.	req.	10	
2. Ask for positive and negative feedback about Step 5.	req.	5	
3. Discuss the supplementary reading from *The Feeling Good Handbook*.	req.	5 – 10	
4. Define a Self-defeating Belief and discuss examples of such beliefs.	req.	5 – 10	
5. Demonstrate how to identify a Self-defeating Belief with the Vertical Arrow Technique.	opt.	20	
6. Exercise in identifying Self-defeating Beliefs with the Self-defeating Belief Scale.	req.	20	
7. Exercise in modifying a Self-defeating Belief with the Attitude Cost-Benefit Analysis.	req.	15	
8. Self-defeating Belief Exercise.	req.	10 – 15	
9. Ask for positive and negative feedback about Step 6.	req.	5	
10. Assign the homework for Step 7.	req.	3	

OVERVIEW OF STEP 6

In today's session the participants will learn how to pinpoint and modify the self-defeating attitudes and beliefs that make them vulnerable to painful mood swings and to difficulties in personal relationships. These attitudes, which are called Self-defeating Beliefs, include the belief that you must always try to be perfect, the belief that it is terrible to fail, the belief that you must always try to get everyone's approval, the belief that you should always be a "nice" person and never upset others by telling them what you want or how you really feel inside, the belief that you should always try to be happy and in complete control of your emotions, the belief that it is terrible when people do not meet all your expectations, the belief that anger and conflict should always be avoided, the belief that life is not worthwhile if you are alone or unloved, and the belief that life *should* be the way you want it to be, as well as others.

A Negative Thought is quite different from a Self-defeating Belief (SDB). A Negative Thought occurs only when someone feels upset, but a Self-defeating Belief is a part of someone's personal philosophy. For example, if people believe, "My worthwhileness depends on my success in life," and they are very successful, they will feel good. But when they experience a failure or career reversal, they may get depressed and tell themselves, "I'm no good. I'm a failure. People will look down on me."

Cognitive therapists believe that these Self-defeating Beliefs make people vulnerable to future episodes of depression, anxiety, and interpersonal conflict. Therefore, when you show people how to change these SDBs, you are working on prevention and personal growth as opposed to symptom relief in the here-and-now.

TIPS FOR LEADERS

DATA COLLECTION

Record the participants' scores on the three self-assessment tests (the BDC, the BAI, and the RSAT) on the Leader's Data Sheet on page 71. Record how much homework they completed using the 3-point rating scale on page 68. Record whether or not they came on time using the 2-point rating scale on page 68.

FEEDBACK AND REVIEW OF HOMEWORK

Ask about the participants' reactions to the Externalization of Voices procedure introduced last week. Ask about their positive and negative feelings about the session. What did they like and dislike about it?

What was their understanding of the Acceptance Paradox? How does it differ from Self-defense? Do they find one strategy more useful for dealing with their own Negative Thoughts? What's the difference between healthy and unhealthy self-acceptance?

Did any of the participants do the optional reading about "Cognitive Therapy in Action" (Chapter 8) or about the Externalization of Voices in *The Feeling Good Hand-*

book? What did they agree or disagree with? Encourage them to ask questions about the reading. Were any passages particularly helpful and interesting? Was there anything they didn't understand?

Ask about the written homework assignment using the Daily Mood Log. Were they able to refute any of their NTs successfully? If so, ask them to give examples. Ask if any participants would be willing to describe their written homework to the group. What problems did they encounter? Did they have some NTs they were not able to refute?

INTRODUCTION TO SELF-DEFEATING BELIEFS

Begin by describing the difference between a Negative Thought and a Self-defeating Belief, as discussed in the overview of this step. Ask the group to read the list of Self-defeating Beliefs on page 147 of the participant's workbook. Ask if any of these beliefs are characteristic of how they sometimes think and feel. Explain that most of these attitudes are widely held in our society, but that they can sometimes create problems in how we feel and relate to other people. Ask if any of the group members can provide examples of how this might work.

THE VERTICAL ARROW TECHNIQUE

Because this exercise requires a little skill, it is optional. However, it is extremely rewarding. Once you have practiced, you will find that the Vertical Arrow Technique is not especially difficult.

The Vertical Arrow Technique has several benefits:

- It nearly always works successfully. There are very few psychotherapeutic techniques with such a high batting average.

- You can do it at any time in an individual or group session, and it rarely takes more than a few minutes.

- It provides a blueprint for the therapy. You will discover the client's most important underlying problems so that you can develop a systematic plan for treatment.

- It identifies the client's Self-defeating Beliefs accurately, regardless of the therapist's orientation.

- It practically never upsets the client.

- It makes therapists appear extremely intelligent!

Explain that there are two ways to identify a Self-defeating Belief. One method is called the Vertical Arrow Technique. This method is described in the exercise on page 147 of the participant's workbook. (More detailed descriptions can be found in Chapter 10 of *Feeling Good: The New Mood Therapy*, as well as pages 122–124 and 144–145 of *The Feeling Good Handbook*.) The other method is to fill out the Self-defeating Belief Scale. Participants will have the chance to do this later on in the session.

Tell them that they can do the Vertical Arrow Technique with any Negative Thought from any Daily Mood Log. This technique will help them discover the deeper attitudes that are hidden underneath their Negative Thoughts. Tell them that most people have only a few Self-defeating Beliefs that lead to mood problems. If they do the Vertical Arrow Technique on several occasions, there's a good chance they will always unearth the same set of Self-defeating Beliefs. This will give them extra confidence that these are the attitudes that usually get them into emotional trouble.

Tell the group to turn to the exercise on page 148 of the participant's workbook. This exercise describes a first-year law student who had panic attacks during classes. Her NT was "If the professor calls on me in class, I might not know the answer to the question."

Tell each group member to imagine that he or she is this student and has written this thought in the Negative Thoughts column of the Daily Mood Log. This thought already appears in the Negative Thoughts column on page 148 of the participant's workbook. Explain that once the student wrote this NT on the DML, you asked her to draw a small vertical arrow directly under it. Tell them that the vertical arrow is a form of shorthand that always stands for the following questions: "If that thought was true, what would it mean to me? Why would it be upsetting to me?"

This is illustrated clearly on page 148 of the participant's workbook. Tell the group to read those two questions out loud together.

When they are doing the Vertical Arrow Technique on their own, they will ask the questions in the *first* person, like this: "If that thought was true, and I didn't know the answer to the professor's question, what would it mean to *me*? Why would it be upsetting to *me*?" When you, as the therapist, are doing the Vertical Arrow Technique with a client, you ask the questions using the *second* person, like this: "If that thought was true, and you didn't know the answer to the professor's question, what would it mean to *you*? Why would it be upsetting to *you*?"

Tell the group that these vertical arrow questions will lead to a new NT. It could be "I might make a fool of myself in front of the other students." Point out that this thought has already been written down underneath the first Negative Thought on page 148 of the participant's workbook.

Tell the group that a small vertical arrow has already been drawn for them under this new thought. Remind them that the vertical arrow means they should ask themselves the same two questions again: "If that thought was true, what would it mean to me? If I made a fool of myself in class, why would it be upsetting to me?"

Tell them to repeat these two questions out loud together: "If that thought was true, what would it mean to *me*? Why would it be upsetting to *me*?" This repetition is helpful for learning.

Explain that as the participants repeat this process over and over, it will lead to a series of additional Negative Thoughts, which they can write down in the NT column. After they write down each new NT, they will draw a vertical arrow under it and ask themselves: "If that thought was true, what would it mean to *me*? Why would it be upsetting to *me*?" That's essentially all there is to it, but it does take a little practice.

Do this exercise with the group now. Tell them to imagine that they are this student.

You can say, "If you were this student, and you made a fool of yourself in front of the other students, why would this be upsetting to you? What would it mean to you?" Each time they come up with a Negative Thought, tell them all to write it down and draw a vertical arrow underneath. Then they will repeat the same two questions again, so as to generate another Negative Thought.

The Negative Thoughts they come up with during the exercise will probably be quite similar to these (they also appear on page 159 of the participant's workbook):

$\downarrow$

3. That would show I was stupid.

$\downarrow$

4. Then no one would like me.

$\downarrow$

5. Then I'd have no friends and I'd be alone.

$\downarrow$

6. That would mean I was a failure.

$\downarrow$

7. Then I'd be worthless and life would not be worth living.

I do this exercise frequently in workshops for mental health professionals and for the general public. It is nearly always well received. However, you may have to do some quick thinking on your feet. Here's a tip that will help. Every now and then someone in the audience will come up with an NT that is off the wall. You can thank that person graciously. Don't write down the NT on the flip chart, because it would derail the process. Instead, ask for other NTs. You can simply say, "That's a thought someone might have. What are some other thoughts someone might have?" When you hear one you like, write it down. Thus, you can do some "editing" when you direct this exercise. This is sometimes necessary to keep things on track.

For example, the second NT of the law student was "I might make a fool of myself in front of the other students." This is written on page 148 of the participant's workbook. When you ask the vertical arrow questions, a member might conceivably raise his hand and say, "This would show she has no business being in law school. She better grow up and face up to the fact that she's in the wrong profession!" (I actually did get this response once during a workshop, and my jaw dropped open.)

This response would make me uncomfortable because it sounds quite judgmental and it misses the point. The law student was, in fact, a top student and well suited for this profession. Her main difficulty was not any lack of talent or intelligence but her brutal perfectionism. She had the belief that it was shameful to be less than perfect. This attitude caused endless stress and panic for her. The professors *purposely* humiliate all the first-year students when they teach! This cross-examination style of teaching, which is called the Socratic method, is designed to toughen up the students and make them think more rigorously.

When I heard this response, I simply said, "Yes, any law student needs to decide if law is the profession they really want to pursue. That's always an important consideration. Let's assume that she's an outstanding student. What other thoughts might she have about making a fool of herself because she couldn't answer the professor's question? Imagine that you are this law student. Why would it be upsetting if you flubbed up in front of your classmates? What would you be thinking if you were her? What would it mean to you?"

Because I responded in this way, I didn't get hung up with the group member who insisted she shouldn't be in law school. I got lots of responses from the other participants that were right up my alley. One participant said, "If I make a fool of myself in front of the other students, they will think I'm stupid and lose respect for me." I wrote this down and drew a vertical arrow under it, and the demonstration proceeded without a hitch.

When you are doing the exercise and you get a response that seems workable, you can say, "Excellent! Let's all write this down as the next Negative Thought." The members can write it in the participant's workbook while you write it on your flip chart. Then you can tell them to draw a vertical arrow under it, and ask what the vertical arrow means. The vertical arrow always means, "If that thought was true, why would it be upsetting to me? What would it mean to me?"

These vertical arrow questions will generate a new NT. It might be "If they think I'm stupid, they'll lose respect for me. I'll be friendless and alone."

Then you can say, "Excellent! Write that down in your workbooks on page 148. You will see that there is already a vertical arrow under it. What does the vertical arrow mean?"

After you have generated a list of five or six Negative Thoughts with the Vertical Arrow Technique, the Self-defeating Beliefs will usually be easy to identify. Tell the group to try to find the law student's Self-defeating Beliefs, using the list of Self-defeating Beliefs on page 147 of the participant's workbook. The law student's Self-defeating Beliefs might include these:

1.   People will like and respect me only if I am a successful, outstanding person.

2.   People are very judgmental and will reject me if I'm not perfect.

3.   I need everyone's love and approval to feel happy and worthwhile.

4.   If I'm alone, I'm bound to feel miserable.

Other examples of the Vertical Arrow Technique can be found in the suggested reading for leaders on page 130. The procedure is quite straightforward. It's an outstanding method to add to your therapeutic toolkit and is well worth the small amount of effort needed to master it.

If you have sufficient time available, you can break up the group into teams of three to six members to practice the Vertical Arrow Technique.

Here are a few upsetting situations that might be suitable. Tell the team members to identify one or two Negative Thoughts they might have in one of these situations, and then use the Vertical Arrow Technique.

You get nervous when you call on a new customer or when you call someone for a date.

Your boss or spouse is feeling irritable and acting bossy.

You've been trying really hard to please a demanding customer who is late paying a bill.

You shout "Hey, George!" to a friend on the other side of the street in a busy part of town. He does not respond to you.

Walk around to supervise the process. Make sure the participants stick to the task and don't begin gossiping. If you let them select their own NTs to work with, make sure you feel comfortable with the ones they have chosen and can picture how they will work. Then you can guide them if they get stuck.

THE SELF-DEFEATING BELIEF SCALE

The second method of identifying a Self-defeating Belief is simply to fill out the Self-defeating Belief Scale on page 150 of the participant's workbook. (Note that this is a new and improved version of the scale that appears in Chapter 10 of *Feeling Good: The New Mood Therapy.* The wording of the items has been modified to make them easier to understand and more obviously dysfunctional.)

Ask the participants to fill out this test and add up their scores on its seven scales, each of which measures a different irrational belief. Each scale is represented by five consecutive items on the test. The seven scales measure attitudes toward approval, love, achievement, perfection, entitlement, self-blame, and hopelessness. To score each scale, participants simply add up their scores on the five test items that measure that mindset. For example, the approval scale score is obtained by adding up the answers to the first five items on the test.

Some members will have done this already because it was part of their homework assignment for today's step. The scoring key for the test is on page 153 of the participant's workbook.

Scores between 11 and 20 on the seven scales are the most self-defeating. Ask if any participants scored between 11 and 20 on any of the scales. Let's assume a man says he scored 15 on the approval scale. You can ask if he ever has problems with disapproval or criticism. Ask if any other members of the group ever get upset or defensive when criticized. Can they think of situations when the fear of disapproval led to emotional or interpersonal difficulties?

Ask them about their reactions to the test, and whether any of the other Self-defeating Beliefs ever caused problems in their lives. See if they can give specific examples. Do they have friends, colleagues, or family members who have had difficulties because of any of these attitudes?

Remember to use the Disarming Technique if any of the participants insist that one of these Self-defeating Beliefs is actually appropriate and healthy. You can tell them that these beliefs are really two-edged swords, with a healthy, constructive edge and an unhealthy, destructive edge.

For example, suppose someone in the group says, "I feel that people really *do* need love and approval to feel happy and fulfilled. In fact, even infants who don't get enough maternal love often fail to thrive and eventually die. Love *really is* a basic human need."

How would you respond to this participant? Think about it for a moment and write down your response before you read on.

_____

_____

_____

_____

I would respond, "You're absolutely right. That's an extremely important philosophical and practical issue, and I'm glad you brought it up. When is it healthy to need another person's love and approval? And when is it unhealthy? Let's examine the benefits of this mind-set first." This response illustrates the Disarming Technique (finding truth in a criticism) and Stroking (expressing respect for the other person in the heat of battle). If you are nondefensive, you will not lock horns and antagonize the member who raised the objection.

Learning how to go with the flow and avoid polarization is a valuable group leadership skill that you can develop over time. I personally find that it is rarely, if ever, productive to get into a battle with a member of a therapy group, or with someone who attends a professional workshop. If the participants feel that it's safe to open up and they know that you will not attack or demean them, no matter how outrageous their comments might sound, they will repay you many times over with enthusiasm, involvement, and respect.

When the group members describe the advantages and disadvantages of needing love and approval, you can list them on your flip chart.

Then you might ask the group, "Can you think of a revised attitude that would maintain the benefits of this belief while getting rid of the disadvantages? Is there a new way to think about the importance of love and approval?" At the end of the demonstration I would again thank the member who raised the objection and emphasize the value of this insight.

HOW TO MODIFY A SELF-DEFEATING BELIEF WITH THE ATTITUDE COST-BENEFIT ANALYSIS

This next exercise begins on page 154 of the participant's workbook. Tell the group to turn to that page now.

Explain that the first step in modifying a Self-defeating Belief involves the Attitude Cost-Benefit Analysis, which was discussed in an earlier session. Ask the group to choose a Self-defeating Belief they wish to evaluate, such as "I must be loved by others to be a worthwhile person" or "My worthwhileness depends on my intelligence and my success in life." They can choose from the list of Self-defeating Beliefs on page 155 of the participant's workbook. If you have completed the exercise with the Vertical Arrow Technique, you can ask them to choose one of the law student's Self-defeating Beliefs instead.

Tell the participants to write down the Self-defeating Belief they have chosen at the top of the Attitude Cost-Benefit Analysis on page 156 of the workbook. Now ask them to list the advantages and disadvantages of this belief in the left-hand and right-hand columns of the form. The emphasis during the exercise is "How will it help me if I think this way? And how will it hurt me?"

Some group members may become confused when they are asked to list the positive and negative consequences of an attitude or a belief. Suppose that the group is listing the advantages and disadvantages of believing, "I need everyone's love and approval to be a worthwhile human being," as mentioned previously. A group member may say, "One advantage is that it would feel *wonderful* to have everyone love me!" This is an error. The group members are *not* being asked to list the advantages and disadvantages of being loved and approved of by everyone. You are asking them to list the advantages and disadvantages of *needing* everyone's love and approval to feel happy and worthwhile. The real question is: What are the advantages and disadvantages of basing my self-esteem on other people's love and approval?

One advantage of this belief would be that when people are nice to you, you'll feel great, because you'll tell yourself that you're worthwhile. In addition, you may value other people's feelings and opinions and work hard to get people to like you.

One disadvantage might be your excessive sensitivity to criticism and the tendency to become depressed when someone doesn't like you. In addition, if you are excessively needy and dependent, you may turn people off.

Once the participants have listed the advantages and disadvantages of a belief, ask them to weigh them against each other on a 100-point scale. If they decide that the disadvantages of the belief outweigh the advantages, they might put a 40 in the lower left-hand circle on the form and a 60 in the lower right-hand circle. Make sure the numbers they put down add up to 100.

If the disadvantages are greater, ask the participants what new value or belief they could replace the old one with. An example of a revised belief could be "It is desirable to have people like me and approve of me, but I don't *need* people's approval to be worthwhile. I care about people and their feelings are important. If someone is upset with me, I can talk to them and try to find some truth in their criticism. This won't ever make me any more or less worthwhile, but it might make me a little wiser." Of course, there are dozens of other revised attitudes that one could also adopt. There are some guidelines on how to revise an SDB on page 154 of the participant's workbook.

If some of the participants decide that the advantages of the belief are greater than the disadvantages, you can say, "It appears that this is not an attitude you want to change just now, because it seems to be more of a benefit than a problem for you. You may have other Self-defeating Beliefs that you would want to work on, and you may decide to modify this one at a later time."

Do *not* get into a power struggle, trying to persuade members that they *should* give up their Self-defeating Beliefs. We are not evangelists, trying to sell people on "right beliefs." We are simply therapists, helping people with what *they* define as problems.

Finally, ask the group to discuss the idea that each Self-defeating Belief has a healthy, productive side and an unhealthy, destructive side. For example, if they believe they must always get everyone's approval, they may be more sensitive to others' ideas and feelings than people who are excessively self-centered. This is the healthy side of the need for approval.

However, they may also be unassertive, lacking in self-esteem, and terrified by conflicts with others. This is the unhealthy side of the Self-defeating Belief. You can ask the group: When is the need for approval healthy? When is it unhealthy?

Similar considerations apply to every other Self-defeating Belief, including the need for love, the need for success, perfectionism, the fear of conflict, and so forth. These attitudes are not simply good or bad, but mixtures of good and bad. Once you understand and acknowledge this—and many clients, sometimes even therapists, struggle with it—most of the conflict and controversy about Self-defeating Beliefs will disappear.

If time permits, divide the group into small teams and ask each one to do an Attitude Cost-Benefit Analysis on a different Self-defeating Belief from the list on page 147, or from the following list, which appears on page 155 of the participant's workbook:

- "I must be productive and successful to be worthwhile."
- "I must be loved to be a worthwhile and happy human being."
- "I should always try to be perfect."
- "I need everyone's approval to be a worthwhile human being."
- "If I'm depressed or unhappy, there's not much I can do about it. My moods result from forces beyond my control."
- "Other people are to blame for most of the problems in my relationships with them."
- "People should meet my expectations, because my expectations are reasonable."

Caution: Make sure the participants list only the advantages and disadvantages of the *belief*. For example, if they are working on the first belief on the list ("I must be productive and successful to be worthwhile"), they should list the advantages and disadvantages of linking their feelings of self-esteem with their success in life. They are *not* supposed to list the advantages and disadvantages of being successful! Emphasize that they are to list the advantages and disadvantages of linking their self-esteem with their success in life.

After the group reconvenes, a spokesperson from each team can summarize their analysis and conclusions.

You may want them to do a Cost-Benefit Analysis together as a group with the sixth attitude on the list above ("Other people are to blame for most of the problems in my relationships with them"). Most people do blame others for the problems in their relationships, so this is an attitude nearly everyone can identify with. The solution to this problem can be found on page 160 of the participant's workbook.

SELF-DEFEATING BELIEF EXERCISE

This exercise is similar in many ways to the previous one, but the format is slightly different. Ask the group to turn to the Self-defeating Belief Exercise on page 157 of the participant's workbook. Divide the group into teams of three to six. Ask each team to spend ten to fifteen minutes writing a paragraph about one of the seven Self-defeating Beliefs from the Self-defeating Belief Scale. They can write this paragraph on page 158 of the workbook. The paragraph should explain why the attitude is irrational and self-defeating and why it can make people vulnerable to depression, anxiety, or anger.

For example, people who believe they must have everyone's approval may be exceptionally sensitive to criticism, and may get defensive or depressed anytime someone is angry or disagrees with them. Has this ever happened to any of the team members? Can they think of a time when they felt inadequate or put down because someone criticized them? Did they become self-critical (the "I'm not good" response), or did they get angry and defensive (the "you're not good" response)? Why are these ways of reacting to criticism self-defeating?

Make sure that different teams work on different Self-defeating Beliefs. (You may want to skip perfectionism, since it will be the focus of Step 8.) You can let people join the team working on the attitude of greatest personal interest to them. Afterward, reconvene the group as a whole and ask a spokesperson from each team to read his or her team's paragraph.

If the group likes this exercise and time permits, you can repeat it. This time, the members can join a team working on a different Self-defeating Belief.

FEEDBACK ABOUT STEP 6

At the end of the session, summarize the ideas that were discussed. Ask the participants what they learned about Self-defeating Beliefs. Ask them about the difference between a Self-defeating Belief and a Negative Thought. How does the Vertical Arrow Technique work? How can the Attitude Cost-Benefit Analysis help them modify a Self-defeating Belief?

Ask what the participants liked and disliked about the session. Tell them to fill out the Evaluation of Step 6 on page 161 of the participant's workbook. Ask if they would be willing to read what they wrote down. Remember to respond nondefensively when they voice criticisms or negative reactions.

SELF-HELP ASSIGNMENTS FOR STEP 7

Before the participants leave, discuss the self-help assignments for Step 7. These assignments are listed on page 162 of the participant's workbook.

STEP 7

SELF-ESTEEM—WHAT IS IT? HOW DO I GET IT?

LEADER'S PREPARATION FOR STEP 7

Activity	Check (√) when done
1. Read the description of Step 7 in the participant's workbook beginning on page 163.	
2. Study the Checklist for Step 7 on the next page of this *Leader's Manual* and the Tips for Leaders beginning on page 145.	
3. Read Chapters 11–13 in *Feeling Good: The New Mood Therapy*.	
4. Concentrate especially on the Four Paths to Self-esteem in Chapter 13, "Your Work Is Not Your Worth," in *Feeling Good: The New Mood Therapy*.	
5. Optional: Read Appendix C, "How to Overcome an Inferiority Complex," in *Intimate Connections*.	

CHECKLIST FOR STEP 7

Activity	Optional or required?	Minimum time (min.)	Check (√) when done
1. Using the Leader's Data Sheet on page 71, record the participants' scores on the three self-assessment tests, along with their points for homework and for attendance.	req.	10	
2. Ask for positive and negative feedback about Step 6.	req.	5	
3. Review the written homework with the Vertical Arrow Technique, the Attitude Cost-Benefit Analysis, and the Daily Mood Log.	req.	5 – 10	
4. Discuss the reading for this step.	req.	5 – 10	
5. Self-esteem Exercise 1.	req.	15	
6. Self-esteem Exercise 2.	req.	10 – 15	
7. Self-esteem Exercise 3.	opt.	10 – 15	
8. Feared Fantasy Exercise.	opt.	10 – 15	
9. Exercise: What Is a Worthless Person? What Is a Worthwhile Person?	opt.	15	
10. Inferiority Exercise.	req.	10	
11. Exercise on the Pleasure-Predicting Sheet.	opt.	15	
12. Exercise on Conditional vs. Unconditional Self-esteem.	req.	10 – 15	
13. Ask for positive and negative feedback about Step 7.	req.	5	
14. Assign the homework for Step 8.	req.	3	

OVERVIEW OF STEP 7

Today's session will focus on self-esteem. Many groups have reported that this was their most successful session. You will see that it is quite long, with many exercises. If you have plenty of time available, you may want to devote two sessions to this topic. If not, you can pick and choose the exercises you like the most. This step represents one of the most important topics in Ten Days to Self-esteem.

You will see that the bottom line in this step is similar in some ways to what you taught in Step 5 on the Acceptance Paradox. As you will recall, in that session you emphasized two ways of refuting Negative Thoughts: Self-defense and the Acceptance Paradox. When we use Self-defense, we talk back to our Negative Thoughts. We defend ourselves against attack and try to build ourselves up. In contrast, when we use the Acceptance Paradox, we accept our shortcomings with ruthless honesty, inner peace, and objectivity.

By the same token, there are two dramatically different ways to achieve self-esteem. We can say, "I am a worthwhile person because . . ." After the "because," we can include some criterion for self-esteem, such as success in life or altruism or the quality of our personal relationships. For example, we can say, "I am a worthwhile person because I have worked hard and done the most I can with my God-given talents and abilities." This kind of reasoning is based on the Calvinist work ethic, which is widespread in our culture.

This or any similar formulation makes self-esteem conditional, and although it may sound quite valid and persuasive, you will show the group that it is fraught with danger. What happens when, in spite of our best efforts, we are not particularly productive or successful? Are people who are tremendously successful more worthwhile than others? What are the consequences of telling ourselves that we are worthless or inferior? No matter how we try to measure or earn our self-esteem, there will be times when we do not fulfill the criterion we have chosen and may sink into depression.

Alternatively, we can make self-esteem unconditional. We can love and respect ourselves because we are human beings, or simply because we have chosen to do so. We can love ourselves because we need the love and support, not because we have earned it. Although it is more difficult to comprehend, this formulation is far more liberating.

Finally, we can adopt an even more radical position: There is no such thing as self-esteem. In addition, there is really no such thing as a worthwhile person or a worthless person. Since a worthwhile person cannot exist, there's no point in trying to become one! Instead of trying to gain self-esteem or trying to be worthwhile, we can discard these notions entirely and refuse to deal with them!

Although this last formulation might sound abstract, mystical, and confusing, it is an immensely practical position reflected in the Pleasure-Predicting Exercise. The participants will see that instead of worrying about whether they are sufficiently worthwhile, they can set goals each day including activities that involve learning, personal growth, helping others, being productive, having fun, being with others, and so forth. This radically pragmatic solution is more in the Buddhist tradition than in the Western one, but it is extremely compatible with the philosophy of cognitive therapy.

TIPS FOR LEADERS

DATA COLLECTION

Record the participants' scores on the three self-assessment tests (the BDC, the BAI, and the RSAT) on the Leader's Data Sheet on page 71. Record how much homework they completed using the 3-point rating scale on page 68. Record whether or not they came on time using the 2-point rating scale on page 68.

FEEDBACK AND REVIEW OF HOMEWORK

Ask about the participants' reactions to the Vertical Arrow Technique and the Self-defeating Belief Scale introduced in the last session. Ask about their positive and negative feelings about the session. What did they like and dislike about it?

Review the ideas presented in Step 6:

- Most people have Self-defeating Beliefs that make them vulnerable to painful mood swings.

- These attitudes get people into trouble only in certain predictable situations. For example, if you believe that you need everyone's approval to be worthwhile, you will feel good when people like and approve of you. However, you may become upset when you are rejected or criticized by someone you care about.

- These Self-defeating Beliefs are not purely good or bad; they have healthy and unhealthy aspects.

- They can be identified with the Vertical Arrow Technique and the Self-defeating Belief Scale.

- They can be modified with the Attitude Cost-Benefit Analysis.

Did any of the participants attempt to use the Vertical Arrow Technique on their own? How did this work out? Were they able to identify any of their Self-defeating Beliefs?

Did any of them do a Cost-Benefit Analysis for a Self-defeating Belief? What was the result of this analysis?

Ask whether they had any additional ideas about Self-defeating Beliefs that they might wish to share. If members of your group have strong religious beliefs, ask about how the last session's ideas can be integrated with their religious orientation. Are there any biblical passages that express ideas that are similar to or different from any of the Self-defeating Beliefs?

Ask about their written homework assignment using the Daily Mood Log. Were they able to refute any of their NTs successfully? If so, ask them to give examples. Ask if any participants would be willing to describe their written homework to the group. What problems did they encounter? Did they have some NTs they were not able to refute?

INTRODUCTION TO STEP 7

You can begin by saying that although every step in this program deals directly or indirectly with self-esteem, the group will deal with this topic in considerable depth today. Ask about their reactions to the assigned reading on self-esteem in Step 7 of the participant's workbook. What did they agree or disagree with? Encourage the group members to ask questions about the reading. Were any passages particularly helpful and interesting? Was there anything they didn't understand?

SELF-ESTEEM EXERCISE 1

You can stimulate a lively discussion of self-esteem by asking the following five questions. Ask the group members to read the answers to these questions that they wrote in Self-esteem Exercise 1 beginning on page 168 of the participant's workbook. If they haven't already done the exercise as homework, you can simply ask them to discuss each question.

1. When participants say they don't have as much self-esteem as they would like, what do they mean? What are the specific situations—like getting rejected or criticized or failing to achieve a goal—that make them feel less worthwhile?

2. What kinds of negative emotions do they have in these situations?

3. What are they thinking in these situations? What do they tell themselves?

4. What are the consequences of low self-esteem? How does it affect their productivity and personal relationships?

5. Have they ever known or read about someone they really liked and admired (other than a romantic interest) who had high self-esteem? What was that person like? What was it that made him or her seem especially worthwhile?

Self-esteem vs. Arrogance

Then ask the participants, "What are the consequences of high self-esteem? Can a person have too much self-esteem? What's the difference between self-esteem and arrogance? When is pride healthy, and when is it narcissistic and excessive?" Tell them to write down their ideas on page 169 of the participant's workbook. Then ask what they wrote down. (The answer to this question can be found on page 189 of the participant's workbook.)

Self-esteem vs. Self-confidence

Next, ask if the participants have ever thought about the differences between self-esteem and self-confidence. Tell them to write down their ideas on page 170 of the participant's workbook. Then ask what they wrote down.

Self-confidence results from people's belief that they will probably succeed at a task, based on their previous successes. For example, a top tennis player would feel self-confident when playing a beginner. In contrast, self-esteem is people's ability to respect and love themselves whether they win or lose, or whether they are loved or rejected.

Point out that people can have self-esteem without self-confidence. If they played tennis against Jimmy Connors, they would not feel particularly self-confident, since their chances of winning would be slim. But they could still have self-esteem if they refused to base their self-esteem on their performance. They could still feel worthwhile and lovable even if they lost.

Ask if the group members agree with this distinction between self-esteem and self-confidence. Can they think of examples of things they are good at that make them feel self-confident? What are those things? What are some things that they are not especially good at? Does it make sense to them to link their feelings of self-esteem with their skill at these various activities? Why or why not?

Do the participants tend to base their feelings of self-esteem on being successful, or on winning, or on being loved or approved of by others? This is not genuine self-esteem. Genuine self-esteem is unconditional. They can have just as much genuine self-esteem whether they win or lose a tennis match, or whether they are successful or unsuccessful in their careers. They cannot earn self-esteem in any way.

(The question about self-esteem and self-confidence is also answered on page 189 of the participant's workbook.)

SELF-ESTEEM EXERCISE 2

Next, ask the group members what they would need in order to feel worthwhile. What is the basis of self-esteem? Some people base their self-esteem on the following characteristics:

- **Looks:** People who are exceptionally attractive, charming, and popular are sometimes considered to be "special" and desirable.

- **Intelligence:** We often think that very brilliant and talented individuals are more worthwhile.

- **Success:** Our culture emphasizes the importance of productivity, accomplishments, and wealth.

- **Personal effort:** We may feel like we are worthwhile as long as we are trying hard and doing the best we can, regardless of how our actual skill or performance compares with that of other people.

- **Fame and power:** Some people think that famous, charismatic, influential people are superior.

- **Love:** We often feel worthwhile if we are loved and cared about.

- **Happiness:** Many people think they are worthwhile as long as they feel happy and satisfied with their lives.

- **Altruism:** We may think that we are worthwhile if we are kind, generous, and loving.

- **Race or religion:** We may think that we are worthwhile because of our race, or because of belief in God or religious beliefs.

There may be other ways that people assess their own or others' worthwhileness. Can the group members think of any?

Explain that many people base their self-esteem on success, or on popularity and external approval. In this exercise the members will examine the positive and negative consequences of these systems with the Attitude Cost-Benefit Analysis.

If they have already completed similar CBAs in the previous step, then you can change the assignment slightly and ask them to examine other criteria for measuring self-esteem from the list above. For example, they could use the CBA to evaluate the positive and negative consequences of basing their self-esteem on their altruism, on their belief in God, on their personal efforts, or on their feelings of happiness and well-being.

Divide the group into two teams. Ask the first team to list the advantages and disadvantages of linking their self-esteem with their achievements and success (or with some other criterion). Tell them to use the Cost-Benefit Analysis form on page 171 of the participant's workbook. Ask them to list ways that it will *help* them if they link their self-esteem with their accomplishments, as well as the ways that it will hurt them. Then ask them whether the advantages or disadvantages are greater.

Tell the team members to put two numbers that add up to 100 at the bottom of the CBA in the two circles. If the disadvantages are greater, they might put a 40 in the left-hand circle and a 60 in the right-hand circle. This would mean that they have concluded that it is not desirable to base their self-esteem on their accomplishments. Ask them what new basis they would have for self-esteem other than their achievements and success. They can list their revised beliefs on page 170 of the participant's workbook. (You can remind them that there are guidelines on how to revise a Self-defeating Belief on page 154 of their workbooks. They can review this material if they need help.)

The second team will have a similar assignment, but they will do the Cost-Benefit Analysis on page 172 of the participant's workbook. They will evaluate the costs and benefits of basing their self-esteem on their popularity or on other people's approval and respect. As an example, this CBA has been filled out on page 190 of the participant's workbook. Tell them not to look there while they are doing the exercise! Once they have completed the CBA, they can put a new, revised belief on page 170 of their workbooks.

Please note the caution I pointed out in the last session: Make sure they list the advantages and disadvantages of the *belief*. For example, the first team should list the advantages and disadvantages of linking their feelings of self-esteem with success in life. They are *not* supposed to list the advantages and disadvantages of *being successful*! Similarly, the second team can list the advantages and disadvantages of linking their feelings of self-esteem with popularity and approval. They are *not* supposed to list the advantages and disadvantages of *having* popularity, approval, and respect!

After ten or fifteen minutes, ask the group as a whole to reconvene so that a spokesperson from each team can report on the conclusions of his or her group.

SELF-ESTEEM EXERCISE 3

This exercise is quite similar to the previous one. It can be done individually or in teams of three to six members. Ask each individual or team to choose one of the beliefs about self-esteem on page 173 of the participant's workbook. Alternatively, the members can list another belief about self-esteem of personal interest. Tell them to write the belief they have chosen on page 174 of the participant's workbook so they can do a Cost-Benefit Analysis, just as they did in the previous exercise.

After they have listed the advantages and disadvantages, ask them to weigh the advantages against the disadvantages on a 100-point scale, just as they did before. If the disadvantages are greater, ask what new basis for self-esteem they could adopt. How could they revise the SDB to eliminate the disadvantages while preserving the advantages?

After ten or fifteen minutes, ask the group as a whole to reconvene so that a spokesperson from each team can report on the conclusions of his or her group.

You may note that so far these exercises have been like peeling the layers off an onion. Each time the participants reject one formulation about self-esteem, they may adopt another formulation, only to discover that it, too, is self-defeating. The goal is to discover that *any* method of measuring self-esteem can be quite hazardous and unproductive.

FEARED FANTASY EXERCISE

After your group completes the Cost-Benefit Analyses, most of the members will see that these formulations of self-esteem are not helpful. However, some of them may protest that they are nevertheless realistic and true.

A woman named Sue in our outpatient Ten Days to Self-esteem group at the Presbyterian Medical Center had always believed that people who are socially successful and popular are more worthwhile than others. After her team completed its CBA, Sue saw clearly that this Self-defeating Belief had caused lots of emotional grief and misery throughout her life. She told the group that she'd felt intensely inferior to the more popular and successful kids ever since she was in junior high school, and she still felt inferior to other people today. In spite of her rational awareness that the disadvantages of this mind-set outweighed the advantages, Sue said she still believed it at the gut level. She said she still felt that socially successful and popular people *really are* superior to other people.

To make Sue more vividly aware of how cruel and unrealistic this notion is, I asked her to do some role playing with another group member. I told her that in this Feared Fantasy exercise, she would enter an Alice in Wonderland nightmare world where she would come face to face with her worst fears. I explained that this would not be assertiveness training, because she and the other volunteer would act far differently from normal human beings. They would be monsters who would say outrageous things that real people might think but would never say.

I placed two chairs in the middle of the group and asked Sue and the other volunteer, a woman named Joan, to sit facing each other. I told Sue to imagine that she was extremely successful and popular. Joan was to play the role of someone who was not especially successful or popular. I told Sue to explain that she was superior to Joan because of all her popularity and success. Even though Sue is a shy and sensitive person in real life, I encouraged her to be as snotty and mean as possible in this exercise.

Of course, Sue was quite reluctant at first. She protested that she was a nice person who couldn't possibly say such mean things to someone else. I reassured her that she would not be a real person but simply a fantasy figure, the projection of her own worst fears. I encouraged her to take a chance, and told her that I would help her by suggesting things to say if she got stuck.

After a little coaching, Sue came up with things like this:

Sue: (*as fantasy figure*) Joan, you probably saw my picture on the cover of *Time* magazine this week as "Woman of the Year." This is only one small tribute to my many incredible achievements. Of course, in addition to being enormously successful in practically everything I do, I'm also gorgeous and charming. In fact, at virtually every social occasion I'm the center of attention. *Everyone* wants to be seen with me, because I'm so *special.*

Joan: (*as ordinary person*) Gee, that must be quite exciting.

Sue: (*as fantasy figure*) Oh, it is. In fact, I go around in a constant state of euphoria when I think of how great I am. But the main thing I wanted to let you know, Joan, is that I'm quite superior to you. You're just ordinary because you don't enjoy even a tiny fraction of my unbelievable success and popularity. So it just logically follows that you're inferior to me, I mean *really* inferior. I'll be looking down on you whenever we're together. I hate to hurt your feelings like this, but I was sure you wanted to know the truth so you wouldn't have any mistaken idea that I considered you my equal!

Once Sue began to talk along these lines, she *really* got into it! I suspect these bottled-up ideas and feelings had never really had the chance to come out. The rest of the group seemed spellbound by her performance!

Once Joan and Sue finished their brief dialogue, I asked the members to process what had just gone on. How did they feel about it? What had they learned?

Sue said that verbalizing this value system made it appear extremely unrealistic. The other members agreed that even if all the claims that the imaginary Sue made were true, she was so obviously self-centered and shallow that the value system lost all its claim to validity.

A college student named Hank said that although it is obviously absurd to believe that the so-called beautiful people are more worthwhile as human beings, he still believed that people who were spiritual or philanthropic, as well as those who contributed a great deal to society through their research and scientific discoveries, *really were* more worthwhile.

Before we go on, ask yourself what you would do as the group leader at this point. What would you say to Hank? Can you see how to use the Feared Fantasy exercise to combat his claim? Think about it for a while before you read on.

I asked Hank to sit in one of the middle chairs and asked another man to sit in the chair opposite him. I explained that they would enter an Alice in Wonderland world where people say things that ordinary people might think but would never dare to say.

I told Hank to imagine that he was one of the most kind and generous people in the world today. In fact, his picture had appeared in this week's *Time* magazine as "Man of the Year" because of his extraordinary philanthropic and scientific contributions to mankind. And because this logically made him a more worthwhile human being, according to his value system, his job was to explain that he was superior to Joe, the volunteer in the other chair. I told Hank that Joe's generosity and contributions to mankind paled by comparison to his own.

Hank *really* got into the role, and the other group members seemed fascinated by what they were hearing. The result was similar to that of the previous role playing. If you say, "Some people are more worthwhile because of their generosity and contributions to mankind," you are in the awkward position of claiming that a few people are superior and that most of the people you know, including your friends and family, are inferior.

You will find that you can do many variations of the Feared Fantasy. You may want the participants to do role reversals, or you may want the one who is being put down to try to defend himself or herself.

If you use this exercise with your group, it's important to have a feeling for the members who volunteer. You would not want to do this with people who are extremely fragile or confused. Emphasize that you are trying to expose the irrationality of these value systems, not trying to put anyone down.

As long as you take these considerations into account, I would recommend this exercise. It can often transform intellectual understanding into real change at the gut level, and it's frequently dramatic and engaging for the participants.

WHAT IS A WORTHLESS PERSON?
WHAT IS A WORTHWHILE PERSON?

Point out that all of these systems for measuring self-esteem suffer from three basic flaws. The first flaw is that there will be times in life when people may no longer fulfill the criteria they have chosen for self-esteem. For example, if they think they are worthwhile as long as they are happy, what will happen if they experience an episode of depression? People who suffer from depression do not feel happy. Does this mean they are no longer worthwhile human beings because they do not feel happy?

The second flaw in any system for measuring self-esteem is that it makes some people better than others, as emphasized in the Feared Fantasy exercise. For example, if success is their criterion for self-esteem, then they may feel inferior to people who have achieved greater success. Will they also feel superior to others who are less successful than they are? Do they want to feel superior to some people and inferior to others? Why or why not?

The third flaw in these systems is that a person is required to rate his or her entire self, as opposed to his or her behaviors. Good (or bad) and worthwhile (or worthless) behaviors exist, but a good or bad human being does not. There's actually no such thing as an inferior or worthless human being, just as there is no such thing as a superior human being.

There are two basic strategies to help people to let go of these systems for rating themselves. One strategy is to say, "Is there any value in measuring my worthwhileness? What are the benefits and what are the costs of basing my sense of self-esteem on my characteristics or my performance? How will this help me, and how will it hurt me?" The Cost-Benefit Analysis exercises used this strategy.

The second strategy is to say, "Is there any such thing as a worthless or worthwhile human being? Are these concepts meaningful or meaningless?" This exercise is based on the second strategy. The goal is to encourage the participants to reject the notion of self-esteem entirely. Then they can stop trying to rate or measure their inherent value as human beings. They will discover that more or less worthwhile behaviors exist, but good or bad human beings do not. We can rate our *traits*, but not our *selves*.

This is an optional exercise because it requires some skill on the part of the leader. If you do it, try to avoid getting into a debate with any member of the group.

One way to demonstrate that there is no such thing as a worthwhile or worthless human being is called Define Terms. Ask the group members to write the definition of a "worthless person" (or an "inferior person" or a "bad person") on page 176 of the participant's workbook. Then ask them to read their definitions out loud, one by one. You can write each definition on the flip chart.

After you write down each definition, ask the group, "Is there anything fishy or suspicious about this definition?" As you lead the discussion, you can show that each definition is useless or meaningless because it has one of these three difficulties:

- The definition applies to all human beings.

- The definition does not apply to any human being.

- The definition is based on all-or-nothing thinking.

For example, let's assume that one of the participants comes up with this definition: "A worthless person is one who can't do anything right."

You can point out that everyone can do *some* things right. Therefore no one is worthless.

On pages 178–180 of the participant's workbook there are a number of additional definitions of a "worthless" or "inferior" human being. Ask the group members to dispute one or two of these definitions in the right-hand column. They can do this exercise individually or in teams. Then ask them to discuss their analyses.

The table on pages 153–154 of this book will show you how to refute several definitions of a "worthless" or "inferior" person. I'm sure you will get many additional ideas as you study these. (This table is a slightly more detailed version of the table on pages 191–192 of the participant's workbook.)

I again want to emphasize that it will not be productive to get into a debate or defend Adolf Hitler as a "worthwhile" person when you do this exercise. Instead, try to guide the group to the idea that all definitions of *worthless* and *worthwhile* tend to be useless, meaningless, and destructive when we apply them in a global way to our entire selves, rather than to our specific behaviors.

Definition of a worthless or inferior person	Rebuttal
1. Someone who does bad things.	Then we're all worthless because we all do some bad things.
2. Someone who fails or makes mistakes.	Then we're all worthless because we all fail and make mistakes.
3. Someone who fails or makes mistakes 51% of the time.	Does this mean that someone who fails 50% of the time is a worthwhile human being and someone who fails 51% of the time is a worthless human being?
4. Someone who does mean, hateful things on purpose to hurt other people.	We all do things that are somewhat mean or hateful at times when we feel hurt and angry. The urge to get back at someone who has wronged us is an unattractive but nearly universal human characteristic. Does it mean that we are all worthless? How many mean, nasty impulses does it take before we become worthless?
5. Someone who is lazy, self-centered, and unproductive, and has no value to society.	We are all lazy and unproductive at times. Does it mean that we are all worthless?
6. Someone whom nobody likes.	Even our greatest heroes, like Abraham Lincoln, had many enemies. By the same token, some of the most destructive people, like Saddam Hussein, Hitler, and Charles Manson, were idolized by many people.
7. Someone who is stupid and untalented.	We're all stupid about most things and untalented in many areas. For example, David Burns, your author, knows little about physics, Greek, or French (and in fact was a lousy French student). He has a drab singing voice, almost no ability to play any musical instrument, etc. According to this definition, all of us are worthless.
8. Someone who does not have *any* talent. To be worthwhile, you have to be good at *one* thing at least.	How good do you have to be, between 0% and 100%, at that *one* thing, to be worthwhile? After all, we all are somewhat talented at dozens of things: walking, talking, listening to music, cooking, drawing, arithmetic, etc.
9. To be worthwhile, you have to be *very* good at *one* thing that is regarded as very important to society. You have to be in the top 5% at that one thing.	According to this definition, a surgeon who is more skillful than 94% of all surgeons would be considered a worthless human being.

Definition of a worthless or inferior person	Rebuttal
10. Someone who does not like himself or herself is not worthwhile. If you feel good about yourself, you are worthwhile.	Most depressed people do not feel worthwhile. They do not like themselves. Low self-esteem is a symptom of depression. Does it follow that depressed people are worthless? Many of the most destructive people, like serial killers, like themselves intensely. Does this make them worthwhile?
11. A murderer is a worthless person because he or she has killed another human being on purpose.	Killing another person is usually seen as a bad, despicable action. But many murders are committed by lovers or spouses as a result of jealousy or marital conflicts. It would not be helpful to label a convicted murderer as a ''bad'' or ''worthless'' person. It would be accurate to say that a convicted murderer is dangerous and has severe difficulties with anger and impulse control.
12. Other: A paranoid like Adolf Hitler who promoted grandiosity, hatred, and violence on a large scale is a bad or worthless person.	There are several issues here. First, this definition is not likely to apply to anyone in your group! Second, there is the question of how you want to use language. Certainly, Hitler had many despicable, immoral, evil thoughts, feelings, and behaviors. But even he also had at least a few good qualities. For example, he started the Volkswagen company and treated his dog well. Did his good traits make him a ''good'' or ''worthwhile'' person?

Do we need to leap from the labeling of someone's actions to the labeling of that person's entire self? What is gained and lost in the process? You can do a Cost-Benefit Analysis, listing the advantages and disadvantages of labeling some human beings as ''bad'' or ''worthless.''

Once you begin this type of labeling, you open a can of worms. The Nazis labeled the Jews as bad. Some Israelis label the Palestinians as ''bad,'' and vice versa. Once you start this labeling process, where does it end? And what are the consequences?

One additional point of interest. Hitler was very committed to this labeling process. He sold the German people on the notion that they were a ''superior'' race and insisted that the Jewish people (as well as many other minority groups) were ''inferior.'' This reasoning led to genocide, a major war, and immense human suffering. |

INFERIORITY EXERCISE

People with low self-esteem feel inferior to others. Although an inferiority complex is usually considered undesirable, there can also be hidden benefits in feeling inferior. Suppose several members of your group believe that they are inferior to others because they are not smart or successful enough. Ask the participants if they can think of any advantages of believing this. When they mention the advantages, ask them to write them down in the left-hand column of the Inferiority Cost-Benefit Analysis on page 182 of the participant's workbook. At the same time, you can list the benefits of feeling inferior on the flip chart. These benefits might include the following:

- If I feel inferior, I won't have to get close to other people and risk rejection.
- I'll have a good excuse for feeling bitter and unhappy.
- I won't have to try new things and fail.
- I can blame my problems on fate.
- I'll feel like I'm being honest and realistic, since I believe with all my heart that I really am inferior to other people.
- I can feel sorry for myself.
- I won't have to be assertive with people.

Next, ask the participants if they can think of any disadvantages of believing they are inferior. Tell them to list these disadvantages in the right-hand column of the Inferiority Cost-Benefit Analysis on page 182 of the participant's workbook. There may be a number of disadvantages:

- I'll feel depressed.
- I'll isolate myself.
- I won't take risks and try new and challenging activities.

After the participants have listed a number of advantages and disadvantages of feeling inferior, ask them whether the advantages or disadvantages are greater. Tell them to put two numbers that add up to 100 in the circles at the bottom of the page.

If the participants decide that the disadvantages of seeing themselves as defective or inferior outweigh the advantages, what new attitude or belief could they substitute for this one? They can put the new attitude on page 181 of the participant's workbook.

THE PLEASURE-PREDICTING SHEET

This exercise may at first seem totally unrelated to the problem of self-esteem. In fact, I originally developed the Pleasure-Predicting Sheet to motivate severely depressed individuals to become more productively involved with life. I subsequently discovered that the Pleasure-Predicting Sheet can also be used to test the accuracy of several of the Self-defeating Beliefs discussed in Steps 6 and 7.

Discuss the following steps in filling out the Pleasure-Predicting Sheet:

- Participants can schedule five or six activities with the potential for pleasure, learning, or personal growth in the first (Activity) column.

- They can indicate with whom they plan to do each activity in the second (Companion) column. Make sure they schedule some activities alone, and some activities with others. Tell them to put the word *self*, not the word *alone*, in this column next to the activities they do by themselves.

- Tell them to predict the satisfaction (on a scale from 0% to 100%) they will get from each activity in the third (Predicted Satisfaction) column. Instruct them to do this *ahead* of time.

- Tell them to record their actual satisfaction (on a scale from 0% to 100%) in the fourth (Actual Satisfaction) column *after* they complete each activity.

When they use the Pleasure-Predicting Sheet, participants can compare how things turned out to their predictions. Depressed people typically underestimate how satisfying things will be. This is one of the reasons they procrastinate and give up on life. Once they see that activities are more enjoyable than anticipated, they often become more motivated and productively involved in life.

There are additional benefits from this exercise:

- The participants can see what kinds of activities really give them satisfaction.

- They can compare the satisfaction they get from being with other people to the satisfaction they get when doing things by themselves.

- They can test Self-defeating Beliefs, such as "If I'm alone, I'm bound to feel miserable," or "I must be a great success to feel happy and worthwhile," or "If I can't do something perfectly, I won't enjoy doing it."

This exercise can sometimes be a real eye-opener for people. For example, I once treated a man named Josh who became severely depressed after his wife left him to live with an exciting attorney she had met. Josh felt worthless and hopeless because he believed that he could never be happy without his wife. He was convinced that if he was alone, he was bound to feel miserable.

People who have been abused or abandoned by a spouse or lover nearly always believe this! They frequently *idolize* the person who mistreated them, and they can be quite committed to the idea that that abusive individual is the source of all their happiness and self-esteem!

Josh portrayed his wife as one of the "beautiful people." He said that his wife had a wonderful personality and a rather glitzy career in fashion design. In contrast, he saw himself as a dull, plain, and sexually unexciting fellow. He apologetically explained that he was only an accountant with a rather boring and tedious job. Josh was convinced that his life could never be the same without his wife.

I asked him to write the following belief at the top of his Pleasure-Predicting Sheet: "Hypothesis: All my happiness in life comes from being with my wife. If I am alone and separated from her, I am destined to feel miserable." He said he was 100% convinced this was true.

I urged him to test this belief by scheduling a variety of activities on the Pleasure-Predicting Sheet. He scheduled some activities by himself, such as jogging and straightening up his desk. I urged him to arrange activities with other people as well, so he agreed to ask out a woman he had met. Finally, he also scheduled an activity with his wife, for purposes of comparison. Josh told me he planned to meet her for lunch in a few days so they could discuss the details of the separation.

I told Josh that he could use the predicted satisfaction and actual satisfaction columns of the Pleasure-Predicting Sheet to test his hypothesis scientifically. After he wrote a brief description of each activity in the first column and whom he would be with in the second, he recorded his prediction of how satisfying each activity would be, on a scale from 0% to 100%, in the third column. He predicted that being with his wife would be *wonderful* and recorded 100% predicted satisfaction for this activity. He predicted that all the other activities, such as jogging, organizing his desk, and going out on a date, would be boring and lonely. Consequently, he predicted less than 10% satisfaction for each of them. He agreed to do all the activities in the next week and to record how they turned out after he had completed them.

Josh was quite surprised to discover that the activities he had done by himself, as well as the date with the woman he had met, were very satisfying. He recorded more than 90% satisfaction for each of these activities in the outcome column.

In contrast, the luncheon with his wife turned out to be a miserable experience. She spent most of the time putting him down and raving about how romantic and sexually fulfilling her new lover was. Since Josh had difficulties with erections from time to time when he and his wife made love, this was extremely humiliating. He recorded 0% satisfaction in the outcome column. The data on the Pleasure-Predicting Sheet were hardly consistent with his belief that all of life's happiness came from being with his wife!

This painful but unexpected revelation gave Josh the strength to begin to let go of her mentally. He scheduled more creative and rewarding activities on his own and began to date more actively. Consequently, he experienced a boost in self-esteem and recovered from his depression. He was able to terminate his treatment after about twelve sessions.

Years later, I learned from a relative of his that Josh and his wife had subsequently divorced. Josh eventually remarried and was doing well. Unfortunately, his ex-wife's love affair turned out to be short-lived and soon disintegrated. She ended up alone and desperately unhappy.

Point out to the participants that using the Pleasure-Predicting Sheet is one of the homework assignments for next week. Tell them to schedule a number of activities in the first column with the potential for pleasure, satisfaction, intimacy, or personal growth. These activities might include learning, doing something productive or creative, helping others, talking to a loved one, or simply having fun with friends. Tell them to list their companion for each activity in the second column and to predict how satisfying each activity will be (from 0% to 100%) in the third column. At the beginning of the next session, they can report how their predicted and actual satisfaction levels compared, and describe what they learned from this exercise.

   If they want to read more about the pleasure-predicting method, you can refer them to pages 127–131 of *The Feeling Good Handbook*.

EXERCISE ON CONDITIONAL VS. UNCONDITIONAL SELF-ESTEEM

Most cognitive therapists believe that the negative thinking of depressed people tends to be quite unrealistic. Cognitive therapists also believe that many deeply held beliefs about the meaning of life and the basis of human worth can be quite illogical and self-defeating. What new and more positive value system do we advocate to replace these negative thinking patterns? What mind-set will lead to greater self-esteem, joy, and productivity?

   When depressed individuals first come to us, they usually feel demoralized and worthless. They may focus on all their shortcomings and overlook their strengths. They often feel unlovable and inadequate. As a first step, some people can achieve greater self-esteem by taking greater pride in what they have accomplished. They can emphasize their good qualities instead of always dwelling on their failures. They may feel better when they resolve personal relationship problems or overcome setbacks in their careers.

   However, this conditional self-esteem may leave them vulnerable to future bouts of depression and anxiety when they once again feel unsuccessful or unloved. Therefore, many therapists try to guide clients to the deeper and more powerful notion of unconditional self-esteem. According to this notion, you do not have to do anything or measure up to any standard in order to be worthwhile. You treat yourself with love and respect simply because you are a human being, in much the same way that you might choose to be compassionate to a beloved friend or child who was troubled and suffering. Your love is not earned but is given unconditionally, because the love is needed.

   The notion of unconditional self-esteem can also have its limits, because the idea that one *should* feel worthwhile may linger. Some clients can get stuck trying very hard to achieve self-esteem, as if it were something they *should* always have. They may also think that they *should* always feel happy and loving.

   Certain clients develop a deeper value system in which they let go of the need for self-esteem entirely. They suddenly comprehend that there is no such thing as self-esteem, just as there is no such thing as a worthwhile person, and so they discard the notion. They can get rid of self-esteem entirely because they realize that they never really needed it in the first place. At the same time, some clients can get rid of their identities as well. They see that the sense of self is just another constricting illusion.

   Of course, these ideas may not be easily conveyed or comprehended at first! Western culture tells us that we *should* try to achieve a great deal so we can be special and worthwhile. The idea that we can be worthwhile even when we have failed or feel abandoned seems alien. The even more radical idea that we do not need self-esteem, or even an identity, may seem bewildering at first.

Once a person comprehends these concepts, they can be incredibly liberating and obvious. They are not mystical mumbo-jumbo but extremely practical, obvious, and healing notions.

Pages 185–188 of the participant's workbook contain an overview of these different approaches to self-esteem. Conditional self-esteem is contrasted with unconditional self-esteem, and the participants are asked to do a Cost-Benefit Analysis of the advantages and disadvantages of unconditional self-esteem.

Ask the participants if they read this section and what their reactions were. Then conduct the CBA for unconditional self-esteem, using your flip chart. List the advantages of unconditional self-esteem in the left-hand column and the disadvantages in the right-hand column. Tell the participants to fill in the blank CBA on page 187 of their workbooks at the same time. Then ask them to balance the advantages against the disadvantages on a 100-point scale at the bottom. Ask about the results of their analysis. Were the advantages or disadvantages greater?

Finally, ask if any of the participants read or thought about the idea of letting go of self-esteem entirely, as discussed on page 188 of the workbook. Do they understand this notion? Does it appeal to them, or do they prefer to maintain the notion of self-esteem? Ask how many participants now favor each of the following:

- Conditional self-esteem: A person can say, "I am worthwhile *because* I am successful (or loved, or kind to others, etc.)"

- Unconditional self-esteem: A person can say, "I am worthwhile simply because I am a human being. Self-esteem is a gift, and I don't have to earn it."

- Letting go of the notion of self-esteem entirely: A person can decide, "Self-esteem is not a useful concept. In fact, there's really no such thing as self-esteem, so I don't have to worry about it. Instead, I can throw away my self-esteem and simply make each day as productive and rewarding as possible."

Emphasize that there is no right or wrong answer, and it's most important to find the value system that will work the best for each participant. This exercise should provide a positive way to integrate the ideas presented in this session and bring it to a close on a positive note.

FEEDBACK ABOUT STEP 7

At the end of the session, summarize the ideas that were discussed. Ask the participants what they learned about self-esteem. Ask them about the difference between conditional and unconditional self-esteem. What's the difference between self-esteem and self-confidence? How does a person develop self-esteem? What are some of the benefits of an inferiority complex? How do you use the Pleasure-Predicting Sheet? What is the purpose of this procedure?

Ask what the participants liked and disliked about the session. Tell them to fill out the Evaluation of Step 7 on page 193 of the participant's workbook. Ask if they would be willing to read what they wrote down. Remember to respond nondefensively when they voice criticisms or negative reactions.

SELF-HELP ASSIGNMENTS FOR STEP 8

Before the participants leave, discuss the self-help assignments for Step 8. These assignments are listed on page 194 of the participant's workbook.

STEP 8

THE PERFECTIONIST'S SCRIPT FOR SELF-DEFEAT

LEADER'S PREPARATION FOR STEP 8

Activity	Check (√) when done
1. Read the description of Step 8 in the participant's workbook beginning on page 195.	
2. Study the Checklist for Step 8 on the next page of this *Leader's Manual* and the Tips for Leaders beginning on page 166.	
3. Read Chapter 14 in *Feeling Good: The New Mood Therapy* and Chapter 7 in *The Feeling Good Handbook*.	

CHECKLIST FOR STEP 8

Activity	Optional or required?	Minimum time (min.)	Check (✓) when done
1. Using the Leader's Data Sheet on page 71, record the participants' scores on the three self-assessment tests, along with their points for homework and for attendance.	req.	10	
2. Ask for positive and negative feedback about Step 7.	req.	5	
3. Discuss the homework on the Pleasure-Predicting Sheet, the Cost-Benefit Analysis, and the Daily Mood Log.	req.	5 – 10	
4. Introduce the topic for this step. Discuss the assigned reading on this step.	req.	5	
5. Discuss perfectionism versus the healthy pursuit of excellence.	req.	5 – 10	
6. Discuss the different kinds of perfectionism.	req.	10 – 15	
7. Perfectionism Exercise 1: the costs and hidden benefits of trying to be perfect.	req.	10 – 15	
8. Perfectionism Exercise 2: the Daily Mood Log.	opt.	10 – 15	
9. Perfectionism Exercise 3: discussion of failure.	req.	10 – 15	
10. Ask for positive and negative feedback about Step 8.	req.	5	
11. Assign the homework for Step 9.	req.	3	

OVERVIEW OF STEP 8

We are constantly bombarded by messages in school, at work, and in the media that tell us how wonderful it is to pursue perfection. Advertisements in magazines and on television promise that we will experience the "thrill of perfection" if only we buy this or that product. Motivational speakers tell us we can achieve *anything* if only we try hard enough and believe in ourselves.

We are less often exposed to the paralyzing shame, inferiority, and despair of believing that we are not good enough. Recent research studies have confirmed a significant link between perfectionistic beliefs and a number of psychiatric disorders such as depression, anxiety, eating disorders, and substance abuse.

I encounter the casualties of perfectionism every day in my clinical practice. A perfectionistic professor once told me, "Sometimes my career seems like a never-ending treadmill. I climb and climb to try to get to the top of the mountain. But when I get there, I just see another, higher peak in the distance, and I feel like I have to keep hiking on. Where's the joy? Where's the reward?"

In spite of the suffering that many perfectionists endure, this mind-set can be addictive and difficult to give up. Many perfectionists take great pride in their relentless self-criticism. They believe that even though perfectionism makes them tense, driven, and irritable, this mind-set will somehow motivate them to try harder and produce a superior product. They are convinced that if they give up their perfectionism they will have to settle for mediocrity and life will lose its luster.

There's actually little or no evidence to support the belief that perfectionism motivates people to achieve. Because perfectionism can lead to anxiety and depression, it may have the opposite effect of reducing creativity and productivity. Many perfectionists probably achieve success in spite of their perfectionism, not because of it.

Another reason for the resistance to change is that many people do not distinguish neurotic perfectionism from the healthy pursuit of excellence. There is certainly nothing wrong with doing one's best or even aspiring to greatness. Where would we be without the achievements of an Einstein or a Mozart? But compulsive perfectionism is quite different from the healthy pursuit of excellence. The perfectionists I am referring to lead driven, joyless lives, they beat themselves up mercilessly whenever they fall short of a goal, and they are deeply convinced that it is somehow shameful—rather than merely human—to fail.

In this step you will discuss the many different kinds of perfectionism and make the members more aware of the costs of perfectionism, along with the hidden benefits of this mind-set. You will show them how to combat perfectionistic attitudes with the Cost-Benefit Analysis and with the Daily Mood Log.

At the end of the session, you will introduce the idea that imperfection can actually be an asset. The real problem is not our imperfection, but our shame. Once we let go of the shame, our brokenness can enable us to form much deeper bonds with others and can help us get in touch with our own spirituality.

Sometimes the understanding of this idea comes after a period of frustration, misunderstanding, and resistance. The idea has to be brought to life with real experience;

otherwise it is like a dry stick without a spark. There's simply no fire or warmth. In my experience, the idea sometimes springs to life during the role playing with the Externalization of Voices, when group members are struggling to talk back to their own Negative Thoughts. Understanding can also sometimes develop when the members begin to trust one another and open up about the painful and shameful experiences in their own lives.

Often, helping group members achieve this kind of trust and understanding can require a lot of patience, empathy, and courage on the part of group leaders. In a recent inpatient group I conducted at the Presbyterian Medical Center, a young man named Benny refused to sit in the group but insisted on standing outside the circle with his arms folded defiantly. Because Benny looked handsome, muscular, and dangerous, and had had lots of run-ins with the law, I wasn't at all in the mood to confront him! When I asked if he'd like to join the group, he scowled at me and I felt a sudden panic. I quickly pointed out that we *never* forced anyone to join a group or open up, and it was perfectly okay if he preferred just to observe. Fortunately, he seemed satisfied with this solution but paced back and forth liked a caged tiger as I started the session.

I began working with a woman who felt guilty and thought that she was a bad mother. She said she thought that her children would hate her and feel abandoned because she had relapsed and had to be rehospitalized. She had carefully written all this out on a Daily Mood Log, and I had her do role playing with another patient who played her Negative Thoughts.

During the role playing, Benny suddenly blurted out in a very aggressive voice, "I get so *sick and tired* of all this *bullshit* about *having to measure up* to some damn *level of success* in order to be somebody and to be worthwhile!"

The room became as quiet as a tomb. If you were the group leader, what would you have said? Think about this for a moment before you read on.

There are lots of people like Benny in the world. You will meet them frequently if you are running groups in hospitals, prisons, or other settings where you will be treating people with a history of drug abuse, criminal behavior, or personality disorders. And even groups of so-called high-functioning people such as corporate executives will challenge you from time to time. Your style of responding will have a big impact on the morale and success of your group. What would you say to Benny?

In this case I said, "Benny, that sounds like Buddhism to me. You know, Benny, that's the whole basis of cognitive therapy. That's just the idea I'm trying to get across, and lots of people don't understand that you don't have to be successful to be worthwhile. But you seem to be enlightened on this point. I wish you could help me teach the other patients about this, because then they wouldn't have to go around feeling like a piece of shit all the time because they aren't smart enough or good enough or successful enough."

Benny said, "Is that right, Doc?"

I said, "That's right, Benny, and it's basically one of the ideas of Buddhism. Tell me, Benny, are you a Buddhist? You seemed to be enlightened."

Benny became quite animated. He leaped into the middle of the circle and said he wanted to role-play just as the other members had been doing. Then he described how his uncle, a man he'd loved and admired greatly, had stood before him and committed suicide with a pistol when Benny was a boy. He said members of his family, including his uncle, had been involved with organized crime, and that he looked up to people who were in the Mafia. He told us how he'd been in and out of prison and had lots of trouble with violence and was a drug addict. Then he said, "My Negative Thought is that I'll *never* change. How're ya gonna handle that one, Doc?"

I said, "Great! Let's write that on the flip chart and do a Cost-Benefit Analysis. Benny, what are the advantages of believing this?"

Benny replied, "There ain't *no* advantages, Doc. I just keep goin' in an' out of prison, and in an' out of the hospital. I'll probably end up dead soon."

I said, "Oh no, Benny, there are tremendous benefits to this thought. Let's list all these advantages of believing you can never change on the flip chart. What are the benefits? Just think about it. You can beat people up, you can use drugs like cocaine and heroin all you want, you can have a real exciting life like James Dean. What could be better?"

Benny said, "Exactly, Doc, exactly! You *really* understand where I'm coming from!"

Benny and several other members of the group were all struggling—although in different ways—with a value system that told them, "You've got to measure up—you've got to be better than you really are—because you're simply not good enough." The woman who thought she was a bad mother had succumbed to the feelings of failure with self-loathing and despair. Others, like Benny, had rebelled with drug abuse and antisocial behavior.

By the end of this ninety-minute session four of the eight participants in the group reported feeling significantly better, and this was reflected in substantial improvements in their scores on the Burns Depression Checklist. There were several reasons for the success of this group. First, I had to be patient and use all my clinical experience with Benny so that he would not be further distanced from the group. When he confronted me, I used the Disarming Technique (I found truth in his statement instead of getting defensive) as well as Stroking (I found something admiring and respectful to say to him, even though he was acting distrustful and aggressive). This clinical style may have helped him to open up.

Second, the ruthlessly honest sharing of several of the participants also contributed to the success of the group. Their openness triggered an infectious camaraderie that was mood-elevating for me as well. We could all feel the exhilaration and warmth as the group evolved.

Finally, they were able to deal with an abstract psychological concept like perfectionism on the level of vivid personal experiences. This prevented the session from being dull and overly academic, and allowed them to see a new and deeper reality with their hearts that they might not have noticed with their intellects alone.

TIPS FOR LEADERS

DATA COLLECTION

Record the participants' scores on the three self-assessment tests (the BDC, the BAI, and the RSAT) on the Leader's Data Sheet on page 71. Record how much homework they completed using the 3-point rating scale on page 68. Record whether or not they came on time using the 2-point rating scale on page 68.

FEEDBACK AND REVIEW OF HOMEWORK

Ask the participants about their reactions to the last session on self-esteem. What did they like and dislike about it? Did their thinking about self-esteem change in any way? What is the difference between conditional and unconditional self-esteem? Which concept do they prefer? Do they think that self-esteem can be earned? Why or why not?

Did the participants do any additional Cost-Benefit Analyses linking self-esteem with love, success, or any other quality? What were the results of these analyses?

Did they use the Pleasure-Predicting Sheet? Can they describe their experience with it? What activities gave them the most and the least satisfaction? How did their estimates of predicted satisfaction compare with the levels of actual satisfaction they recorded in the right-hand column?

Ask about the written homework assignment using the Daily Mood Log. Were the participants able to refute any of their NTs successfully? If so, ask them to give examples. Ask if any of them would be willing to describe their written homework to the group. What problems did they encounter? Did they have some NTs they were not able to refute?

PERFECTIONISM VS. THE HEALTHY PURSUIT OF EXCELLENCE

Ask the group members to discuss what they liked and disliked about the assigned reading on perfectionism.

Ask them about the problems that can result from perfectionism. These problems can include:

- stress at work or school
- mood swings, like depression and anxiety
- loneliness and difficulties in forming intimate relationships
- excessive frustration, anger, and conflicts in personal relationships
- problems in learning from criticism, failure, or mistakes
- procrastination as well as difficulties sticking with jobs that are tough

As the members come up with additional problems, you can write them on the flip chart. Ask them to list these problems on page 200 of their workbooks at the same time. Ask if they can think of some personal examples of these problems in their own lives. Did they ever feel discouraged when they failed to achieve a goal? Did they ever feel inferior to friends or colleagues who were more intelligent or successful?

Ask if the participants can think of any differences between perfectionism and the healthy pursuit of excellence. The differences are explained in the table on page 201 of the participant's workbook. If they can think of any more differences between perfectionism and the healthy pursuit of excellence, write them on the flip chart. Ask the participants if this distinction strikes them as an abstract, philosophical notion or if it could be useful in their daily lives.

KINDS OF PERFECTIONISM

Read the definition of each type of perfectionism from the table on page 202 of the participant's workbook. As you read each definition, ask the members if they can recognize that problem in themselves or in a family member, friend, or colleague.

You should be able to stimulate considerable discussion as you do this exercise. When members respond positively, ask how it feels to have that kind of perfectionism or to interact with someone with that mind-set. See if they can supply some personal examples.

1. **Physical perfectionism:** These perfectionists think they must have a perfect face or figure to be desirable and appealing.

2. **Achievement perfectionism:** These perfectionists feel it would be terrible to make a mistake, to fail, or to fall short of a personal goal in their career or studies.

3. **Perceived perfectionism:** These perfectionists believe that they have to impress people to be liked and respected. They are convinced that others will look down on them if they fail, look foolish, or make a mistake.

4. **Emotional perfectionism:** Emotional perfectionists feel ashamed of negative and vulnerable feelings such as loneliness, depression, anger, anxiety, or panic. They believe that others would not accept and love them if they knew how they really feel inside. They may believe that they should always feel happy and in control of their emotions.

5. **Self-esteem perfectionism:** These perfectionists believe they aren't sufficiently worthwhile. They feel inferior to people who are more intelligent, attractive, or successful.

6. **Relationship perfectionism:** These perfectionists believe that people who care for each other should never fight or argue. They avoid conflicts in personal relationships, thinking they should always get along with everyone.

7. **Romantic Perfectionism:** Perfectionists in romance find it difficult to form lasting intimate relationships because other people are never quite good enough for them. They become preoccupied with the shortcomings of others.

8. **Entitlement:** These perfectionists are quite demanding and get extremely upset when other people do not measure up to their expectations. They may get excessively angry or frustrated if a train is late, if traffic is slow, or if others do not treat them with sufficient respect.

9. **Obsessive-compulsive tendencies:** People with these tendencies feel their house must always be immaculate and they spend excessive amounts of time cleaning, organizing, checking things, counting, or doing other rituals.

10. **Other:** Ask if the members can think of any other kinds of perfectionism.

PERFECTIONISM EXERCISE 1

Divide the group into teams of three to six members. Each team will evaluate the advantages and disadvantages of one of the following beliefs on the Attitude Cost-Benefit form on page 205 of the participant's workbook:

- I must always try to be perfect.

- People will think less of me if I fail or make a mistake.

- I must be outstanding to be worthwhile and loved by others.

Members can ask themselves, "How will it help me, and how will it hurt me, if I believe this?"

Each team can first list some of the hidden benefits of perfectionism in the left-hand column. These may include:

- I will try very hard.

- I will not settle for mediocrity.

- I may feel "special" because I have such high personal standards.

- Others will admire me because I am so ambitious and devoted to my work.

- When I do a good job, I may feel especially worthwhile.

- I can avoid risky, frightening situations that involve the possibility of failure.

For example, if a student thinks she has to have a *perfect* paper, she may work on it endlessly to reduce the chances that her efforts will be criticized. If a man thinks he has to find someone "perfect" to date, he can avoid flirting and asking women out, because no one will ever seem quite good enough for him. He won't have to risk getting rejected or getting close to others.

Participants can also list the disadvantages of perfectionism in the right-hand column. Will perfectionism cause problems in their lives? What are the problems? The costs of perfectionism could include:

- I will have difficulties in coping with criticism or disapproval.

- I may procrastinate.

- I may have more anxiety and depression.

- I may have low self-esteem when I feel I'm not perfect.

- I may feel lonely and have difficulties getting close to others.

- I may be prone to anger and frustration when circumstances do not live up to expectations.

Ask the team members to balance the advantages against the disadvantages of perfectionism on a 100-point scale at the bottom of the Cost-Benefit Analysis. For example, if the advantages of perfectionism are higher, they might put a 60 in the circle on the left and a 40 in the circle on the right.

When people feel that the disadvantages of an attitude are greater than the advantages, then the circle on the right will have the larger number. In this case, ask the participants what new attitude they could substitute for the old one. They can write the revised attitude in the space provided in the participant's workbook.

Afterward, reconvene the group as a whole and ask a spokesperson from each team to read the Cost-Benefit Analysis and summarize the conclusions of his or her group. (A completed CBA appears on page 212 of the participant's workbook.)

PERFECTIONISM EXERCISE 2

Point out that perfectionism, like depression, results from illogical Negative Thoughts. Even though perfectionists always try to be right, their thoughts are often quite illogical and distorted.

The commonest distortion is all-or-nothing thinking: If a perfectionist doesn't perform perfectly, he or she may feel like a total failure, a complete zero. Other common distortions include "should" statements ("I shouldn't have screwed up"), mind reading ("Everyone will think less of me"), emotional reasoning ("I feel like a failure; therefore I must be one"), and mental filter (dwelling on one's errors and overlooking one's accomplishments), to name just a few.

Ask the members if they can think of a specific time when they felt upset because they had failed in some aspect of their lives—in their careers, in their parenting, in their intimate relationships, in their attempts to diet or quit drinking, or in other areas. Ask them to write a brief description of the experience in Step One of the Daily Mood Log on page 207 of the participant's workbook. Ask several members to read what they wrote down.

Ask them to record their negative emotions in Step Two of the Daily Mood Log. Were they feeling frustrated? Put down? Inferior? Discouraged? Tell them to rate each negative emotion on a scale from 0% (the least) to 100% (the most).

After the participants have discussed their experiences and emotions, ask what they were telling themselves that made them feel upset. Tell them to record their Negative Thoughts and number them sequentially in the left-hand column of the Daily Mood Log. Remind them to put an estimate of how strongly they believed each Negative Thought on a scale from 0% (not at all) to 100% (completely).

Now ask the members to identify the distortions in their NTs using the list on page 50 of the participant's workbook. After several minutes, ask them to discuss the distortions they found in their thoughts. This should make them more aware of how unrealistic these perfectionistic thoughts can be.

Finally, see if they can substitute Positive Thoughts using the strategies listed on page 109.

PERFECTIONISM EXERCISE 3

Many perfectionists believe that they must earn other people's love and approval by being outstanding. An alternative philosophy would be that our vulnerabilities and flaws—not our successes and strengths—ultimately make us lovable and human. People can be admired or resented—but never loved—for their successes and achievements.

To care for someone in a deep and genuine way, we must be aware of that person's pain and shortcomings. A person who was truly perfect and never made any mistakes would be unlovable. Our "brokenness" is essential to being human. Failure and despair can be opportunities for growth, for intimacy, for spiritual awareness, and for self-acceptance. What do they think about this idea? Does it make any sense? Or does it seem like nonsense?

After the group discusses these ideas, see if a volunteer can describe a failure in his or her career, or a painful personal experience that he or she would like to share with the other group members. You can suggest a variety of nearly universal problems that would be appropriate for this discussion:

- being criticized by a colleague or family member
- failing in attempts to achieve a personal goal
- problems with children
- being rejected in a romantic relationship
- any interpersonal conflict
- shame about a personal habit such as alcoholism or overeating
- feelings of inadequacy about a sexual problem
- feeling nervous about public speaking or shy in social situations

Ask the group members to discuss the positive and negative consequences of these negative experiences. Would they be better off having perfect lives? Or do these moments of despair and self-doubt actually enhance their lives? In what way?

FEEDBACK ABOUT STEP 8

At the end of the session, summarize the ideas that were discussed. Ask the participants what they liked and disliked about it. Tell them to fill out the Evaluation of Step 8 on page 213 of the participant's workbook. Ask if they would be willing to read what they wrote down. Remember to respond nondefensively when they voice criticisms or negative reactions.

SELF-HELP ASSIGNMENTS FOR STEP 9

Before the participants leave, discuss the self-help assignments for Step 9. These assignments are listed on page 214 of the participant's workbook.

STEP 9

A PRESCRIPTION FOR PROCRASTINATORS

LEADER'S PREPARATION FOR STEP 9

Activity	Check (√) when done
1. Read the description of Step 9 in the participant's workbook beginning on page 215.	
2. Study the Checklist for Step 9 on the next page of this *Leader's Manual* and the Tips for Leaders beginning on page 174.	
3. Read Chapters 9 and 10 of *The Feeling Good Handbook*.	

CHECKLIST FOR STEP 9

Activity	Optional or required?	Minimum time (min.)	Check (√) when done
1. Using the Leader's Data Sheet on page 72, record the participants' scores on the three self-assessment tests, along with their points for homework and for attendance.	req.	10	
2. Ask for positive and negative feedback about Step 8.	req.	5	
3. Discuss the written homework with the Daily Mood Log.	opt.	5 – 10	
4. Discuss the assigned reading and introduce today's topic.	req.	5 – 10	
5. The Procrastination Test.	req.	15	
6. The Procrastination Cost-Benefit Analysis and the Action Cost-Benefit Analysis.	req.	10 – 15	
7. The Devil's Advocate Technique.	req.	10 – 15	
8. The TIC-TOC Technique.	req.	10 – 15	
9. Exercise: Little Steps for Big Feats (the Antiprocrastination Sheet).	req.	10 – 15	
10. Exercise: Make a Plan.	req.	10 – 15	
11. Summary of Step 9.	opt.	5	
12. Ask for positive and negative feedback about Step 9.	req.	5	
13. Assign the homework for Step 10.	req.	3	

OVERVIEW OF STEP 9

Today's session will differ from the past several sessions in three respects. The previous groups have focused primarily on thoughts and attitudes, whereas today's will focus more on motivation and on action. Previous sessions emphasized the importance of self-acceptance, whereas today's deals with personal responsibility. Finally, the teaching methods in the previous sessions were relatively straightforward, whereas this step emphasizes paradoxical methods.

At the end of this step, the participants should be able to

- recognize specific examples of procrastination in their own lives
- identify the ten causes of procrastination
- understand the hidden benefits of procrastination
- combat procrastination with the Procrastination Cost-Benefit Analysis, the Devil's Advocate Technique, the TIC-TOC Technique, and the Antiprocrastination Sheet

TIPS FOR LEADERS

DATA COLLECTION

Record the participants' scores on the three self-assessment tests (the BDC, the BAI, and the RSAT) on the Leader's Data Sheet on page 72. Record how much homework they completed using the 3-point rating scale on page 68. Record whether they came on time using the 2-point rating scale on page 68.

FEEDBACK AND REVIEW OF HOMEWORK

Ask about the participants' reactions to the last session on perfectionism. What did they like and dislike about it? Did their thinking about perfectionism change in any way? What are the different kinds of perfectionism? What is the difference between perfectionism and the healthy pursuit of excellence?

Ask about the written homework assignment using the Daily Mood Log. Were the participants able to refute any of their NTs successfully? If so, ask them to give examples. Ask if any of them would be willing to describe their written homework to the group. What problems did they encounter? Did they have some NTs they were not able to refute?

THE CAUSES OF PROCRASTINATION

Ask for the participants' reactions to the assigned reading on procrastination. Ask if procrastination has ever been a problem for them. What are the things they procrastinate about? Did they write descriptions of what they procrastinate about on page 220 of the participant's workbook? They may mention day-to-day examples of tasks they avoid such as straightening up their desks or balancing their checkbooks, as well as more significant problems such as not studying for exams until the last minute, not completing projects at work on time, not applying for a new job, not flirting or asking someone for a date, or not getting started on a diet.

Ask the members to take the Procrastination Test on page 221 of the participant's workbook. Tell them to score the test using the instructions on page 223 of the workbook. Their scores on each of the ten causes of procrastination can range between 0 and 6. Lower scores are better and higher scores are worse. The causes of procrastination include: putting the cart before the horse, the mastery model, the fear of failure, perfectionism, a lack of rewards, "should" statements, passive aggression, unassertiveness, coercion sensitivity, and lack of desire.

As you discuss each pattern with the group, you can ask, "Does this pattern describe you or a family member or colleague?"

THE BENEFITS OF PROCRASTINATION

Ask each group member to think about one thing that he or she procrastinates about. If they can think of something they are currently procrastinating about, it will give the session more meaning. If they can't think of anything, they can write down something they used to procrastinate about. It is important that the example be a *specific* one. For example, one group member may lie around on the couch eating junk food and watching TV on Saturdays instead of fixing the screen on the porch. Another member may procrastinate about doing the self-help exercises between group sessions!

Ask each member to write a brief description of one specific thing he or she procrastinates about at the top of the Procrastination Cost-Benefit Analysis on page 226 of the participant's workbook. Ask people to describe what they wrote down.

Ask the participants if they can think of any advantages of procrastinating about that task today. Tell them to try to identify the obvious advantages as well as the hidden ones. Ask them to list the advantages in the left-hand column of the CBA. Draw a line down the middle of your flip chart from top to bottom and list the advantages in the left-hand column at the same time.

The advantages of procrastination may not be entirely evident to the participants at first, since people usually think of procrastination as a "problem." There are, nevertheless, *many* obvious as well as hidden benefits, and they need to bring these out. They may come up with a list like this one:

- Procrastination is easy.
- I have too many other important things to do today.
- I can avoid feeling upset.
- I can avoid doing something unpleasant.
- I can live for the moment and do more pleasurable things.

- It's fun to lie around and be lazy.

- I can get back at the people who are making demands on me.

- I can feel special, like a prince or princess who doesn't have to do any hard work.

- If I act passive and helpless, people will learn not to expect too much of me.

- I might get other people to do my chores for me, since they will realize it's easier than waiting around for me.

While you list the advantages of procrastination on your flip chart, remind the members to list them in the left-hand column of the Procrastination Cost-Benefit Analysis on page 226 of their workbooks.

Now ask them to list the disadvantages of procrastinating in the right-hand column of the Procrastination Cost-Benefit Analysis. Ask them to think about the down side—what is the price they pay for procrastinating? When they mention the disadvantages, write them in the right-hand column of your flip chart.

Once you have a good list of the advantages and disadvantages of procrastinating, ask the participants to weigh the advantages against the disadvantages on a 100-point scale. Ask them to put two numbers that add up to 100 at the bottom of the CBA on page 226 of the participant's workbook to indicate the results of this analysis.

For example, if the advantages of procrastinating today are somewhat greater, they might put a 60 in the left-hand circle at the bottom of the page and a 40 in the right-hand circle. If, in contrast, the disadvantages seem very much greater, they might put a 35 in the left-hand circle and a 65 in the right-hand circle. Ask how many people felt the advantages were greater? How many felt the disadvantages were greater?

Since it is socially correct to think of procrastination as a weakness or bad character trait, we can assume that most of the participants will come to the conclusion that the disadvantages of procrastination are greater. At the same time, we know that most procrastinators are extremely stubborn and hide their motives from themselves. If the disadvantages were *really* greater, we wouldn't have any procrastinators! That's why the Procrastination Cost-Benefit Analysis is only a first step. To see some real changes, we may need some stronger medicine.

Tell the participants that they have to pass at least one more acid test of their motivation before they can make the decision to stop procrastinating and to get started. In order to be really sure of how they feel, tell them to list the *disadvantages* of getting started *today* in the right-hand column of the Action Cost-Benefit Analysis on page 227 of the workbook. Please notice that this Action CBA is on the *next page* after the one they just used. This may be confusing, so please spell it out.

When the participants mention disadvantages, list them in the right-hand column of a new Cost-Benefit Analysis on your flip chart. The disadvantages of getting started are quite abundant. They may include these:

- The job will be difficult and boring.

- It will take time and effort.

- I can just as easily do it some other day.

- There are more rewarding things to do instead.

- Once I'm done, other people may expect more of me so I may have to keep it up and work even harder.

- Life may feel less magical and more ordinary and humdrum.

- I may end up doing more and more things I don't really want to do.

This is a paradoxical strategy. Instead of persuading the group members to become more productive, you are trying to make them more aware of the many reasons they procrastinate.

This is an important exercise because most procrastinators appear to have little insight into why they put things off. They act as if it were all a big mystery. They may appear helpless and confused. Behind this facade there is usually a powerful and systematic game plan. People cannot usually develop the motivation to change until they come to terms with the fact that they are intensely committed to maintaining the status quo. Paradoxically, once they admit that they really have almost no intention of changing, they often begin to behave more productively and responsibly.

Once the participants have listed the disadvantages of getting started today, ask them about the advantages. List the advantages of getting started today in the left-hand column of your flip chart while they list them in the left-hand column of the Action CBA on page 227 of the participant's workbook.

Finally, ask them to weigh the advantages against the disadvantages of getting started today on a 100-point scale. Tell them to put two numbers adding up to 100 in the two circles at the bottom of the Action CBA on page 227 of the participant's workbook, just as they did before. For example, if the disadvantages of getting started today are slightly greater than the advantages, they could put a 45 in the left-hand circle and a 55 in the right-hand circle.

Ask about the results of their evaluation. How many participants felt the advantages of getting started were greater? How many of them felt the disadvantages were greater? What did they learn? Did this help them understand why they are procrastinating? Do they still want to get started today, once they take all these disadvantages into account?

This technique is usually effective only when it is used paradoxically. Emphasize the many benefits of procrastinating, and the many disadvantages of getting started, when you direct the exercise. Members who conclude that they want to give up procrastination may have missed the point. They may still be deceiving themselves. Many experienced procrastinators have no intention to change—now or in the foreseeable future! The participants who discover that they really are committed to procrastination will have the best chance to change.

If you are an idealist and you believe that you can use logic or reason to persuade an entrenched procrastinator to change, you may be in for a disappointment. Procrastinators will usually be quite pleasant and agree politely with your recommendations. They will tell you they have *every intention* of changing. When you see them next, they will often act embarrassed or evasive and will confess that they "forgot" or "didn't have time" to get started. This pattern is so predictable that I have switched to more forceful and less straightforward strategies, such as the paradoxical CBA exercises that I just described.

I do not intend to make you cynical or overly pessimistic about the prognosis for group members who procrastinate. I simply hope you will understand that this problem may require a sophisticated approach. In my practice, I have found that the paradoxical strategies can be helpful to clients. In addition, they empower me as the therapist, because I do not put myself in the position of "helping" or giving advice and then being disappointed when the client fails to follow through.

The next exercise is designed to intensify the motivation of those participants who claim that they want to stop procrastinating. You will be holding their feet to the fire by using a role-playing technique designed to make them vividly aware of their commitment to procrastination.

THE DEVIL'S ADVOCATE TECHNIQUE

Ask for a volunteer to help demonstrate a new method called the Devil's Advocate Technique. The volunteer will pretend to be a man named Michael who keeps procrastinating about cleaning up his garage. The garage has been disorganized and junk has been piling up for years.

To make matters worse, Michael's wife keeps nagging him to clean the garage. He tells her he will clean it up but never seems to get around to it. This is a source of constant irritation in their marriage. Michael is puzzled about why he can't seem to get around to it. He acts as if there were an invisible barrier that mysteriously holds him back, in spite of his intense determination and most strenuous efforts. He says he hopes that the group can help him with his problem.

According to his Cost-Benefit Analyses, Michael sees lots of advantages in cleaning out the garage, and lots of disadvantages in procrastinating any longer. And yet, in spite of his best intentions, he has put off cleaning it out for eighteen months (or approximately five hundred days in a row). How can this be?

Whenever Michael thinks about cleaning up the garage, he has lots of Negative Thoughts like the ones below. Ask the volunteer to read them out loud for the group. (These Negative Thoughts appear on page 228 of the participant's workbook.)

1. I really *should* do it, but I'm not in the mood.

2. I can do it a little later. I'll wait until I feel more like it.

3. Just think of all the junk in the garage! There must be a mountain of it.

4. It will take forever.

5. Even if I do get started it will just be a drop in the bucket. I need to wait until I have several free days in a row.

6. I have other, more important things to do right now. I can relax and have a beer and watch the football game on TV.

7. It will really be exhausting.

8. Once I'm done, it will just get messy again.

9. Why is my wife such a nag? Why is she so compulsive? What's so important about the garage anyway? It's fine the way it is.

10. Why don't we have sex more often? I shouldn't have to clean the garage if we don't have sex!

Ask the group members if they ever have Negative Thoughts like these when they procrastinate. Ask what their thoughts are. When someone describes a thought, you can say something like this: "Good. That's an excellent procrastination thought! Do any of the rest of you have similar thoughts when you procrastinate?" This will help them identify their own Negative Thoughts, which they will work on later in the session when you introduce the TIC-TOC Technique.

After a brief discussion, tell the volunteer that he will play the role of Michael's Positive Thoughts. Tell the volunteer that you will play the role of Michael's Negative Thoughts and will try to convince him to procrastinate. You can use your intuition and your knowledge about the hidden benefits of procrastination when you do the role playing. Try your hardest to persuade him to keep procrastinating.

When the volunteer plays the role of Michael's Positive Thoughts, he will try to persuade you that he would really like to clean out the garage. He will argue that he is committed to getting started on it when he goes home from the group *today*.

You will play the role of the Negative Thoughts and so you will use the second person ("you") in the role playing, as illustrated in the sample dialogue below. The volunteer must talk back to you using the first person ("I"). He can insist that in spite of your objections he really is determined to get started on the garage today. Emphasize that even though the role playing may sound like two people talking, they are really just the two parts of Michael's mind: the negative, lazy part and the positive, responsible part.

To get this demonstration rolling, you and the volunteer can read the dialogue below, which is reproduced on page 229 of the participant's workbook:

Leader: (*as Devil's Advocate*) It's really too late to get started on cleaning out the garage today. You're tired. Tomorrow will be a better day.

Volunteer: (*as PTs*) Well, I really *should* get started.

Leader: It's really late and you can't get much done today anyway.

Volunteer: Even if I only work in there for fifteen minutes, at least I will get started. That would be something.

Leader: That would only be a drop in the bucket. Besides, it will be cold and dark by the time you get home from the group meeting. You'll be all tired out and it will be more fun to have a beer and watch a little TV. There may be a good game on. You can wait until the weekend to do the garage. Then you'll feel more in the mood and you can get a whole lot done.

Volunteer: Yes, but my wife has been nagging me and I can get her off my back if I get started.

Leader: Yes, but your wife is a real nag and she doesn't seem to appreciate you very much. If you have a couple of beers you won't mind so much. Why should you break your butt for her?

Volunteer: But this is ruining our marriage. She's annoyed and we practically *never* have sex.

Leader: Yes, but you shouldn't have to do housecleaning just to have sex with your wife. After all, you slave away sixty hours a week at the office and all she does is gripe at you when you get home. You deserve better. Besides, the garage can wait for a better day.

You can continue to ad lib for a couple of minutes if you like. The key to the success of this exercise is to *try hard* to persuade Michael to keep procrastinating. If the volunteer who plays Michael's Positive Thoughts gets stuck and gives up, you can do a role reversal. Tell the volunteer to play the role of the NTs while you (or another volunteer from the group) play the role of the PTs.

After you have completed the exercise using the imaginary example with the garage, you can repeat the exercise using an actual example from a group member. Ask for a second volunteer. Choose someone who has done a reasonably good job of completing the previous assignment with the Procrastination Cost-Benefit Analysis. (Let's assume it is a woman this time.) Make sure there is something specific she has been procrastinating about, and that she has concluded that she wants to get started on it *today*.

Whenever she thinks about doing the task, she has lots of Negative Thoughts. What does she tell herself? Write her thoughts down on the flip chart. Review her lists of the advantages of procrastinating and the disadvantages of getting started from the Procrastination and Action CBAs. Ask the participants if they can think of any other advantages of procrastinating.

Then begin the Devil's Advocate Technique again. As before, you will play the role of the Negative Thoughts. Remember to use the second person ("you") just as in the example above. The volunteer must talk back to you using the first person ("I"). She can try to insist that, in spite of your objections, she really is determined to get started today.

TIC-TOC TECHNIQUE

By now the participants should be aware of the fact that when they procrastinate they give themselves negative messages that get in the way. The messages are called TICs, or Task-Interfering Cognitions. (A TIC is just a Negative Thought with a cute name.) There is a sample TIC on page 230 of the participant's workbook in a form that looks like this:

TICs (Task-Interfering Cognitions)	Distortions	TOCs (Task-Oriented Cognitions)
1. *There's so much to study. I'll never learn it all.*		

Ask the participants to identify the distortions in this TIC. Tell them to list the distortions in the middle column of the TIC-TOC form on page 230 of the workbook. Then ask them to write a TOC, or Task-Oriented Cognition, in the right-hand column of the TIC-TOC form. (A TOC is just a Positive Thought with a cute name.) There is an example of how to do this on page 231 of the workbook. Ask them what they wrote down. Were they able to come up with a convincing TOC?

Now ask the participants to identify some of their own TICs. What do they tell themselves when they are procrastinating? Tell them to write these TICs on the blank TIC-TOC form on page 232 of the participant's workbook. Write them on the flip chart at the same time. Then tell the group to identify the distortions in their TICs using the checklist on page 50 of the participant's workbook. Finally, ask how they could talk back to these TICs. Tell them to write their TOCs in the right-hand column while you write them on the flip chart.

Next, break up the group into teams of two or three members so they can practice the Devil's Advocate Technique. This time they will use the actual thoughts they have when they are procrastinating about a specific task. One member will play the role of the TICs and the other will play the role of the TOCs. They can use the TICs they just wrote down in their workbooks.

It will be most useful if the person who plays the role of the TOCs is the one who is procrastinating. This will prevent the others from helping or giving advice. The idea is to force the participants to challenge their own TICs.

The box on page 182, which appears in the participant's workbook on page 230, summarizes the Devil's Advocate procedure.

Walk around and supervise the exercise, which can be quite challenging. Make sure the team members don't talk in a general fashion. Encourage them to stay focused on the assignment.

When they are done, ask them what the role playing was like. What worked and what did not? Did they experience any difficulties? Were they able to win the argument with the Devil who tempted them to procrastinate?

DEVIL'S ADVOCATE TECHNIQUE

1. Make a list of your Negative Thoughts when you procrastinate. Think of all the advantages of procrastinating. Write down what you tell yourself when you procrastinate, such as "I'm not really in the mood." These Negative Thoughts are sometimes called TICs, or Task-Interfering Cognitions.

2. Select a partner. The two of you face each other.

3. Tell your partner to read your Negative Thoughts, one by one, using the second person ("you" statements). Tell your partner to try to tempt you or persuade you to procrastinate. Tell your partner to be as persuasive as he or she can possibly be.

4. Talk back to your partner using the first person ("I" statements). Try to refute his or her arguments. Don't give in, fight back! Argue that it really would be to your advantage to get started today. These Positive Thoughts are sometimes called TOCs, or Task-Oriented Cognitions.

5. If you get stuck, do a role reversal.

LITTLE STEPS FOR BIG FEATS

People who are highly productive rarely try to tackle a difficult job all at once. More often, they break a task down into its smallest component parts, and then they do these, one small step at a time.

There are two ways to do this. The simplest solution is just to work in small time chunks, such as fifteen minutes. The rationale is that it's relatively easy to do something if you know you can quit after fifteen minutes. Of course, once you get started, you will often get more in the mood and end up doing additional work.

Nearly all procrastinators stubbornly refuse to follow this advice. They give themselves excuses such as these:

1. Fifteen minutes is barely enough time to get started.

2. I'll wait until I have time to get the job done right.

3. It would be pointless just to do a little bit.

Ask the group members if they can think of any other excuses a person might have for refusing to spend fifteen minutes on a difficult task.

The second solution is to organize the task into small steps that all follow one another in a logical sequence. For example, suppose that Michael has decided to clean out the garage. He might list the following steps:

1. Go into the garage and look around.

2. Purchase or locate some trash bags.

3. Load several bags with trash.

4. Repeat Step 3 several times.

5. Organize the things we need to keep.

6. Sweep the floor.

Let's assume a single man in your group has the problem of shyness. He is afraid to flirt or to ask women out for fear of looking foolish or being rejected. Here's how he might solve the problem by breaking it into small steps:

1. During the next week I can smile and say hello to fifteen strangers just for practice. (They can be men or women of any age.)

2. Once I have accomplished this, I can smile and say hello to five attractive women I'd like to date. However, I don't have to talk to them or ask them out.

3. Next, I can start small, innocuous conversations with several strangers (men or women of any age) just for practice.

4. Next, I can start small, innocuous conversations with several attractive women I meet in places like the lunch counter or the elevator of my building.

5. Then I can ask for the phone number of at least one attractive woman I'd like to date.

6. I can repeat Steps 3, 4, and 5 over and over.

Divide the group into teams and ask each team to break a complex task into its smallest possible parts using the Antiprocrastination Sheet on page 234 of the participant's workbook. The team members can use a task they are actually procrastinating on, or tasks that you assign. Tell them to number each small step of the task in the left-hand column of the Antiprocrastination Sheet. Then they can predict how difficult and how satisfying (on a scale from 0% to 100%) each little step will be. They can record these predictions in the second and third columns of the sheet.

After about five minutes, you can ask a spokesperson from each team to summarize the work they did. You can suggest that the participants use the Antiprocrastination Sheet for homework, and you will discuss the results with them at the next session. Tell them to break a task down into small steps and to predict how difficult and how satisfying (on scale from 0% to 100%) each step will be, in the second and third columns. In the fourth and fifth columns of the sheet, they can record how difficult and how satisfying (on a scale from 0% to 100%) each small step of their task actually turns out to be.

MAKE A PLAN

Participants who wish to stop procrastinating will need a specific plan for getting started. This plan will spell out precisely *what* they are going to do, *how* they are going to do it, *when* they are going to do it, and how they are going to overcome the many predicable obstacles that will arise the moment they start.

First, ask the group members to write a brief description of a specific task they would like to complete on page 235 of their workbooks.

Next, ask them to write a brief description of the very first thing they have to do to get started on this task. Ask if they would be willing to make the first step a small one that can be completed in fifteen minutes or less, as described in the previous section.

Ask them to write down the specific time when they intend to take the first step toward completing the task.

Ask what problems they anticipate that could cause them to procrastinate at that time. They can list one or two likely problems in the participant's workbook while you list them on your flip chart. For example, if they intend to study for fifteen minutes starting at 3:00 P.M., they may coincidentally get a phone call from a friend at just that time; or they may suddenly feel tired or bored and decide they need a nap or a snack; or they may remember that they need a book at the library.

Now, ask them to write down solutions to these problems. (For example, if someone calls, the participants can say they are busy and offer to call back in fifteen minutes.)

SUMMARY OF STEP 9

People often maintain that procrastination is a problem they want help with. In reality, they usually are deeply committed to their procrastination, for much the same reason that someone who is overweight eats instead of dieting. They eat because they *want* to eat—this is far more pleasurable than dieting! People who say they want to lose weight are saying something that is probably untrue. They do not want to lose weight, they want to eat goodies! They may fantasize about being slim and sexy, but they aren't really attracted to the rigors of dieting!

In this session, you used the Cost-Benefit Analysis and the Devil's Advocate Technique to help the participants identify conscious and hidden reasons for procrastinating. These are paradoxical strategies, because you tried to sell the participants on the benefits of procrastinating. If, instead, you tried to persuade them to stop procrastinating, you would be in the position of a parent. Although they might agree with you in a polite way, they would be likely to rebel passively between sessions by forgetting to follow through.

These paradoxical procedures are intended to increase the participants' motivation and to enhance the likelihood that the other techniques, such as the TIC-TOC Technique or the Antiprocrastination Sheet, will be helpful to them.

The five-step plan that follows is similar to the chart on page 237 of the participant's workbook. Discuss this list and ask the participants which ideas and techniques seem the most helpful.

HOW TO BEAT PROCRASTINATION

1. **Don't put the cart before the horse:** Instead of waiting for motivation, they can get started. Action comes first, and motivation comes second.

2. **Make a specific plan:** Instead of telling themselves they'll get started one of these days, participants can make a specific plan. Would they like to get started today? At what time today? What will they do first?

3. **Make the job easy:** Instead of telling themselves they have to do it all at once, participants can make the task easy if they break it down into small steps. They can remind themselves that they only have to do the first step today (little steps for big feats). After the first small step, they can quit with a clear conscience, or they can do more if they like. But one tiny step gives them full credit for the day.

4. **Think positively:** Participants can identify the Negative Thoughts (called TICs) that make them feel guilty and anxious, and substitute other thoughts (called TOCs) that are more positive and realistic.

5. **Give yourself credit:** Instead of noticing everything they didn't accomplish, participants can give themselves a pat on the back for what they did accomplish.

FEEDBACK ABOUT STEP 9

At the end of the session, ask the participants what they liked and disliked about it. Tell them to fill out the Evaluation of Step 9 on page 238 of the participant's workbook. Ask them if they would be willing to read aloud what they wrote down. Remember to respond nondefensively when they voice criticism or negative reactions.

SELF-HELP ASSIGNMENTS FOR STEP 10

Before the participants leave, discuss the self-help assignments for Step 10. These assignments are listed on page 239 of the participant's workbook. Remind them to do one or more small steps of some task they've been procrastinating about, and to record the predicted and actual difficulty and satisfaction of their accomplishments on the Antiprocrastination Sheet.

STEP 10

PRACTICE, PRACTICE, PRACTICE!

LEADER'S PREPARATION FOR STEP 10

Activity	Check (√) when done
1. Read the description of Step 10 in the participant's workbook beginning on page 240.	
2. Study the Checklist for Step 10 on the next page of this *Leader's Manual* and the Tips for Leaders beginning on page 189.	
3. Complete any reading you may not have finished from previous assignments.	

CHECKLIST FOR STEP 10

Activity	Optional or required?	Minimum time (min.)	Check (√) when done
1. Using the Leader's Data Sheet on page 72, record the participants' scores on the three self-assessment tests, along with their points for homework and for attendance.	req.	10	
2. Ask for positive and negative feedback about Step 9.	req.	5	
3. Discuss the homework with the Antiprocrastination Sheet and the Daily Mood Log.	req.	5 – 10	
4. Evaluate the progress that the participants have made in this program.	req.	15	
5. Exercise: An Ounce of Prevention (relapse prevention).	req.	20	
6. Exercise: The Key to Recovery.	opt.	10 – 15	
7. Exercise: Self-esteem and Spirituality.	opt.	10 – 15	
8. Practice, Practice, Practice!	opt.	20	
9. Review of Ten Days to Self-esteem.	req.	20	
10. Feedback and sharing about Ten Days to Self-esteem.	req.	10 – 15	
11. Ask the group to complete the participant evaluation form for Ten Days to Self-esteem.	req.	5	

OVERVIEW OF STEP 10

This is the last session of the program and there are a number of important tasks:

- The participants will evaluate how much progress they have made so far—and assess areas where there is room for further growth. You will present a number of options for members who are still depressed, as well as those who would like additional training.

- The exercise on relapse prevention will show the participants how to deal with feelings of hopelessness and overcome episodes of depression in the future, after they have recovered. This topic is quite important, because sooner or later nearly everyone who is depressed begins to feel better. However, these spurts of improvement, which can be quite exhilarating, are frequently followed by sudden and unexpected relapses. These relapses are quite dangerous because some people feel enormously disillusioned and hopeless. Many become suicidal. If you plan for these relapses ahead of time, they lose most of their sting. They can usually be turned around rather quickly if the participants will reapply the same techniques that helped them recover the first time. When they recover from a relapse, their confidence in what they have learned usually deepens. They see that the first improvement was not a fluke but the direct result of the skills they have learned to use.

- This process of preventing serious relapses is made somewhat easier by the fact that most people become depressed about one specific type of problem. One person's bad moods may always be triggered by criticism or disapproval. Someone else may get upset whenever things don't go as expected. By the same token, the key to each person's recovery tends to be unique and specific to that individual. One person may recover when she does something she's been avoiding. Someone else may feel better when he does a Cost-Benefit Analysis on needing approval, or when he responds to criticism nondefensively. In this session you will help the members identify the keys to their recovery. This will represent the essence of what each person has learned—the single idea or technique that will make the biggest impact on his or her life.

- You will lead a discussion of the relationships between what the participants have been learning in this program and their own values and spiritual beliefs. If your group has a religious orientation, you can help the members integrate these ideas with their religious beliefs and discuss areas of compatibility as well as any conflicts they may sense.

- You will emphasize the importance of ongoing paper-and-pencil practice after the participants leave the group. In fact, they can use techniques such as the Daily Mood Log for the rest of their lives whenever they are upset. You will direct an exercise with the Daily Mood Log in the group.

- You will conduct a systematic review of several ideas and techniques they have learned about in this program.

- The participants will get a chance to talk about what this experience has meant to them on a personal level.

- They will fill out an evaluation form for Ten Days to Self-esteem. This will give you invaluable information about what they liked and disliked. You will identify the teaching methods that worked best, as well as those that fell a little flat. You can use this information to revise the program and make it more and more rewarding each time you present it.

TIPS FOR LEADERS

DATA COLLECTION

Record the participants' scores on the three self-assessment tests (the BDC, the BAI, and the RSAT) on the Leader's Data Sheet on page 72. Record how much homework they completed using the 3-point rating scale on page 68. Record whether or not they came on time using the 2-point rating scale on page 68. You can either refund their deposit at this point, or tell the group that their deposits will be refunded by mail.

FEEDBACK AND REVIEW OF HOMEWORK

Ask for positive and negative reactions to the last session, on procrastination. Did any of the participants do any of the optional reading on procrastination from *The Feeling Good Handbook* (Chapters 9 and 10)? Do they have any questions about this material? Did they use the Antiprocrastination Sheet between sessions? Did they encounter any resistance when they tried to do something they'd been putting off? What were they thinking and feeling? Did they use the TIC-TOC Technique and find it helpful?

Did any of the participants work on the Daily Mood Log as homework? Do they have any questions or personal reactions they wish to share with the group?

EVALUATION OF PROGRESS

The most straightforward way to evaluate the participants' progress is to compare their scores on the three self-assessment tests in Step 10 with their scores the first time they took these tests, in Step 1. Ask them to record both sets of scores in the following box, which appears on page 245 of the participant's workbook. (They can find their initial scores on pages 21, 23, and 27 of the participant's workbook. You should also have this information on your Leader's Data Sheet.)

Ask how many people's scores on the depression, anxiety, and personal relationship tests have improved. Ask if the results seem valid—do they feel that the scores accurately reflect how they are feeling? Can any of them give examples of differences in how they are now thinking, feeling, and behaving?

Another way the participants can evaluate their progress is to review their personal

Test	Step 1 score	Step 10 score	Optimal score
Burns Depression Checklist			less than 5
Burns Anxiety Inventory			less than 5
Relationship Satisfaction Scale			greater than 35

goals for this experience. Remind them about the three types of goals for the program that were discussed at the first session:

- **psychological:** understanding their moods and learning to deal more effectively with negative feelings

- **interpersonal:** getting to know others with similar interests and concerns

- **philosophical and spiritual:** examining their attitudes, beliefs, and personal values.

On page 28 of the participant's workbook they listed their own personal goals for this experience. Ask them to take a look at those goals now. Ask how much progress they have made so far. Have they accomplished some of their goals? Do they have goals they will continue to pursue in the future through their own studies or through participation in additional modules?

Ask the participants to write a brief description of what they have achieved and indicate any areas where there may still be some room for improvement on page 245 of their workbooks. Ask if they would be willing to share these assessments of their progress with the group.

Some members may feel that their mood scores on the three self-assessment tests have not yet improved sufficiently, and some may not have achieved all of the personal goals they outlined in Step 1. You can reassure them that this is quite normal, since everyone develops at a different rate. Some people recover rapidly and others require a persistent effort over a longer period of time.

Emphasize that recovering slowly is *not* unusual or shameful. This does *not* mean these members are hopeless or different from other people. It only means that they still need to keep working with these ideas and techniques. There are a number of options open to members who would like to continue their program of personal growth after they complete this session:

- They could repeat Ten Days to Self-esteem. Many people find that repeated practice and exposure to these ideas can be helpful. Sometimes when they work with a concept over a period of time and hear it expressed a little differently, it suddenly begins to make sense. The longer they work with these ideas, the more deeply they will comprehend them. Further work could be especially useful to members who attended the groups without doing the self-help assignments between sessions.

- They could participate in another module, such as the one on personal relationship problems, which will be published later. This module is a nice complement to what they have learned in Ten Days to Self-esteem, since the ideas and methods are quite different.

- They could obtain a consultation with a psychologist or psychiatrist to see if individual psychotherapy or treatment with an antidepressant medication would be helpful.

- They could join a self-help group such as the local chapter of the National Depressive and Manic Depressive Association.

You can ask if any of the participants feel discouraged or have Negative Thoughts about their progress. These thoughts would be excellent grist for the mill. Some members may feel inferior and compare themselves to others in the group. Some of them may feel perfectionistic and self-critical because they have not achieved all of their goals. Some may feel angry and entitled to a better result.

It's important not to get defensive when they voice these concerns. Remember to use the Disarming Technique and to respond with a respectful attitude. Ask if other members sometimes feel this way as well.

If time permits, you can do a group exercise with these Negative Thoughts on the flip chart. Make three vertical columns and label them as they appear on a Daily Mood Log. Ask the participants what kinds of thoughts they might have in this session if they haven't yet improved sufficiently. Record the Negative Thoughts in the left-hand column, and ask the participants to write them in their workbooks on a blank Daily Mood Log, as in this example:

Negative Thoughts	Distortions	Positive Thoughts
1. There must be something wrong with me. 100%		
2. I should have recovered by now. 75%		
3. I'm a hopeless case. 75%		
4. The other members probably look down on me. 75%		

You can ask the group to identify the distortions in the Negative Thoughts and to suggest Positive Thoughts for the right-hand column. This exercise will allow the members who have improved to provide helpful and compassionate feedback to those who still feel upset. This can boost the morale of the group by making negative reactions seem less shameful and unusual.

AN OUNCE OF PREVENTION

In this exercise the participants will look at the other side of the coin. What should they do if they have improved and are feeling a whole lot better?

Explain that most of the people who are depressed, including those who have been severely depressed for a long time, begin to improve sooner or later. Sometimes this improvement occurs early in treatment and sometimes it takes many months or even a year or more of hard, persistent therapy. But sooner or later, improvement nearly always occurs, if they will hang in there and keep trying.

When people recover, and their Burns Depression Checklist scores fall below 5, they often feel better than they have in years. Some people tell me they feel better than they ever felt in their entire lives. It's a heady experience. The pain and agony of hopelessness and depression may have seemed overwhelming and nearly unbearable. When these feelings suddenly lift, some people get an entirely new lease on life.

Many become euphoric. They suddenly feel worthwhile again—and this is a shock! They may even tell themselves, "Hey, my problems are over. I'm okay after all. My depression was based on faulty thinking. It was a hoax. Now that I've finally got the dragon licked, I'll feel good forever!"

Ask if any members of the group have ever had this experience when they started to feel better. Then ask if they know what typically happens next. Someone may say, "You may be in for a relapse, a big letdown." Tell the group that's absolutely correct and ask them to estimate what percentage of people who recover from a depression relapse.

After they guess, you can tell them that the number is 100%, or nearly 100%. Explain that practically *everybody* who recovers from a depression will relapse sooner or later, and it's usually sooner. Often, it's within a few weeks of the first recovery. Since relapse is incredibly common, many members of this group will almost certainly experience the same thing after they recover. This need not be a problem—indeed, it can be an advantage—if, *and only if*, they *expect* the relapse and *prepare* for it ahead of time. But if it catches them by surprise, look out! The pain, bitterness, and disillusionment can be intense, and many people will conclude they are hopeless after all and become suicidal.

Fortunately, there's a good way to prepare for these relapses. The first step is for the participants to predict that they *will* happen and to make a plan for dealing with them. The second step is to write down the Negative Thoughts that the participants will have when they relapse so they can practice talking back to them. They need to do this *now*, before the relapse occurs.

Explain that nearly everyone has exactly the same Negative Thoughts during a relapse. This makes the job of talking back to these thoughts much easier. They will find the Daily Mood Log of a woman who has relapsed on page 248 of their workbooks.

Tell the group members to imagine that they are this woman. After years of chronic depression, she experiences a dramatic improvement in her mood and feels the happiest she has felt in decades. After an angry exchange with her husband during a tennis match, she suddenly experiences a relapse of depression. She feels overwhelmingly depressed, self-critical, and demoralized again.

In the emotions section of the Daily Mood Log she records her negative feelings. The group will see that she feels hopeless, inferior, sad, frustrated, angry, and defeated.

Next, she records these Negative Thoughts in the left-hand column of the Daily Mood Log:

1. I feel worse now than I ever did. I'm back to the zero point. 100%

2. These techniques can't really help me after all. 100%

3. My improvement was just a fluke. I was just fooling myself. 100%

4. This proves that I'm hopeless after all. 100%

5. I'll never really improve. I'll be depressed forever. 100%

6. I'm a worthless nothing. 100%

Almost everyone has NTs that are similar to these during a relapse. Ask the members to put themselves in this woman's shoes and to select one of her thoughts. Write it on the flip chart, and put "100%" after it. Ask them to identify the distortions in the Negative Thought. Write the distortions in the middle column while the participants write them on page 248 of their workbooks. Then ask them how they might talk back to that thought, using some of the techniques listed on page 251 of the workbook.

Tell the participants to write a Positive Thought in the right-hand column of their Daily Mood Logs and to estimate how strongly they believe it, on a scale from 0% (not at all) to 100% (completely). At the same time, you can record their PTs on your flip chart. Finally, ask them to reestimate how strongly they now believe the NT, from 0% to 100%. Draw a line through the original estimate, and replace it with the new, lower estimate.

Emphasize these points while the participants do the exercise:

1. Remind them about the importance of using percentages when they do the DML.

2. Only PTs that are believable and valid will help them. Phony rationalizations won't help.

3. Their moods will not improve until their belief in each NT has been reduced to nearly 0%. This may not happen right away, and often it is not easy. If someone feels certain that he or she is a hopeless loser and has felt this way for many years, it may require many weeks of hard work using a lot of different types of PTs to put the lie to this belief.

4.   The Daily Mood Log must be done on paper. Thinking things out in your head is
      not likely to be helpful.

Let's assume that the group chooses to work on the fourth negative thought, "This
proves that I'm hopeless after all." Ask how they would attack this thought with the
techniques listed in Fifteen Ways to Untwist Your Thinking on page 251 of the workbook. Here are some ideas:

1.   **Identify the Distortions:** This thought contains a number of distortions such as
      all-or-nothing thinking, overgeneralization, mental filter, discounting the positives,
      fortune-telling, magnification, and emotional reasoning.

Once the participants identify these distortions, you can point out that feelings of
hopelessness always stem from all-or-nothing thinking. Ask the group to explain why
hopelessness results from this particular distortion. (Answer: It's because the woman is
thinking that she's either totally cured or totally hopeless. In reality, our moods go up
and down, like a roller coaster. No one can be totally happy or completely depressed
all the time.)

2.   **The Straightforward Approach:** What could she tell herself that would be more
      compassionate and realistic?

3.   **Thinking in Shades of Gray:** She can remind herself that her moods have changed
      continually during her life, and that this happens to all human beings. Right now
      she's in a bad patch, and a week or two ago she was feeling a whole lot better.
      Instead of insisting that she's hopeless, which is quite unrealistic, she could pinpoint
      what's making her upset and think of a plan for dealing with it.
           Since her relapse followed an argument with her husband, this gives us an
      important hint about what triggers her depressions. When she gets angry, she
      may pout and hold her feelings in. She may withdraw into depression instead of
      confronting the problem. She thereby avoids the conflict, feels sorry for herself,
      and punishes the person she's mad at.

4.   **The Double-Standard Technique:** Would she tell a depressed friend who had a
      relapse that she was hopeless? Why or why not?

5.   **The Cost-Benefit Analysis:** What are the advantages and disadvantages of giving
      up and insisting things are hopeless?

6.   **The Experimental Method:** She could test her belief that things are hopeless by
      working hard to make things better for the next several weeks. She can take the
      BDC test twice a week to see how much she is improving.

7.   **Define Terms:** What's the definition of a hopeless person? Each definition will turn
      out to be invalid. For example, she could define a hopeless person as someone

who feels completely depressed all of the time. But no one has been "completely depressed" every minute of every day since birth. She might then define a hopeless person as someone who is depressed some of the time. But nearly everyone has had at least some periods of feeling angry, unhappy, or discouraged. According to this definition, nearly everybody would be hopeless, and that obviously doesn't make sense. No matter how she defines hopelessness, her definition will always crumble.

8. **The Semantic Method:** Instead of telling herself she's hopeless, she could tell herself that she's suffering and needs some support.

9. **The Pleasure-Predicting Method:** She could schedule a series of activities with the potential for pleasure, learning, and personal growth, and predict how satisfying each one will be on a scale from 0% to 100%. Then she can record how satisfying it turned out to be. She will probably discover that many activities are more rewarding than she predicted. This is not consistent with her belief that she is hopeless, since there are many things she can do to improve the way she feels.

10. **Reattribution:** We know that her self-critical Negative Thoughts and feelings of despair followed an argument with her husband. Instead of using up her energy in telling herself she's hopeless and no good, she could acknowledge that they both got defensive. She could try to talk things over with him. She may discover that her tension will diminish when she deals with the problem instead of avoiding it.

This list of ten interventions is not a complete list of strategies by a long shot! When one technique does not work the participants can try another, and then another, until they finally put the lie to the Negative Thought. The way to success is persistence and creativity, along with some compassion and support from others.

Emphasize that the participants can prepare for relapse ahead of time by writing down the thoughts they might have when they suddenly take a turn for the worse. If they prepare ahead of time, then a relapse can be a golden opportunity to overcome depression again, using the very same techniques that helped them in the first place. This will prove that their improvement was no fluke and will give them confidence that they can use these techniques for the rest of their lives whenever they feel discouraged.

If time permits, you can break the group into teams of two or three to practice the Externalization of Voices method they learned in earlier sessions. This would be extremely useful for review and practice. One participant can play the role of the Negative Thoughts on the Daily Mood Log on page 248 of the workbook, and another can play the role of the Positive Thoughts. They can use either the Double-Standard Technique or the Confrontation Technique. You may recall that in the Double-Standard Technique the person who plays the Negative Thoughts uses the first person. In the Confrontation Technique, the person who plays the Negative Thoughts uses the second person, as described in this table:

	The person who plays the Negative Thoughts uses:	The person who plays the Positive Thoughts uses:
Double-Standard Technique	the *first* person ("I feel worse than I ever did before. I'm back to the zero point.")	the *second* person
Confrontation Technique	the *second* person ("You feel worse than you ever did before. You're back to the zero point.")	the *first* person

For this exercise on relapse prevention, I prefer the Confrontation Technique, since it packs more punch.

Make sure you conclude this discussion of relapse prevention on a note of solid hope and optimism. Try not to create the impression that the participants are doomed to a life of constant relapse and misery! Remind them that even though the road to recovery may feel bumpy at times, the prognosis for continual growth and steady improvement is excellent.

In my practice, I strongly encourage all my clients to prepare for relapses ahead of time by writing down their Negative Thoughts. Then we practice talking back to these thoughts with the Externalization of Voices procedure. This preventive medicine pays off handsomely. When the relapse comes, the client usually remembers, "Dr. Burns told me this would happen, and although it seems terrible, he said I could probably turn it around quickly if I use the techniques again." In the vast majority of cases, these relapses are extremely short-lived and prove to be invaluable opportunities to reaffirm the value of the cognitive methods.

The real key to recovery is not *feeling* better but *getting* better. Getting better means that the group members understand the causes of their bad moods and have mastered techniques to deal with their feelings more effectively. With persistent effort, they can gain greater control over their bad moods and experience longer and longer periods of happiness and productivity.

THE KEY TO RECOVERY

Explain that people seem to experience recovery in different ways. Some people may notice a difference in their attitudes and in the way they think when they begin to feel happy. For example, they may suddenly realize that they don't need everyone's approval to feel happy and worthwhile. If someone is critical or angry with them, instead of getting defensive and feeling devastated, they may tell themselves, "Hey, there's probably some truth in the criticism. Let's see what I can learn from this." This new mind-set may improve their self-esteem and lead to better relationships with other people.

Ask if any members have noticed a significant change in their attitudes or thinking patterns during Ten Days to Self-esteem. Ask them to describe these changes.

Other people notice a change in their behavior when they recover. They may typically put things off and avoid personal problems when they get upset. For them, recovery may simply involve confronting the problem or task that they were avoiding. Ask if any members have noticed a change in the way they behave as a result of Ten Days to Self-esteem. Do they procrastinate less? Do they relate to other people in a different way? Are they more open and honest about how they feel?

The key to recovery for each person is usually a little different. Recovery is frequently based on one simple idea or technique. However, each person has an individual key. Do any of the members have an idea yet about what the key to recovery may be for them? Can they identify one or two ideas or methods that have been particularly helpful to them during the past nine steps?

Once they have discovered this key, it will very likely help them over and over again in the future. They probably won't have to go through a long process of figuring out what to do every time they're depressed.

SELF-ESTEEM AND SPIRITUALITY

Although psychotherapy and religion have been at odds during much of the twentieth century, the ideas and techniques presented in this program are quite compatible with a wide variety of religious and philosophical orientations. This exercise is designed to make the participants more aware of these connections. This can strengthen their own religious convictions and make their recovery more meaningful.

The purpose of this exercise is not to promote any specific religion, or even religion in general. It is not necessary for group leaders to have a religious orientation that is similar to that of most members of their groups. However, leaders would do well to respect the religious and spiritual beliefs of the participants. In this exercise, you will encourage the participants to integrate the new ideas and methods they have been learning with their own beliefs.

For example, they may be able to relate the following Old Testament passage to what they learned during the second step:

Proverbs 23:7: "For as he thinketh in his heart, so is he."

The meaning of the passage is similar to the idea that our thoughts—not external events—create our moods. Ask if any of the participants can see similarities between this biblical passage and the principles of cognitive therapy.

This program has focused on self-esteem because the lack of self-esteem is one of the most painful symptoms of depression. In Step 7 you led a discussion of several ways to develop self-esteem. These approaches to self-esteem are quite compatible with the basic tenets of the Jewish and Christian religions, as well as the Eastern religions such as Buddhism. The material on pages 255–260 of the participant's workbook describes these similarities. This discussion of the spiritual and philosophical aspects of self-esteem summarizes and strengthens many of the ideas that have been presented so far in this program. If you read those pages prior to leading this step, it will be easy to spark a stimulating discussion with your group.

Ask if the participants' own attitudes and values have changed as a result of the past nine steps. Have they begun to think about the meaning and purpose of life in a new and different way? Can they describe any changes in their personal philosophies? Have any of them experienced a deeper understanding of their own religious faith? Which ideas in this program are most compatible with their own spiritual beliefs?

The participants were asked to write brief answers to these questions on pages 258–259 of the workbook. See if any of them would be willing to read what they wrote down as they discuss these questions.

Can the participants think of anything they have learned that seems in conflict with their spiritual beliefs? If any of them raise areas of conflict between psychotherapy and their own beliefs, ask the group if they can think of any way to reconcile the conflict. For example, some Christian Fundamentalists might feel a mistrust of secular psychotherapy and argue that only a belief in Christ as one's personal savior can help a person with emotional difficulties. However, the following biblical passages could be interpreted to suggest that spiritual healing and psychological therapy need not be at odds:

John 1:14: "And the Word was made flesh and dwelt among us. . . ."

John 3:16: "For God so loved the world that he gave his only begotten Son, that whosoever believeth in him should not perish, but have everlasting life."

One way of thinking about these passages is based on the idea that clergy and psychotherapists share the goal of understanding and relieving human suffering. In these New Testament passages, Saint John tells us that redemption is the result of God's spiritual work in the world. Jesus lived and worked among us as a flesh-and-blood human being. Christians believe that God loved the world and sent his son to work *in the world* to interact with people and to provide healing and salvation.

Similarly, psychological healing occurs through human interaction. This healing is a gift that occurs in the context of a compassionate and caring relationship between people. Psychotherapy can be the expression of a spiritual commitment, even if the therapist does not believe in God or make any reference to prayer or to religious ideas in his or her daily practice.

PRACTICE, PRACTICE, PRACTICE!

Self-help is an important key to recovery from depression and anxiety. Remind the participants that they will be far more likely to continue to make progress, and to maintain those gains in the future, if they remember to *practice, practice, practice* with their Daily Mood Logs whenever they feel upset!

You can recommend that the participants use the DML for ten to fifteen minutes per day whenever their scores on the BDC are greater than 5. Whether or not they are receiving therapy, this procedure can be invaluable. Remind them that there's always a temptation just to do the DML in one's head. This rarely works. Doing the exercise on paper is the key to success!

In today's group, members can share Negative Thoughts they have recorded on their Daily Mood Logs and use cognitive techniques to generate Positive Thoughts. If a group member has experienced a rejection in a love relationship, he or she may feel sad and discouraged because of Negative Thoughts such as these:

1. It's all my fault.

2. I'm unlovable.

3. I'll never find anyone like him (or her) again.

Write these thoughts on the flip chart one at a time. Ask the group to identify the distortions in each thought and suggest several Positive Thoughts to replace each of them.

If the group is not successful in turning around a Negative Thought, tell them to review the list of Fifteen Ways to Untwist Your Thinking on page 251 of the participant's workbook. They can also review the Troubleshooting Guide on page 87 of the workbook.

Remind the participants that there are extra copies of the DML in the Appendix. If they leave at least one copy blank, they can photocopy extras whenever they need them.

REVIEW OF TEN DAYS TO SELF-ESTEEM

Toward the end of this step you can review what the participants have learned in Ten Days to Self-esteem. First, ask them about the basic principles of cognitive therapy. Ask what they wrote on page 263 of the participant's workbook as an answer to this question. Some of these principles are:

1. Your thoughts—not actual events—create your moods.

2. Specific kinds of negative feelings—such as guilt, anger, depression, and anxiety—result from specific kinds of Negative Thoughts.

3. Some negative emotions are healthy and some are unhealthy. If negative feelings are healthy and appropriate, then people can express them or take action based on them. If the negative feelings are unhealthy and inappropriate, people can change them with the Daily Mood Log.

4. Unhealthy feelings—such as depression, neurotic anxiety, and destructive anger—result from Negative Thoughts that are distorted and illogical. However, these thoughts frequently seem absolutely valid, so we are not aware that we are feeling ourselves.

5. Self-defeating attitudes, such as perfectionism and the need for approval, can make people vulnerable to depression, anxiety, and conflicts in personal relationships.

6. When people change the way they think, they can CHANGE the way they FEEL.

Ask the group members to discuss their reactions to these ideas. Do they understand each of them? Do they have any questions about them? (A shorter version of these ideas appears on page 267 of the participant's workbook.)

On page 263 of the participant's workbook the members were asked to list four differences between healthy and unhealthy negative emotions. Ask them to read their answers to this question while you list them on your flip chart. Some of these differences include the following:

1. Depression, in contrast to healthy sadness, often involves a loss of self-esteem. Depressed people may feel like inferior, worthless losers.

2. Unhealthy feelings are often associated with a loss of respect for other people as well. For example, people with unhealthy, destructive anger may view others as totally bad, malignant jerks who deserve rejection, punishment, or retaliation.

3. Unhealthy feelings nearly always result from thoughts that are distorted and illogical. In contrast, healthy negative feelings usually result from realistic thoughts.

4. Unhealthy feelings often involve hopelessness. You feel certain that your problems can never be solved and your misery will go on forever.

5. Healthy negative feelings usually result from a stressful event that would trigger similar feelings in most people. An example of this would be grief after the death of a loved one. Unhealthy negative feelings can be incredibly intense even when there is no clearly negative event that triggered them. An example of this would be a panic attack while standing in a grocery store line.

6. Healthy negative feelings are limited in time. Unhealthy negative feelings, such as a chronic depression, sometimes go on and on for years no matter what happens.

7. Unhealthy negative feelings often lead to a loss of functioning and giving up on life. Unhealthy feelings may also be associated with destructive actions such as overeating, drug abuse, or violent behavior. In contrast, healthy negative feelings lead to constructive action. If you are mad at a friend, you may talk the problem over in a tactful, respectful way so that you can resolve the problem and end up even better friends.

After the group has discussed several of these ideas, ask why it is important to make this distinction between healthy and unhealthy feelings. (Some of these ideas are stated briefly on page 268 of the participant's workbook.)

Ask the participants if they can describe the steps in filling out a Daily Mood Log. The steps are:

1. **Describe the upsetting event:** The participants write a brief description of what happened. It must be specific about person, place, and time.

2. **Describe your emotions:** The participants record their negative feelings and rate each one on a scale from 0% to 100%.

3. **Triple-Column Technique:** The participants write down their NTs in the left-hand column and rate how strongly they believe each one on a scale from 0% to 100%. Then they identify the distortions in the NTs and substitute other thoughts that are more realistic and positive in the right-hand column. They rate how strongly they believe each PT on a scale from 0% to 100%, and reevaluate how strongly they believe each NT on a scale from 0% to 100%. When they have put the lie to all the NTs, they reestimate the strength of their negative feelings on a scale from 0% to 100%. This will show whether and how much they have improved.

Ask the participants to name several techniques for refuting NTs. As they name the techniques, write them on the flip chart. The following techniques, as well as others, may be included:

- Identify the Distortions
- The Straightforward Approach
- The Vertical Arrow Technique
- The Cost-Benefit Analysis
- Examine the Evidence
- The Experimental Technique
- The Survey Method
- The Double-Standard Technique
- Thinking in Shades of Gray
- Be Specific
- The Semantic Method
- Define Terms
- The Pleasure-Predicting Sheet
- The Externalization of Voices
- Reattribution
- The Devil's Advocate Technique
- The Acceptance Paradox

When the participants mention each technique, ask them to give an example of how it would work. Be sure to compliment them for their efforts. You can rephrase the example a little if it does not initially seem to illustrate a particular technique adequately. Try to make the group members look good so they will feel some self-confidence and pride in what they have learned.

Ask them to name the different types of Cost-Benefit Analysis. A Cost-Benefit Analysis can be used to evaluate the advantages and disadvantages of:

- a negative emotion, such as guilt, hopelessness, anxiety, or anger
- a Negative Thought, such as "It's all my fault"
- a Self-defeating Belief, such as "I need everyone's approval"
- a self-defeating behavior, such as procrastination, overeating, or going out on dates with unsuitable people (for example, married men or women)

Remember that a Cost-Benefit Analysis can be done in a straightforward way (for people who are cooperative) or in a paradoxical way (for people who are resistant and oppositional).

Ask the group about the difference between a Self-defeating Belief and a Negative Thought. (The answer can be found on page 146 of the participant's workbook.)

Ask about the difference between Self-defense and the Acceptance Paradox. (The answer can be found on page 131 of the participant's workbook.)

Tell the group members to write a Positive Thought to substitute for the Negative Thought "I'm a total loser," using the Self-defense technique. They can write their Positive Thoughts on page 265 of the participant's workbook. Ask what they wrote down. (The answer can be found on page 268 of the workbook.)

Now ask the members to write another Positive Thought for the same Negative Thought on page 265 of the participant's workbook, using the Acceptance Paradox. Ask what they wrote down. (The answer can be found on page 268 of the workbook.)

Ask which approach was more useful to the participants. Do they prefer the Self-defense style or the Acceptance Paradox when they talk back to their Negative Thoughts?

Ask them to list five or more different kinds of perfectionism. (The answer can be found on pages 202–203 of the participant's workbook.)

You can ask, "What is self-esteem? How can a person develop self-esteem? What is the difference between self-esteem and arrogance? Between self-esteem and self-confidence? What is the difference between conditional and unconditional self-esteem? How can a person develop better self-esteem? Do we really need self-esteem?" (These are general discussion questions that do not appear in the workbook.)

Encourage the group members to continue studying these concepts and practicing. Remind them to use the Daily Mood Log when they feel upset. Consistently doing ten or fifteen minutes per day of written homework is often the key to recovery.

FEEDBACK AND SHARING ABOUT TEN DAYS TO SELF-ESTEEM

Make sure you leave at least ten minutes at the end so the participants can talk about their experiences during Ten Days to Self-esteem. Ask what they liked the most about the sessions. What did they learn? Was the reading helpful to them? Which sessions, ideas, or techniques were the most relevant and useful?

Was the leader helpful? Was it useful to open up and get to know the other members of the group? Did any particular member make a positive impact on the others? In what way?

Give each participant the opportunity to make a closing statement of a personal nature about what the group has meant to him or her.

FEEDBACK ABOUT THE PROGRAM

At the end, ask the participants to fill out the Participant Evaluation Form for Ten Days to Self-esteem from pages 270–271 of the participant's workbook. Also, ask the participants to fill out the Empathy Scale, which appears on page 272 of the workbook. Ask them to fill out these forms from their workbooks and turn them in to you before they leave. If you don't want them to have to tear pages out of their workbooks, you can photocopy the evaluation forms, which appear on the next few pages.

A tabulation and thoughtful review of the results will give you invaluable information about the group's perceptions of you, the other members, and the overall experience. You can use this feedback to make the next group even more effective. If you use the same evaluation form every time you run this program, you will be able to compare the effectiveness of different groups and chart your own personal development as a group leader.

PARTICIPANT EVALUATION FORM

Date: _____ Name: _____

Circle the number to the right that best describes how you feel.	Agree strongly	Agree	Neutral	Disagree	Disagree strongly
1. The overall objectives of the program were met.	5	4	3	2	1
2. My personal goals for this experience were achieved.	5	4	3	2	1
3. The sessions were clear, understandable, and well organized.	5	4	3	2	1
4. The teaching methods were helpful to me.	5	4	3	2	1
5. The facility was comfortable and pleasant.	5	4	3	2	1
6. The program was a valuable learning experience.	5	4	3	2	1
7. This experience will be helpful in my personal life.	5	4	3	2	1
	Every day	Frequently	Occasionally	Almost never	Never
8. How often did you do the self-help exercises between sessions?	5	4	3	2	1
9. How often did you do the reading in *Ten Days to Self-esteem*?	5	4	3	2	1
	Very helpful	Helpful	Neutral	Somewhat unhelpful	Very unhelpful
10. How helpful was the workbook (*Ten Days to Self-esteem*)?	5	4	3	2	1
11. How helpful were the self-help assignments between sessions?	5	4	3	2	1
12. How helpful were the discussions during the sessions?	5	4	3	2	1
13. How helpful were the group exercises?	5	4	3	2	1
14. How helpful and supportive was the group leader?	5	4	3	2	1

PARTICIPANT EVALUATION FORM (page 2)

Circle the number to the right that best describes how you feel.	Very helpful	Helpful	Neutral	Somewhat unhelpful	Very unhelpful
15. How helpful and supportive were the other group members?	5	4	3	2	1
16. How helpful was the program in understanding your moods?	5	4	3	2	1
17. How helpful was the program in learning to change your moods?	5	4	3	2	1
18. How helpful was the program in developing better self-esteem?	5	4	3	2	1
19. How helpful was the program overall?	5	4	3	2	1

20. Please explain any low rating: _____

_____

_____

21. What did you like the *least* about the program? _____

_____

_____

22. What did you like the *most* about the program? _____

_____

_____

23. What did you learn that will be the most helpful to you? _____

_____

_____

24. General comments: _____

_____

_____

_____

EMPATHY SCALE*

Circle the number to the right of each statement that best describes how strongly you agree with it.	Not at all	Somewhat	Moderately	A lot
1. I felt that I could trust the group leader during the sessions.	0	1	2	3
2. The leader felt I was worthwhile.	0	1	2	3
3. The leader was friendly and warm toward me.	0	1	2	3
4. The leader understood what I said during the sessions.	0	1	2	3
5. The leader was sympathetic and concerned about me.	0	1	2	3
Total Score on Items 1–5 $\rightarrow$				
6. Sometimes the leader did not seem completely genuine.	0	1	2	3
7. The leader pretended to like me more than he or she really does.	0	1	2	3
8. The leader did not always seem to care about me.	0	1	2	3
9. The leader did not always understand the way I felt inside.	0	1	2	3
10. The leader seemed condescending and talked down to me.	0	1	2	3
Total Score on Items 6–10 $\rightarrow$				

APPENDIX A:
ADDITIONAL LEADER'S
DATA SHEETS

LEADER'S DATA SHEET

Name of participant	Preliminary testing date: ___			Step 1 date: ___					Step 2 date: ___				
	BDC (0–45)	BAI (0–99)	RSAT (0–42)	BDC (0–45)	BAI (0–99)	RSAT (0–42)	HOME-WORK (0–3)	ON TIME? (0–2)	BDC (0–45)	BAI (0–99)	RSAT (0–42)	HOME-WORK (0–3)	ON TIME? (0–2)

LEADER'S DATA SHEET (Continued)

Name of participant	Step 3 date: _____					Step 4 date: _____					Step 5 date: _____				
	BDC (0–45)	BAI (0–99)	RSAT (0–42)	HOME-WORK (0–3)	ON TIME? (0–2)	BDC (0–45)	BAI (0–99)	RSAT (0–42)	HOME-WORK (0–3)	ON TIME? (0–2)	BDC (0–45)	BAI (0–99)	RSAT (0–42)	HOME-WORK (0–3)	ON TIME? (0–2)

LEADER'S DATA SHEET (Continued)

Name of participant	Step 6 date:___					Step 7 date:___					Step 8 date:___				
	BDC (0–45)	BAI (0–99)	RSAT (0–42)	HOME-WORK (0–3)	ON TIME? (0–2)	BDC (0–45)	BAI (0–99)	RSAT (0–42)	HOME-WORK (0–3)	ON TIME? (0–2)	BDC (0–45)	BAI (0–99)	RSAT (0–42)	HOME-WORK (0–3)	ON TIME? (0–2)

LEADER'S DATA SHEET (Continued)

Name of participant	Step 9 date: _____					Step 10 date: _____					Follow-up date: _____				
	BDC (0–45)	BAI (0–99)	RSAT (0–42)	HOME-WORK (0–3)	ON TIME? (0–2)	BDC (0–45)	BAI (0–99)	RSAT (0–42)	HOME-WORK (0–3)	ON TIME? (0–2)	BDC (0–45)	BAI (0–99)	RSAT (0–42)	HOME-WORK (0–3)	ON TIME? (0–2)

APPENDIX B:
PERSONAL HISTORY FORM
FOR INTAKE EVALUATIONS

This appendix contains a Personal History Form you can use for initial participant evaluations. This form is suitable for an individual psychotherapy practice as well as the Ten Days to Self-esteem groups. Feel free to modify it to make it more useful in your particular setting.

The form requires approximately one hour to administer. You will be asked to record *DSM-III-R* diagnoses near the end of the evaluation. If, like many clinicians, you are not clear about the names, codes, or diagnostic criteria for the various disorders, you can consult the *Diagnostic and Statistical Manual of Mental Disorders*, 3rd ed. rev., *DSM-III-R* (Washington, D.C.: American Psychiatric Association, 1987).

PERSONAL HISTORY FORM
Identification and Referral Source

Name		Age	Date / /
Address			
Home phone	Work phone		
Do you live in a house or an apartment?		Race	
With whom do you live?			
Who referred you for treatment?			

Marital Status

Single?		Married?		Cohabiting?	
If married or cohabiting, for how long?					
Your first marriage?			Spouse's first?		
Separated?		Divorced?		Widowed?	
How long since you were separated, divorced, or widowed?					
Names of children					
Ages of children					

Education and Employment

Last year of schooling completed	
Occupation	
Length of employment	Current salary
If unemployed, why?	
Partner's occupation	Partner's salary

Insurance and Disability Status

Are you receiving or seeking disability payments?	
Type of disability	
What portion of the fee will you collect from insurance?	
Is the fee for the program appropriate? Will there be any financial problems?	

Emergency Contact Person

Whom can we reach in an emergency?	
Friend? Relative?	Phone

Initial Psychological Testing

Test	Score	Test	Score
Burns Depression Checklist		Relationship Satisfaction Scale	
Burns Anxiety Inventory		Other	

Reason for Seeking Treatment

Describe current problems in this individual's life, including difficulties at work and conflicts in personal relationships. Ask about recent stressful events. Describe symptoms such as guilt, depression, anxiety, irritability, etc.

Why did this individual decide to come to therapy *at this particular time*? Find out if he or she feels motivated to be in treatment, or if someone is pressuring him or her to be here.

_____

_____

_____

_____

Reason for Seeking Treatment (Continued)

Reason for Seeking Treatment (Continued)

_____

_____

_____

_____

_____

_____

_____

_____

_____

_____

_____

_____

_____

_____

Perception of Group Therapy

If this individual appears suitable for the group, you can ask, ''Have you ever been in a therapy group before? Was it a positive or negative experience?''

_____

_____

_____

_____

If he or she has had unpleasant experiences with groups, it can be helpful to point out some of the features of Ten Days to Self-esteem: Participants are not put on the spot, but learn specific techniques to overcome depression and enhance self-esteem in an upbeat and supportive atmosphere.

Medication Survey
Current Nonpsychiatric Medications

	Medication	Dose	Purpose	How long on this medication?
1.				
2.				
3.				

Current Psychiatric Medications

	Medication	Dose	How long on this medication?	How effective is it?	Describe any side effects
1.					
2.					
3.					

Past Psychiatric Medications

List them chronologically, starting with the first medication he or she received.

	Medication	Dose	Starting date and duration	How effective was it?	Describe any side effects
1.					
2.					
3.					
4.					
5.					
6.					
7.					
8.					
9.					
10.					

Summary of Prior Psychotherapy

List therapists chronologically, beginning with the first therapist this individual ever consulted.

Name of therapist and degree	Starting date, duration, and frequency	Reason for seeking treatment	What type of therapy? Was it helpful? Any negative reactions?
1.			
2.			
3.			
4.			
5.			

Family History

Has any blood relative ever had any psychiatric disturbance, including depression, mania, schizophrenia, suicide, nervous breakdown, mental retardation, drug abuse, alcoholism, trouble with the police, hallucinations, psychosis, or any other emotional difficulty?

Relative	Symptoms and diagnosis

Sexual History

1. Sexual preference: (circle one)	heterosexual	homosexual	bisexual

2. How are this individual's current sexual relationships? Describe any inhibitions or problems, such as lack of interest, lack of sexual experience, difficulty with erections, difficulty reaching orgasm, pain during intercourse, premature ejaculation, or sexual fantasies or practices that he or she is uncomfortable with:

_____

_____

_____

_____

_____

_____

_____

3. Did this individual have any sexual difficulties in previous relationships?

_____

_____

_____

_____

4.   Describe any other relevant sexual experiences, problems, or concerns:

_____

_____

_____

_____

_____

_____

Sexual, Physical, or Psychological Abuse

Has this individual ever experienced any kind of sexual, physical, or psychological abuse as a child or as an adult? Has he or she ever had sexual activity with a family member or relative? Has he or she ever been raped or beaten?

_____

_____

_____

_____

_____

_____

Other Information

Are there any other emotional or behavioral difficulties, such as loneliness, marital conflict, or work or legal problems, that have not been mentioned?

_____

_____

_____

_____

_____

_____

Quality of Information During the History

Ask if there is anything this individual was unable to tell you about due to feelings of shame or embarrassment? This could include problems such as drug or alcohol abuse, violent outbursts, suicidal feelings, or sexual abuse. Did he or she feel free to be completely candid during the entire history?

Try to be alert to hidden agendas that could influence the quality of the information.

_____

_____

_____

_____

_____

_____

_____

Goals for Therapy

If this individual had a magic wand and could solve all of his or her problems, what would be on the wish list? If the therapy was tremendously successful, how would you know? How would this person's life be different? What are this person's goals for the therapy?

If the individual has trouble identifying goals, you can suggest problems that were mentioned during the history. You can also explain that some participants want to develop greater self-esteem or personal productivity, overcome depression, improve relationships with others, etc.

1. _____

2. _____

3. _____

4. _____

5. _____

6. _____

7. _____

Summary of DSM-III-R Axis I Disorders

Diagnosis*	Yes	No	Date (from)	Date (to)
1. Alchohol Dependence 303.90				
2. Alcohol Abuse 305.00				
3. Psychoactive Substance Dependence 304.XX				
4. Psychoactive Substance Abuse 305.XX				
5. Organic Mental Disorder 290.21 = Alzheimer's with depression				
6. Schizophrenia 295.X				
7. Bipolar Disorder 296.4 = manic 294.5 = depressed 294.6 = mixed				
8. Major Depressive Episode 296.2 = single; 296.3 = recurrent				
9. Dysthymia 300.40				
10. Panic Disorder Without Agoraphobia 300.01				
11. Panic Disorder with Agoraphobia 300.21				
12. Agoraphobia Without History of Panic Disorder 300.22				
13. Social Phobia 300.23				
14. Simple Phobia 300.29				
15. Obsessive-Compulsive Disorder 300.30				
16. Post–Traumatic Stress Disorder 309.89				
17. Generalized Anxiety Disorder 300.02				
18. Ajustment Disorder 309.24 = with anxiety 309.00 = with depression				
19. Anorexia Nervosa 307.10				
20. Bulimia Nervosa 307.51				
21. Other Axis I disorders (specify):				
22.				

*See the *Diagnostic and Statistical Manual of Mental Disorders,* 3rd ed. rev., *DSM-III-R* (Washington, D.C.: American Psychiatric Association, 1987), for the Axis I diagnostic criteria.

Summary of DSM-III-R Axis II Disorders

Diagnosis*	Yes	Possible	No
1. Avoidant Personality Disorder 301.82			
2. Dependent Personality Disorder 301.60			
3. Obsessive-Compulsive Personality Disorder 301.40			
4. Passive-Agressive Personality Disorder 301.84			
5. Self-defeating Personality Disorder 301.90			
6. Paranoid Personality Disorder 301.00			
7. Schizotypal Disorder 301.22			
8. Schizoid Personality Disorder 301.20			
9. Histrionic Personality Disorder 301.50			
10. Narcissistic Personality Disorder 301.81			
11. Borderline Personality Disorder 301.83			
12. Antisocial Personality Disorder 301.70			
13. Personality Disorder Not Otherwise Specified (NOS) 301.90			

*See the *Diagnostic and Statistical Manual of Mental Disorders,* 3rd ed. rev., *DSM-III-R* (Washington, D.C.: American Psychiatric Association, 1987), for the Axis II diagnostic criteria.

DSM-III-R Axis III: Physical Disorders and Conditions

Describe any current illnesses. Ask about any symptoms (such as fever, pain, or unexplained weight loss) that might require medical attention.

_____

_____

_____

_____

_____

_____

_____

DSM-III-R Axis IV: Psychosocial Stresses

Describe any stressful events immediately before the current psychological problem began that may have triggered the symptoms:

_____

_____

_____

_____

_____

Circle one	Degree of stress at onset of current episode of distress*
99	inadequate information
1	none (no stressful events immediately before the current episode)
2	mild (broke up with boyfriend; graduated from school)
3	moderate (marriage; separation; loss of job; miscarriage)
4	severe (divorce; birth of first child)
5	extreme (death of a spouse; serious illness; rape)
6	catastrophic (death of child; suicide of spouse)

*Adapted from the *Diagnostic and Statistical Manual of Mental Disorders*, 3rd ed. rev., *DSM-III-R* (Washington, D.C.: American Psychiatric Association, 1987).

DSM-III-R Axis V: Global Assessment of Functioning Scale

Circle one	Degree of impairment in functioning*
81 – 90	absent or minimal symptoms with good functioning in all areas
71 – 80	transient symptoms with only slight impairment in work or social functioning
61 – 70	some mild symptoms or mild impairment in functioning
51 – 60	moderate symptoms or difficulty functioning
41 – 50	serious symptoms (suicidal ideas, severe obsessional rituals) or any serious impairment in functioning
31 – 40	some impairment in reality testing (speech illogical) or major impairment in judgment, thinking, mood, or functioning
21 – 30	behavior considerably influenced by delusions or inability to function in almost all areas with serious impairment in judgment
11 – 20	significant danger of hurting self or others, or failure in hygiene (e.g., smears feces) or capacity to communicate (e.g., mute)
1 – 10	persistent danger of severely hurting self or others

*Adapted from the *Diagnostic and Statistical Manual of Mental Disorders*, 3rd ed. rev., *DSM-III-R* (Washington, D.C.: American Psychiatric Association, 1987).

Administrative Checklist	Check (√) when discussed
1. **Self-help:** Does this individual understand that daily self-help assignments between sessions are required? Would he or she prefer to be referred to a therapist who does not require self-help assignments?	
2. **Premature termination:** Would this individual agree to attend an additional session if he or she becomes dissatisfied and decides to drop out prematurely? Does this individual understand that he or she will be billed for the entire program if he or she drops out prematurely?	
3. **Legal matters:** Is therapy to be part of a current or contemplated lawsuit, a disability claim, or a divorce proceeding?	
4. **Financial arrangements:** Inquire about any financial problems. Does this individual understand the payment schedule? Can he or she afford the cost of the program?	
5. **Last-minute cancellations:** Explain your late-cancellation policy. In individual therapy, 24 hours' advance notice is usually required to cancel a session without a fee, regardless of the reason for the cancellation. In Ten Days to Self-esteem, participants typically pay a set fee for the program regardless of the number of sessions actually attended. Does he or she understand these arrangements?	
6. **The Deposit System:** If you are using this system, explain that participants are required to pay a deposit above and beyond the cost of the group. This deposit can be earned back entirely by attending on time and by doing the self-help assignments between sessions.	
7. **Emergencies:** Explain the emergency on-call policy and procedures. Will you be available for emergencies between group sessions? What types of emergencies? How can you be reached?	
8. **Negative feelings:** Encourage the individual to complain to you if he or she feels dissatisfied with you or the program at any time. Ask about any positive or negative feelings he or she may have had so far.	
9. **Commitment to the group:** Does the individual understand that inconsistent attendance, habitual lateness, premature termination, or a failure to do the self-help assignments will be disruptive to the group?	
10. **Other:** Were additional administrative issues discussed? What were they?	

APPENDIX C:
ADDITIONAL PROGRESS NOTES

TEN DAYS TO SELF-ESTEEM
Progress Note

Patient name: _____

Date of session: _____ Session number: _____

BDC score =   BAI score =   RSAT score =

Goal: _____

_____

Progress toward goal: _____

_____

_____

_____

_____

_____

_____

_____

_____

_____

_____

_____

_____

_____

_____

_____

_____

_____

_____

_____

signature

TEN DAYS TO SELF-ESTEEM
Progress Note

Patient name: _____

Date of session: _____ Session number: _____

BDC score =   BAI score =   RSAT score =

Goal: _____

_____

Progress toward goal: _____

_____

_____

_____

_____

_____

_____

_____

_____

_____

_____

_____

_____

_____

_____

_____

_____

_____

_____

_____

_____
signature

APPENDIX D:
SAMPLE CONSENT FORMS

This section contains two different consent forms for Ten Days to Self-esteem. Participant Agreement A on pages 231–232 refers to the Deposit System. The actual amount of the deposit is left blank so that you can fill in a suitable amount for your group.

Participant Agreement B on page 233 does not refer to the Deposit System. You can use this form if the Deposit System is not appropriate for your group.

Feel free to choose the form that is most appealing to you, and to modify it. You can give two copies of the consent form to each participant prior to the first session or at the first session. Ask the participants to return one copy to you for your files, and keep the other copy.

PARTICIPANT AGREEMENT A FOR TEN DAYS TO SELF-ESTEEM

I, _____ (*print your name*), agree to participate in Ten Days to Self-esteem. I understand that I will be asked to attend ten sessions dealing with mood and personal relationship problems. I understand that during each session I will participate in group exercises that are designed to help me develop more positive thinking patterns and improved self-esteem.

I understand that once I have made a commitment to participate in Ten Days to Self-esteem, the morale of the group will depend in part on my consistent attendance and involvement. I understand that if I drop out prematurely or attend inconsistently, this will be disruptive and may hurt the morale of the other group members.

Please check the box below that best describes how you feel about attending consistently:

- ☐ I definitely plan to attend all ten sessions in this series.
- ☐ I anticipate that I may not be able to attend all the sessions.

I understand that I will be asked to do daily self-help assignments between sessions in a workbook entitled *Ten Days to Self-esteem*. These assignments will consist of activities such as reading, taking self-assessment tests to evaluate my progress, keeping a journal of negative thoughts and feelings, becoming more productive, and trying new and more effective ways of relating to other people.

I understand that my learning will depend on the amount of time I spend doing self-help assignments between sessions, and that I will need to do approximately thirty minutes of homework per day. I understand that my failure to do this homework will diminish any learning or growth that I might experience during this program.

Please check the box below that best describes how you feel about the homework assignments:

- ☐ I am definitely willing and able to spend an average of thirty minutes per day doing the self-help assignments.
- ☐ I am not sure that I will be able to do the homework assignments consistently.
- ☐ I am not willing to do the homework assignments consistently.

I agree to make a deposit of $_____ at the beginning of the program. I understand that I can earn some or all of this deposit back by attending sessions consistently and by doing the self-help assignments between sessions. I understand that if I arrive late or miss sessions or if I fail to complete the assignments between sessions, I will lose some or all of this deposit.

I understand that my refund at the end of the program will be calculated in the following manner. I will receive points for attending sessions on time and for completing the self-help assignments between sessions. I understand that my refund at the last session will be based on the total number of points I earn. If I attend all the sessions on time and do all the assignments, my entire deposit will be refunded.

If I miss a session due to illness or some other factor beyond my control, I agree to give the group leader notification at least twenty-four hours in advance. If I give twenty-four hours' advance notification and do all the self-help assignments for a session I missed due to factors beyond my control, I will not lose any points for failing to attend that session.

I have read this form and I have had the chance to ask questions about the purpose of Ten Days to Self-esteem as well as the nature of my participation. I agree to participate along the lines described here.

_____

sign your name

_____

today's date

PARTICIPANT AGREEMENT B
FOR TEN DAYS TO SELF-ESTEEM

I, _____ (*print your name*), agree to participate in Ten Days to Self-esteem. I understand that I will be asked to attend ten sessions dealing with mood and personal relationship problems. I understand that during each session I will participate in group exercises that are designed to help me develop more positive thinking patterns and improved self-esteem.

I understand that once I have made a commitment to participate in Ten Days to Self-esteem, the morale of the group will depend in part on my consistent attendance and involvement. I understand that if I drop out prematurely or attend inconsistently, this will be disruptive and may hurt the morale of the other group members.

Please check the box below that best describes how you feel about attending consistently:

☐ I definitely plan to attend all ten sessions in this series.
☐ I anticipate that I may not be able to attend all the sessions.

I understand that I will be asked to do daily self-help assignments between sessions in a workbook entitled *Ten Days to Self-esteem*. These assignments will consist of activities such as reading, taking self-assessment tests to evaluate my progress, keeping a journal of negative thoughts and feelings, becoming more productive in my work, and trying new and more effective ways of relating to other people.

I understand that my learning will depend on the amount of time I spend doing self-help assignments between sessions, and that approximately thirty minutes of homework per day will be required. I understand that my failure to do this homework will diminish any learning or growth that I might experience during this program.

Please check the box below that best describes how you feel about the homework assignments:

☐ I am definitely willing and able to spend an average of thirty minutes per day doing the self-help assignments.
☐ I am not sure that I will be able to do the homework assignments consistently.
☐ I am not willing to do the homework assignments consistently.

I have read this form and I have had the chance to ask questions about the purpose of Ten Days to Self-esteem as well as the nature of my participation. I agree to participate along the lines described here.

_____
sign your name

_____
today's date

TRAINING FOR GROUP LEADERS

If you need information about treatment or training for group leaders, you may contact the author at the following address:

David D. Burns, M.D., and Bruce Zahn, M.A.
c/o Presbyterian Medical Center of Philadelphia
39th and Market Streets
Philadelphia, PA 19104

INDEX

Page numbers in **bold** refer to charts and tables.

ABOUT THE AUTHOR

David D. Burns, M.D., a clinical psychiatrist, is one of America's foremost authorities on mood and personal relationship problems. He is the author of several popular books, including the best-selling *Feeling Good: The New Mood Therapy*, which has sold more than two and a half million copies. He has published numerous original research papers in scientific journals and has also appeared on many radio and television programs, such as *Donahue*. Dr. Burns is a clinical associate professor of psychiatry at the University of Pennsylvania School of Medicine and practices at the Presbyterian Medical Center of Philadelphia, where he has served as acting chief of the Division of Psychiatry.

ORDER FORM FOR
TEN DAYS TO SELF-ESTEEM
AND
TEN DAYS TO SELF-ESTEEM: THE LEADER'S MANUAL

In *Ten Days to Self-esteem,* Dr. Burns provides hope and healing for people suffering from low self-esteem and unhappiness. Use this form to order a copy of *Ten Days to Self-esteem* for a friend, a family member, a class, or a therapy group.

Ten Days to Self-esteem: The Leader's Manual will show you how to create a revolutionary self-esteem group training program to help people in a wide variety of settings: hospitals and clinics, schools and universities, HMOs and EAPs, churches and synagogues, corporations, and correctional institutions. *Ten Days to Self-esteem: The Leader's Manual* will be treasured by any clinician or educator who is looking for new, creative ways to meet the need for cost-effective, time-limited treatment programs!

Please return this form to the address below with your *check or money order* for the purchase price ($12.95 for each copy of *Ten Days to Self-esteem* or $23.00 for each *Leader's Manual*), plus $3.00 shipping and handling for the first book and $1.50 for each additional book, plus appropriate sales tax (or include tax exempt/resale number here: _____).
Make your check payable to William Morrow and Company. Please allow four weeks for delivery.

Enclosed is a check for $_____ to bill to a/c 99110.

Name _____

Shipping address _____

_____

City _____ State/ZIP _____

Phone (___) _____ Date of order _____

How many copies? *Ten Days to Self-esteem* ____ *The Leader's Manual* ____

Mail to: William Morrow and Company, Inc.
Special Sales Department
1350 Avenue of the Americas
New York, N.Y. 10019

Call toll-free 1-800-821-1513 for discounted bulk orders of ten copies or more for organizations planning to form groups based on *Ten Days to Self-esteem.*

Please note: Prices and availability are subject to change without notice.